Exemplars, Imitation, and Character Formation

This volume examines the role and relevance of exemplars and the practice of imitation in character development and formation. While the role
of exemplars and imitation in spiritual and moral formation has been an
integral part of many religious and wisdom traditions, in recent times there
has been limited theological and philosophical investigation into it and a
dearth of interdisciplinary discussion. The book brings together relevant
research and insights from leading experts within philosophy, psychology,
and theology, with an emphasis on Christian approaches to exemplars
and imitation, especially given the reflection on these themes throughout
the history of the Christian intellectual and mystical tradition. Many of the
contributions display an interdisciplinary approach to these issues; hence,
this volume will be of interest to philosophers, psychologists, theologians,
and others who work in moral psychology and character formation.

Eric Yang is Associate Professor of Philosophy at Santa Clara University, USA.

Routledge Science and Religion Series
Series editors:
Michael S. Burdett, *University of Nottingham, UK*
Mark Harris, *University of Edinburgh, UK*

Science and religion have often been thought to be at loggerheads but much contemporary work in this flourishing interdisciplinary field suggests this is far from the case. The Science and Religion Series presents exciting new work to advance interdisciplinary study, research and debate across key themes in science and religion. Contemporary issues in philosophy and theology are debated, as are prevailing cultural assumptions. The series enables leading international authors from a range of different disciplinary perspectives to apply the insights of the various sciences, theology, philosophy and history in order to look at the relations between the different disciplines and the connections that can be made between them. These accessible, stimulating new contributions to key topics across science and religion will appeal particularly to individual academics and researchers, graduates, postgraduates and upper-undergraduate students.

Julian of Norwich and the Ecological Crisis
Restoring Porosity
Claire Gilbert

Progress in Theology
Does the Queen of the Sciences Advance?
Edited by Gijsbert van den Brink, Rik Peels and Bethany Sollereder

Perspectives on Spiritual Intelligence
Edited by Marius Dorobantu and Fraser Watts

Exemplars, Imitation, and Character Formation
A Philosophical, Psychological, and Christian Enquiry
Edited by Eric Yang

For more information and a full list of titles in the series, please visit: https://www.routledge.com/religion/series/ASCIREL

Exemplars, Imitation, and Character Formation

A Philosophical, Psychological, and Christian Inquiry

Edited by Eric Yang

Routledge
Taylor & Francis Group

LONDON AND NEW YORK

First published 2025
by Routledge
4 Park Square, Milton Park, Abingdon, Oxon OX14 4RN

and by Routledge
605 Third Avenue, New York, NY 10158

Routledge is an imprint of the Taylor & Francis Group, an informa business

© 2025 selection and editorial matter, Eric Yang; individual chapters, the contributors

British Library Cataloguing-in-Publication Data
A catalogue record for this book is available from the British Library

ISBN: 978-1-032-63935-2 (hbk)
ISBN: 978-1-032-64834-7 (pbk)
ISBN: 978-1-032-64839-2 (ebk)

DOI: 10.4324/9781032648392

Typeset in Sabon
by KnowledgeWorks Global Ltd.

For Peter and Sue Yang and Tim and Lynette Tidwell,
exemplars par excellence

Contents

Contributors

Lily M. Abadal is a Visiting Assistant Professor of Philosophy at the University of South Florida.

Alfred Archer is an Associate Professor at Tilburg University in the Netherlands, affiliated with the Tilburg Center for Moral Philosophy, Epistemology and Philosophy of Science (TiLPS).

Kendall Cotton Bronk is the Principal Investigator for the Adolescent Moral Development Lab and a Professor of Psychology in the Division of Behavioral and Social Sciences at the Claremont Graduate University.

Aaron Cobb is a Professor of Philosophy and Chair of the Department of English and Philosophy at Auburn University at Montgomery.

Emily Dumler-Winckler is an Assistant Professor of Christian Ethics and Constructive Theology at Saint Louis University.

Bart Engelen is an Associate Professor at Tilburg University in the Netherlands, affiliated with the Tilburg Center for Moral Philosophy, Epistemology and Philosophy of Science (TiLPS).

Heidi M. Giebel is a Professor of Philosophy at the University of St. Thomas in St. Paul, Minnesota.

Mark Graves is a Research Associate Professor in the School of Psychology at Fuller Theological Seminary and a Research Director of AI & Faith in Seattle, Washington.

Grace Hibshman is a doctoral candidate in philosophy at the University of Notre Dame.

Sabrina B. Little is an Assistant Professor in the Department of Leadership and American Studies at Christopher Newport University.

Thomas Jay Oord directs the Center for Open and Relational Theology and a doctoral program at Northwind Theological Seminary.

Timothy Reilly is an Assistant Professor of Psychology at Ave Maria University.

Brother John Baptist Santa Ana, O.S.B., is a Benedictine monk of St. Andrews Abbey and a graduate student at the University of Notre Dame.

James A. Van Slyke is an Associate Professor and Director of the undergraduate psychology program at Fresno Pacific University.

Eric Yang is an Associate Professor of Philosophy at Santa Clara University.

Linda Zagzebski is the George Lynn Cross Research Professor Emerita and Kingfisher College Chair of the Philosophy of Religion and Ethics Emerita at the University of Oklahoma.

Acknowledgments

This work was primarily funded by the New Visions in Theological Anthropology (NVITA) at the University of St. Andrews. Through the NVITA fellowship, a workshop was hosted at Santa Clara University during the Spring of 2023, gathering a handful of the philosophers, psychologists, and theologians who have contributed to this volume, where the fruit of their interdisciplinary labor is on display here. Additionally, most of the chapters in this volume exemplify a sensitivity to the research in other fields, and so the work in this volume has sought to be exemplary with respect to interdisciplinary engagement.

I am grateful to John Perry, Joanna Leidenhag, and the whole NVITA team for awarding me a fellowship and providing funds to support this project. Without them, this volume would probably not have seen the light of day. I would also like to thank Laura Clark, my editorial assistant, whose labor and careful attention to each chapter have made this work much better than it would have been had I done this alone. And my home institution, Santa Clara University, provided me with a grant to support finishing the editing of this volume. Finally, I am grateful to all of those people who have served as moral and spiritual exemplars for me, and I hope these theoretical and practical discussions will actually help me and anyone else who genuinely desires to become a good person.

Introduction

Eric Yang

Exemplarism and Imitation in Philosophy, Christian Theology, and Psychology

Some moral theories center their account on rules or obligations, and others focus on calculating what the best result would be—or at least providing a rough estimate. Corresponding practices emphasize obedience or adherence to these rules or acting in ways to bring about the best expected outcomes. However, there is a long history of philosophical and religious thought that focuses less on duties and consequences and more on good people. In some of these traditions, we identify a good person and seek to become like them by copying a lot of what they do in order to acquire some of their personality or character traits that we deem morally good. These good people are exemplars, that is, examples or models that people may have positive emotions toward as it relates to morality. And given their exemplarity, some people naturally emulate them, whereas others intentionally strive to imitate them in order to become more like them or to become more morally virtuous. While there is a long history that emphasizes exemplars and the practice of imitation (more of this anon), there has been a scarcity of systematic analysis or evaluation of this approach in contemporary philosophy (though there are notable exceptions).

For example, as of November 2023, there has been no entry on *exemplarism* or *imitation* (or their cognates) in either the *Stanford Encyclopedia of Philosophy* (probably the most reputable online reference in philosophy) or the *Internet Encyclopedia of Philosophy*. We can, however, see the role and relevance of exemplars in early western and non-western philosophy. In ancient Greek philosophy, Socrates was often regarded as the paradigmatic exemplar of philosophical inquiry and philosophical way of living. But it was Aristotle who offered a more systematic treatment, where his virtue-theoretic approach can be seen as having a role for exemplars or good people to play, though it is contentious exactly what their role is supposed to be (cf. Hampson 2019). In ancient Chinese philosophy, Confucius is not only seen as the most "complete and compelling exemplar" (Olberding 2012, 105), but the *Analects* may also be interpreted as either offering (or having

DOI: 10.4324/9781032648392-1

as an underlying basis) an exemplarist moral theory. While the concept and language of virtue is pervasive throughout philosophical history, it was not until the resurgence of virtue ethics in the 20th century (with luminaries such as Elizabeth Anscombe, Alasdair MacIntyre, Philippa Foot, and Rosalind Hursthouse) that talk of exemplars was primed and ready. Drawing on both religious traditions and psychological research, the most extensive investigation and defense of exemplarism came from the work of Linda Zagzebski. The initial approach was formulated in her book *Divine Motivation Theory*, which offered a normative ethical theory that regarded God as the primary exemplar—though she also included an alternative secular approach that was in the same vein. Her view was further developed and defended in *Exemplarist Moral Theory*, providing the richest treatment of exemplarism and the practice of imitation in contemporary philosophy, which has yielded interdisciplinary studies and critical reflections on exemplarism.

There is also a long history of reflection on exemplars and imitation in different religions, with a notably high level of engagement by Christian thinkers. This should not be surprising, as there are a large number of passages within Christian Scripture that attest to Christ as the central exemplar for Christians. There are also many passages in Christian Scripture that charge the reader or listener to practice imitating God, Christ, the apostle Paul, etc. (Ephesians 5:1, John 13:15, 1 Peter 2:21, Matthew 11:28-30, 1 Corinthians 10:31-1:1, Philippians 3:12-17, 1 Corinthians 4:14-17, 2 Thessalonians 3:7-9). The Benedictines, perhaps the oldest monastic order, adhere to the *Rule of St. Benedict*, which is not only compatible with exemplarism but arguably best fits with such an approach to spiritual formation (Santa Ana & Yang forthcoming). Christ's role as an exemplar is also central to Peter Abelard's account of the atonement, versions of which have contemporary defenders (Page & Thornton 2021). There are also themes of imitation appearing in Thomas à Kempis (with the aptly named work, *The Imitation of Christ*) and in Kierkegaard (cf. Cockayne 2022). Some recent Christian theological work addresses how someone can imitate an exemplar, such as Christ, who is not present or directly observable to us, with solutions that appeal to joint or shared attention (Cockayne 2017) or to observation and imitation of members in a local ecclesial body (Yang 2022).

While psychology as a scientific discipline is relatively new on the scene (at least when compared to philosophy and theology), considerable research and study have utilized and investigated exemplars and the practice of imitation. For example, some developmental psychologists have proposed a methodology that intentionally selects exemplars or paradigmatic examples, i.e., individuals who significantly differ from what we would expect in typical individuals, in order to study some of the more advanced developments in character or personality (Bronk 2012; Bronk, King & Matsuba 2013). Regarding imitation, we find a more nuanced discussion among psychologists, some of whom distinguish between imitation, emulation, and mimicry as different kinds of copying behaviors (Boesch & Tomasello 1998; Fridland

& Moore 2015). Psychologists have also paid considerable attention to the social and communal elements involved in imitation (McIntosh 2006; Over & Carpenter 2013; Tickle-Degnen 2006). Recently, Van Bergen et al. (2023) have written *Imitation: The Basics*, an excellent and accessible introduction to imitation in developmental and social psychology.

Until recently, most of these discussions on exemplars and imitation have occurred in disciplinary isolation, with very little interaction between philosophers, psychologists, and theologians. Happily, in recent years, there has been a significant rise in interdisciplinary interaction on various moral topics (humility, honesty, wisdom, etc.), and one of the chief aims of this volume is to introduce and propagate more interaction across these fields when studying the function, characteristics, and relevance of exemplars and imitation in moral development and character formation.

Summary of Chapters

This volume is divided into three parts, presenting philosophical, psychological, and Christian inquiry into exemplars and the practice of imitation. Regarding philosophical contributions, Heidi Giebel investigates the notion of moral charisma (or the classical Confucian notion of *dé*) as possessed by exemplars in Chapter 1, showing that it can serve as a bridge concept that is beneficial to interdisciplinary discussions between philosophers, theologians, and psychologists. In Chapter 2, Aaron Cobb argues for the importance of considering exemplar communities (and not just individuals) in our discussion of exemplarism, claiming that doing so may illuminate important moral truths. Bart Engelen and Alfred Archer distinguish between imitation and emulation in Chapter 3, arguing that the emulation of exemplars can avoid worries of indoctrination and problematic forms of moral deference that beset the practice of imitation, especially when it comes to exemplar education. In Chapter 4, I argue that real people should not be regarded as our immediate exemplars since we are ignorant of many important facts about real people and we may select a bad person as an exemplar; instead, we should take our conceptual model of a person as our immediate exemplar, which avoids these worries. Sabrina Little considers the emotion of admiration of exemplars in Chapter 5, showing some of the limitations of admiration regarding spiritual development (especially from a Christian framework) and considering the ways in which other emotions such as contrition, gratitude, and awe can bolster admiration in the process of spiritual formation.

The next part highlights psychological contributions in investigating exemplars and the practice of imitation. In Chapter 6, James Van Slyke argues that moral exemplars have an emotional appraisal system, especially the emotion of empathy, that distinguishes them from non-exemplars and enables them to carry out morally praiseworthy behavior, and he focuses on holocaust rescuers to support his case. Kendall Cotton Bronk employs an exemplar methodology to investigate family purpose in Chapter 7, which yields several interesting results and insights into family purpose and the relational features in exemplar families. In Chapter 8, Timothy Reilly considers spiritual formation in light of traditional Catholic thought and developmental psychology, showing that the interdisciplinary approach from these two domains attends to unexplored or underexplored ideas (e.g., relational exemplarity, redemptive exemplarity) and exposes the need for future investigation. In Chapter 9, Mark Graves considers recent methods employed in psychology to investigate sociotechnical systems within communities that ground practical wisdom and discernment, highlighting some of the ways these are exhibited in exemplars and are acquirable by imitation.

The final part considers theological inquiry into exemplars and imitation, specifically from a Christian approach. In Chapter 10, Emily Dumler-Winckler avers that exemplarity requires radical love, which requires being an extremist, demonstrating this through the example of Jesus and Martin Luther King Jr. Thomas Jay Oord considers the Christian charge to imitate God in Chapter 11, which he argues requires loving in the manner that God loves; and Oord criticizes an account of love by Augustine and Thomas à Kempis, instead defending an account of love based on open and relational theology. In Chapter 12, Lily Abadal challenges Aristotle's thesis that only a small number of privileged people are capable of becoming virtuous, and Abadal argues that taking Jesus Christ as a moral exemplar (along with Abelard's theory of atonement) makes the possibility of becoming virtuous more accessible than just to a privileged few. In Chapter 13, Brother John Baptist Santa Ana considers the lives of St. Antony and St. Augustine as a case study to argue for the advantages of having numerous exemplars as well as the benefits of having exemplars that exhibit various weaknesses and disadvantages. In Chapter 14, Grace Hibshman considers a puzzle of imitating exemplars (such as saints) whose behavior would appear to be inappropriate for many of us, and Hibshman addresses the puzzle by offering a model of engagement with exemplars that involves a three-way relationship between an individual, an exemplar, and God, whereby the individual need not imitate exactly what the exemplar does.

This volume concludes with an Afterword by Linda Zagzebski, whose influence on the discussion over exemplars and the practice of imitation is noticeably felt. In the Afterword, Zagzebski offers some remarks on the future direction of philosophical, psychological, and theological investigation into these topics on exemplars and imitation.

The hope is that the work found in this volume will generate interdisciplinary dialogue and continued investigation into the role of exemplars and the practice of imitation that will be beneficial not only with respect to our moral theorizing but also to our moral practice and character formation.

References

Boesch, Christophe and Michael Tomasello. 1998. "Chimpanzee and Human Cultures." *Current Anthropology* 39: 591–614.

Bronk, Kendall Cotton. 2012. "The Exemplar Methodology: An Approach to Studying the Leading Edge of Development." *Psychology of Well-Being* 2: 1–10.

Bronk, Kendall Cotton, Pamela Ebstyne King, and M. Kyle Matsuba. 2013. "An Introduction to Exemplar Research: A Definition, Rationale, and Conceptual Issues." *New Directions for Child and Adolescent Development*, 2013, no. 142: 1–12.

Cockayne, Joshua. 2017. "The Imitation Game: Becoming Imitators of Christ." *Religious Studies* 53: 3–24.

Cockayne, Joshua. 2022. "Imitation and Contemporaneity: Kierkegaard and the Imitation of Christ." *Heythrop Journal* 63: 553–66.

Fridland, Ellen and Richard Moore. 2015. "Imitation Reconsidered." *Philosophical Psychology* 28: 856–80.

Hampson, Margaret. 2019. "Imitating Virtue." *Phronesis* 64: 292–320.

McIntosh, Daniel N. 2006. "Spontaneous Facial Mimicry, Liking, and Emotional Contagion." *Polish Psychological Bulletin* 37: 31–42.

Olberding, Amy. 2012. *Moral Exemplars in the Analects: The Good Person Is That*. New York, NY: Routledge.

Over, Harriett and Malinda Carpenter. 2013. "The Social Side of Imitation." *Child Development Perspectives* 7: 6–11.

Page, Meghan and Allison Thornton. 2021. "Have We No Shame?: A Moral Exemplar Account of Atonement." *Faith and Philosophy* 38: 409–30.

Santa Ana, John Baptist and Eric Yang. Forthcoming. "Achievement through Humility: Wild Lessons from Benedictine Monasticism." In *Mind Over Matter*, edited by Rod Nicholls and Heather Salazar, Leiden: Brill.

Tickle-Degnen, Linda. 2006. "Nonverbal Behavior and Its Functions in the Ecosystem of Rapport." In *The SAGE Handbook of Nonverbal Communication*, edited by V. Manusov and M. L. Patterson, 381–99. Thousand Oaks, CA: Sage.

Van Bergen, Naomi, Allard R. Feddes, Liesbeth Mann, and Bertjan Doosje. 2023. *Imitation: The Basics*. New York, NY: Routledge.

Yang, Eric. 2022. "Can Psychology Help Resolve the Problem of a Putatively Non-present Christ?" *Theological Puzzles* 10.

Zagzebski, Linda. 2004. *Divine Motivation Theory*. Cambridge: Cambridge University Press.

Zagzebski, Linda. 2017. *Exemplarist Moral Theory*: Oxford: Oxford University Press.

Part I

Philosophical Inquiry into Exemplars and Imitation

1 Moral Charisma

Why We (Almost) Can't Help Imitating Virtue

Heidi M. Giebel

Introduction: Moral Charisma as a Bridge Concept

Among my fondest professional memories is a student-faculty reading group on moral development, which I co-led for several years with a psychologist colleague. She and I had similar research interests, and she was generally game for pursuing joint projects; the students were bright and engaged and made great research assistants. However, I have to confess that some of the psychology articles we read together made me want to tear my hair out. Not because I couldn't follow the statistical analysis (that was true too, but the students delighted in explaining it to me), but because on a conceptual level, they seemed hopelessly confused. The authors frequently failed to explain, or maybe even think about, what they meant by fundamental terms like "ethics," "virtue," and "moral development"—even though their studies claimed to show what was most effective at promoting those very things. What these articles needed (and, to their credit, what others had) was good use of bridge concepts.

As philosopher Aaron Stalnaker points out, any comparative study faces two simultaneous challenges: it must bring distinct vocabularies and approaches "into interrelation and conversation, and it must simultaneously preserve their distinctiveness within the interrelation."[1] Bridge concepts enable us to preserve this delicate balance of distinction and commonality. Both broad enough and informative enough to be used across multiple texts, approaches, and even disciplines, these concepts provide "a way to thematize their disparate elements and order their details," highlighting both "similarities and differences, and even more subtle similarities within differences, and differences within similarities."[2] The study of moral and spiritual development—of growth in character, grace, and virtue—is just the sort of comparative and interdisciplinary study best facilitated by bridge concepts' plentiful yet careful deployment. Inspired by classical Confucianism, I propose that moral charisma is just the sort of idea we need: a key bridge concept for philosophers, theologians, and psychologists discussing moral and spiritual formation.[3]

DOI: 10.4324/9781032648392-3

Moral Charisma in Philosophical Ethics

In classical Chinese thought, the term *dé* has more nuance than its common English translation as "virtue" might suggest. Originally meaning "power" or "influence" more generally, by Confucius's time, the word came to mean something like "moral charisma." Not just any sort of power, *dé* is "a power over others, but one that … paradoxically cannot be used to manipulate others for one's own private ends."[4] PJ Ivanhoe, a contemporary scholar of Confucianism, describes moral charisma as "the natural attraction one feels toward morally great individuals, the same kind of feeling that people claim to have experienced in the presence of Mahatma Gandhi or Martin Luther King, Jr."[5]

Along with "moral portraits" of exemplars such as Confucius,[6] we see the attractiveness of virtue described (and likely overstated) in Confucius's account of good government in the *Analects*. To take just a few representative examples:

> The Master said, "One who rules through the power of Virtue is analogous to the Pole Star: it simply remains in its place and receives the homage of the myriad lesser stars."[7]

> The Master said, "If you try to guide the common people with coercive regulations and keep them in line with punishments, the common people will become evasive and will have no sense of shame. If, however, you guide them with Virtue, and keep them in line by means of ritual, the people will have a sense of shame and will rectify themselves." (2.3)

> The Virtue of a gentleman is like the wind, and the Virtue of a petty person is like the grass—when the wind moves over the grass, the grass is sure to bend.[8] (12.19)

Indeed, classical Chinese history tells of ancient (even to Confucius!) sage kings who did not have to use laws or threats to gain the people's compliance—they were so virtuous that people instinctively followed them.

Although descriptions of moral charisma and its effectiveness tend not to be quite so dramatic in the classical Western tradition, at least in its concrete interpersonal manifestations, the intelligibility and attractiveness of goodness is foundational to the theories of Plato and Aristotle as well as their medieval successors. Plato's *Republic* speaks of the Form or Idea of the Good as an ultimate reality in which everything else participates—and resembles it to a greater or lesser degree. Aristotle famously begins *Nicomachean Ethics*, his principal ethical work, with "The good is that which all things seek."[9] Virtues, then, being good character traits, should be obvious objects of our seeking. Relatedly, in the interpersonal sphere, Aristotle discusses emulation (*zelos*) as a learner's virtue in his *Rhetoric*:

> Emulation is pain caused by seeing the presence, in persons whose nature is like our own, of good things that are highly valued and are

possible for ourselves to acquire; but it is felt not because others have these goods, but because we have not got them ourselves. It is therefore a good feeling felt by good persons, whereas envy is a bad feeling felt by bad persons. Emulation makes us take steps to secure the good things in question, envy makes us take steps to stop our neighbour having them. ... [Emulation] is accordingly felt by the young and by persons of lofty disposition. ... Further, since all good things that are highly honoured are objects of emulation, moral goodness in its various forms must be such an object, and also all those good things that are useful and serviceable to others.[10]

As philosopher Kristján Kristjánsson points out, emulation, just as an emotion (pain or distress at another's having achieved a worthy good that we have not yet achieved), can't be considered a virtue—like many moral virtues, the virtue of emulation (or emulousness) involves a combination of appropriate emotion, intention, and action. Kristjánsson ultimately identifies four aspects of this virtue:

(1) the emotion of distress at the relative absence amongst ourselves of desired, honoured goods which someone else possesses; (2) the zeal to make efforts to acquire (deservingly) similar goods without taking them away from the emulated other; (3) true self-understanding and rational persuasion, which directs us towards goods that are attainable for us and, thus, towards future honours of which we can realistically become worthy; and (4) a striving for goods that are "appropriate attributes of the good."[11]

Like other virtues, emulousness is a mean between two extremes: "excessive eagerness to emulate others" and "too little will to improve."[12] Emulousness involves a more moderate reaction to our inferiority compared to others, along with morally appropriate steps to remedy it. Thus, its status as a learner's virtue—one who is already fully virtuous need not emulate others; rather, s/he will be a fitting object of others' emulation.

Contemporary philosophical ethics also addresses the moral charisma of exceptionally virtuous people. Vanessa Carbonell, in response to an article infamously claiming that moral sainthood is undesirable and unattractive,[13] gives the extended counterexample of humanitarian physician Paul Farmer, who "attracts friends and followers like a magnet."[14] Farmer, she says, "is obsessed but not fanatical, ascetic but not self-righteous. He is sarcastic and cynical without being resigned. He is funny and fun, and no less morally admirable for it."[15] In short, he is just the sort of person that we want to be—and be around. Linda Zagzebski is well-known for her exemplarist virtue theory, in which the nature of virtue itself is known through the admiration we feel toward moral exemplars, which leads us to emulate them.[16] Building on Zagzebski's moral theory and connecting it with Confucian ethics and aesthetics, Ian Kidd gives an account of the moral beauty of virtuous exemplars: "Such beauty is a form of energy, radiance, or charisma that can make the moral life attractive in the very literal sense of making those who live it attractive."[17] And when working on my own book project, I couldn't help but notice, even over the phone, the attractiveness of several of the exemplars I interviewed.[18]

Moral Charisma in Christianity

As a non-theologian observer and practicing Christian, I can't help but notice an obvious role for moral charisma in Christianity: the exemplarity of Jesus Christ. This small-town carpenter persuaded both simple fishermen and wealthy tax collectors to drop everything and join him—just by calling them.[19] Thousands of people would follow him into the wilderness just to hear him preach. Crowds threw their cloaks on the road in front of him, singing his praises and hoping to crown him king. (That is, until they decided to have him executed instead.)

People still find Jesus charismatic—and not just in the healing and praying in tongues sense.[20] In a more encompassing way, many people hearing Jesus's story and teachings find him attractive. Just to take a couple of examples, Lisa Nigro, an interviewee of mine, considers herself Christian not for doctrinal reasons but because she sees Jesus as a rebel and a champion of the poor and weak. Don Schoendorfer, another interviewee and a very linear-thinking engineer, turned to Jesus to help him navigate the parts of life he couldn't predict or control—and for inspiration in using his engineering skills to help others. And Aiden, a high school senior and a good friend of my kids, was raised with no religious background but suddenly decided to start coming to Mass with us; he was baptized at the Easter Vigil this year. If you ask him why, he won't give you a theological answer—he just felt like Jesus was calling him.

So, Jesus certainly exemplifies charisma. Is it *moral* charisma? I think even non-Christians generally recognize that it is people of many religions and no religion call him a "great moral teacher." Gandhi is often approvingly misquoted as saying he admires Jesus Christ (but not Christians). After the movie *The Passion of the Christ* came out, there were numerous stories of people vowing to reform their lives—sometimes beginning with confessing their crimes[21]—because his story moved them so strongly. Perhaps more to the point, Jesus exemplifies the kind of moral charisma the Confucians extolled: he just has to be himself, exemplifying his exceptional virtue, and people want to fall in line. And it's been that way since the beginning, as far as I can tell. Jesus himself advises his disciples to imitate both his actions and his character: "Take my yoke upon you and learn from me, for I am meek and humble of heart; and you will find rest for yourselves."[22] Thomas à Kempis's work, *The Imitation of Christ*, is the all-time most popular work of Christian spiritual formation outside the Bible itself. And, of course, many of us remember the 1990s when Christians asked themselves—and each other— "What would Jesus do?" (Some of us even wore "WWJD" wristbands.)

To a lesser but still noteworthy extent, several great Christian saints have exemplified a similar sort of moral charisma. For example, St. Francis of Assisi is held up as a model of humility, material simplicity, and caring for the Earth; St. Nicholas inspires generosity, especially at Christmas; and even St. Valentine manages to persuade us to send nice cards once a year. (Poor St. Patrick: although he was also a great Christian exemplar, somehow his legacy seems to be green beer.) Some of us imitate saints more consciously and systematically as well. In the Catholic Church, there are orders of priests, nuns, and even laypeople dedicated to following the examples of St. Francis, St. Dominic, and several others. As von Balthasar famously said, "the saint is the apology for the Christian religion"[23]—that is, when we observe saintly people, we find their lives attractive and want to imitate them.[24]

Moral Charisma and Psychology

In addition to being a philosopher (and a physician and a zoologist), Aristotle was something of a psychologist; his observations on imitation (*mimesis*) in learning are a good place to start: "The instinct of imitation is implanted in man from childhood, and through imitation [he] learns his earliest lessons; and ... to learn gives the liveliest pleasure.... Imitation, then, is one instinct of our nature."[25]

In the modern psychological literature, we've seen study of imitative learning at least since Bandura and his poor, abused Bobo dolls.[26] As proponents of social learning theory have observed, behavior can be learned solely through imitation (without the influence of external rewards or punishments)—particularly if it is observed attentively, remembered accurately, and accompanied by motivation to replicate it.[27] Further, the tendency to attempt a given behavior depends heavily on one's perceived ability to succeed, and that perceived efficacy, in turn, is influenced by whether its successful completion has been modeled by relevantly similar others.[28] As those famous Bobo dolls studies show, behaviors can also be *reinforced* vicariously: we are more likely to imitate behavior that has resulted in good outcomes for others—especially those with whom we identify.

In addition to the vast literature on learning via imitation, we're also blessed with a growing body of literature on moral exemplars. Just to take a few favorite examples, Anne Colby and Bill Damon's groundbreaking 1992 book, *Some Do Care*, dug into the lives and works of 23 carefully selected exemplars and the "paradoxes" of their moral commitment.[29] (For example, they tended to enjoy unshakeable certainty regarding their fundamental values while remaining surprisingly open to influence from colleagues and beneficiaries.) The same authors later wrote on famous twentieth-century exemplars, emphasizing their truthfulness, humility, and faith.[30] And Larry Walker traveled across Canada (probably several times!) interviewing recipients of the Caring Canadian Award.[31]

Empirical questions regarding the moral charisma of exemplars seem to land at (or at least near) the intersection of research on imitation and moral exemplars. Psychologist Hyemin Han has found that exemplars we find especially attainable and relevant are more effective in promoting voluntary service behavior than are extraordinary moral heroes.[32] Further, relatable and attainable exemplars promote elevation,[33] a warm and pleasant feeling caused by witnessing acts of virtue or moral beauty, motivating the observer to act more virtuously as well.[34]

In addition to imitation *of* exemplars, it seems worth observing imitation *by* exemplars—perhaps there is an exemplary way to learn by imitation. (As Kristjánsson argues, there are certainly better and worse ways: understanding and emulating an exemplar's virtues is clearly superior to blind hero worship.[35]) Although I know of no quantitative studies examining this topic, I can offer a couple of qualitative tidbits. One of Colby and Damon's interviewees, a businessman-turned-statesman, said, "What we got from our parents was this basic, fundamental understanding that you do what's right and you don't do what isn't. I can't remember them preaching. ... None of that got said, *but that's how they lived.*"[36] He and his brothers, he said, all hoped to have a similar effect on their own children. Other exemplars set out to emulate extraordinary moral heroes (in Han's terms): one hung a quote from Martin Luther King on his wall; another put up a picture of Mother Teresa.[37] One of my own exemplar interviewees, Noah Levinson, similarly sought to emulate Mother Teresa, even working at her Home for Dying Destitutes. Later, somewhat in contrast to Mother Teresa's approach but very much in the spirit of her love for the poor and neglected, he started a preventive health-care organization in Kolkata.[38] So Levinson seemed to achieve a mean of emulousness, emulating Mother Teresa's compassion without uncritically copying her methods of exercising it.

Just one last observation before we turn to questions and puzzles: learning through imitation is a species of learning from *actions*. As parents and teachers everywhere have observed, sometimes with a touch of despair, words have limited effectiveness in practical teaching. Aristotle warned us millennia ago that arguments won't make people virtuous—we need to perform relevant actions to develop virtuous habits. And it may be worth noting that Jesus himself, although he was a great moral teacher and had been teaching his disciples for *years*, couldn't even get them to recognize him as he taught them for *hours* on the road to Emmaus. How did they finally figure out it was him? Through his actions: in the breaking of bread.[39]

Philosophical and Practical Questions

Thus far, we have seen several interesting features of moral charisma in philosophy, theology, and psychology: it's built into the very notion of virtue in Confucianism and is a natural fit with the attractiveness of the good in classical Western philosophy. It's also a helpful description of so many people's willingness to follow Jesus (both when he literally called them and throughout history), and even of their willingness to follow great saints' *ways* of following Jesus. And it resonates with at least two major areas of psychological study: social learning and exemplar studies. Together, these disciplines seem poised to offer a fuller explanation of what moral charisma is and how and why it works. For example, what exactly is it about exemplars that makes us want to emulate them? What moral and spiritual benefits can we expect from doing so? And how can we more effectively showcase exemplars for others' (and our own) imitation?

Before we plunge into such a large-scale project, though—one well beyond the scope of this short essay—it seems important to acknowledge some puzzles in need of our attention. In this section, I'll note just a few, along with a bigger-picture reflection on the implications of our resolutions to them.

Question 1: Is unconscious and/or indirect imitation of exemplars effective in moral and spiritual formation? This question is mostly empirical, although what counts as moral or spiritual formation is the purview of philosophers or theologians. While I'm not aware of any studies directly and systematically addressing the effect of unconscious imitation on moral or spiritual formation, I strongly suspect the answer is "Yes, but not nearly as effective as explicit, conscious imitation." The social learning literature seems clearly applicable here (humans routinely learn through unconscious imitation),[40] and of course anecdotal evidence abounds—indeed, most of us probably have anecdotes regarding our own, or our children's or students', imitating others' traits to good (or bad) effect. At the very least, I think we can say with great confidence that having moral exemplars readily available for such imitation can't hurt.

The question of indirect imitation is at least partly a conceptual question regarding whether imitation is transitive: that is, whether, given that *A* imitates *B* and *B* imitates *C*, we can conclude that *A* imitates *C*. And the answer is … it depends. Like a good medieval philosopher, we need to make some distinctions. If by "imitation" we mean "intentional copying," then it's obviously not transitive: in imitating *B*, who is imitating *C*, *A* (who has never met or heard of *C*) is not imitating him. But if instead we mean something more like "resembling" or "following a pattern," then imitation can be transitive as long as what *A* imitates in *B* is a quality *B* imitates in *C*. If not (e.g., if *A* imitates *B*'s bravery while *B* imitates *C*'s fashion sense), then transitivity obviously doesn't apply. Where imitation *is* transitive, indirect imitation of a moral exemplar presumably can be effective in moral and spiritual formation. Indeed, it seems that's what Colby and Damon's interviewee (quoted above) seemed to count on: he emulated his virtuous parents with the hope that his own children would emulate the same good qualities in him.

Question 2: Can exemplars be too good—and their virtue too seemingly unattainable—to inspire emulation? This is a fair question, and support for skepticism can be found both in philosopher Immanuel Kant's well-known "ought implies can" principle and in the common phenomenon of our own disinclination to attempt the impossible. While the details are surely complex, I think the simple answer is "no"—there can't be "too good" a moral exemplar. As I noted earlier, we do have some empirical evidence that attainable moral exemplars are *more* effective (in the circumstances studied) in inspiring emulation (of the obvious kind studied). However, even if those results generalize and more "ordinary exemplars" universally inspire more emulation, that doesn't mean "extraordinary moral heroes" inspire *no* emulation. And, as we've also already seen, both my and Colby and Damon's more "ordinary" exemplars did in fact emulate famous moral heroes.

Here is a working hypothesis harmonizing the data: for those of us just beginning our ethical journey (and perhaps that's most of us), our standards for "attainable" are quite modest. In this case, "ordinary" moral exemplars are especially useful for helping us to see the virtuous life as not only desirable but achievable. As we progress in virtue, however, we gradually come to see more of the actions and traits we previously thought of as "heroic" as being attainable by ordinary people like us. At that point, "extraordinary" exemplars may become increasingly emulable (and decreasingly "extraordinary") in our view.[41] Another way to come to see "heroes" as more emulable is to learn more about them: with a fuller picture of exemplars' stories and motivations, their actions and traits may not seem so inaccessible.

Question 3: Speaking of our perceptions, to what extent does charisma itself depend on the observer rather than just on the observed?[42] This question is also fair; it is well established that our perceptions can vary significantly. For example, ten eyewitnesses of the same car accident might give ten different accounts of what happened. And in the case of imitating a virtuous exemplar, doing so (at least consciously) seems to require noticing the exemplar's behavior and/or character, interpreting it as virtuous, and applying it to one's own situation. So, it seems that charisma, which implies attraction, must depend to a significant extent on the observer.

How, then, can an objective account of moral charisma, such as those seen in Confucius's *Analects* or Plato's *Republic*, get off the ground? Although a complete answer is well beyond the scope of the current essay, I propose (following Plato and Aristotle, among many others) that the commonalities of our human nature ground an objective answer to the question of which character traits (e.g., generosity, courage) are good for us to have and which ones (e.g., cowardice, dishonesty) are bad. And this objectivity with regard to traits grounds at least a range of possible examples of moral charisma. Thus, while the degree to which a particular individual finds a particular exemplar inspiring or "charismatic" may vary according to factors like culture, age, and interests (hence Han's findings regarding "relatable" exemplars), there remains significant conceptual space for objectivity regarding the characteristics of an exemplar and what counts as *moral* charisma. Just as eyewitness accounts can be not merely different but wrong (e.g., by claiming that the accident was caused by brain-snatching aliens), one's perception of moral charisma can be wrong when it targets an agent outside the ethically good range (e.g., by "inspiring" her to emulate a "virtuous" serial killer). So, while there is room for *some* observer relativity in moral charisma, its status is far from "anything goes."

Question 4: If virtue is naturally attractive, why do we seem just as apt to imitate vice? To answer this question, we'd first have to determine *whether* we really are just as apt to imitate vice. That's a mostly empirical question (and the Bobo dolls would probably vote "yes"!), but it depends on significant conceptual analysis of what virtues and vices are, how they're exercised, and what counts as imitation of them. That would make for a fascinating interdisciplinary study; to pull it off (and do so ethically) would require more clever methodology than I'm capable of devising. For now, let's remain agnostic regarding the "just as apt" claim but acknowledge that we are indeed *significantly* apt to imitate vice. (That much seems uncontroversial; any parent with vices has surely seen them reflected in her children.)

So, why are we apt to imitate vice, and what does that say about moral charisma and the attraction of goodness in general? Some psychologists might simply propose that social learning is ethically neutral—we're apt to imitate the character dispositions that we observe, especially if we see them rewarded in some way, whether they're ethically good or bad.[43] A mimetic theorist like René Girard might point to our (also inherently neutral) tendency to imitate each other's desires—which can lead to competition and even violence when the objects of desire are scarce.[44]

Christian theology offers a handy explanation for our misdirected desires in the story of the Fall—we were originally created for good, but when sin entered the world, our desires became misdirected and unreliable. This basic historical explanation fits nicely with the stories of imitation in Augustine's *Confessions*—before his conversion, he finds himself imitating, and even fabricating, all sorts of misdeeds for the sake of fitting in with his companions. And even the natural desire to imitate God, he says, can be twisted into a perverse desire to *be* a god.

So how do we embrace the power of imitation while avoiding its dark side? A key insight from Christian theology, as Jessica Hooten Wilson observes in her reading of Augustine's *Confessions*, is that mimetic desire for spiritual goods rather than this-worldly ones eliminates scarcity and the need to compete, providing a safer and more pleasant basis for emulation:

Book VIII, in which the conversion occurs, has layers upon layers of imitation. Although St. Augustine initially desires to become a Christian follower, after hearing of Victorinus, he does not act upon this inclination until he hears the influence that the life of St. Antony, the Egyptian monk, has had on others. When his African compatriot Ponticianus visits unexpectedly, he relates the story of how Antony converted him to Christianity; Antony was transformed by the gospel story in which Jesus tells a rich young ruler to sell everything he owns and follow him (see Matt. 19:16-22). The first model is Christ who gives up everything to follow the will of his Father. Then, Antony imitates Christ, who is imitated by Ponticianus, who inspires St. Augustine to imitate him. Whereas the desire for earthly goods leads to competition rather than imitation, the renunciation of earthly goods by each of these followers encourages others to imitate them.[45]

Despite our aptness to imitate vice, then, it seems there is something especially attractive about virtue—something that could make us *especially* apt to imitate it. As I mentioned earlier, virtuous moral exemplars promote elevation in their observers, which provides extra motivation to emulate them. Virtue, in other words, is not just imitable but inspiring. So, although we can expect imitation of vice (or any trait) if it's the only salient example or if it's observed to lead to extrinsic rewards, virtue has an additional, intrinsic attractiveness. As such, it should provoke emulation not just in these limited circumstances but in *all* circumstances—at least absent significant distractors and disincentives. (As I noted above, confirming this claim empirically would be complicated. For now, I propose it as a working hypothesis.)

Plato and Aristotle have (non-historical and non-theological) explanations for our tendencies toward vice, involving disharmony between reason and desire as well as nearer goods competing with more important ones for our attention. This explanation, like the theological one above, has the advantage of retaining the attractiveness of goodness—it's just that nearer goods, even if lesser, can have a stronger pull. And maybe I've just been reading Aristotle for too long, but that sounds right to me: what attracts us about anything is some good we see in it, and if we can train ourselves (and our kids and our students) to prefer the higher good to the nearer one, we'll reliably imitate virtue rather than even the most exciting vice.[46]

Last question: What do our responses to Questions 1–4 imply regarding real-life issues like moral education, evangelization, and how we categorize each other? While there are probably more implications than I can even wave a hand at, let me mention a few especially salient ones, limiting the domain to Christianity and Christian virtue.

Working my way through the questions, it seems to me that the transitivity of imitation may have direct implications for how we approach evangelization. If following moral exemplars who follow Jesus is sufficient for being Christian (even in those who have no or negative beliefs regarding Jesus and/or Christianity), then there seems little reason to persuade disciples of Mother Teresa or Martin Luther King of the merits of Christian discipleship. On the other hand, if the old saying that "God has no grandchildren" is correct, then following even the greatest of saints doesn't make one a Christian. If that's the case, then (assuming Christian is a desirable thing to be) it's worth our time to encourage others to explicitly embrace Christianity rather than remain simply followers of followers.[47]

But that's not to say that indirect imitation is not also worthwhile. Even if it doesn't make one a Christian, such imitation can help one exemplify Christian virtues, which is a great thing in itself. For example, Noah Levinson, my interviewee who (partly) emulates Mother Teresa, is Jewish; that didn't deter him from working with her, admiring her, and being inspired by her compassion and generosity. But it also didn't lead him to endorse all of her specific methods—or all of her theological beliefs. Further, it seems even unconscious, implicit imitation could help bring about Christian-like virtues in those of other faiths or no faith.[48] And, if Pascal was right,[49] acting like a Christian can predispose one toward belief in Christianity. If that's true, it could mean that following a saint's example can make one a Christian after all—but this time in a causal rather than definitional sense of "make."

Regarding the second question, a Christian had better not say that an exemplar can be "too good" to imitate, since that would rule out imitating Jesus. (And, among other catastrophic effects of that conclusion, children of the 90s would have to throw out those "WWJD" wristbands.) I think both methods I proposed for emulating extraordinary exemplars could apply here: Christians can start by emulating more ordinary role models and work their way up to emulating Jesus himself, or they can render him more accessible by familiarizing themselves with his story.

Regarding Question 3, the dependence of the attraction of moral charisma on the "attractee" as well as on the attractor seems to apply to Christian moral exemplars like great saints and even Jesus himself as much as it applies to any other exemplar. This phenomenon has obvious implications for effective religious education and transmission: it will involve presenting Jesus in a way that (1) is accurate and (2) the intended audience perceives as charismatic. Missionaries bringing the message of Christianity to new cultures and peoples have taken great pains to do this sort of thing; similar methods may be increasingly needed within our own cultures. (With other Christian exemplars, such as saints, the task may be easier—one can simply present the exemplars s/he thinks the audience will find most appealing.)

And finally, regarding the question about our aptness to imitate vice, I'm fairly confident in my Aristotelian belief that the good really is what we all seek. But I'm also painfully aware that lesser goods like pleasure and ease abound and manage to compete successfully with greater ones: as with gravity, the force of the pull depends on both the "mass" of the good and its proximity to us. So, while our attraction to virtue is real, it is also fragile.

That brings us full circle to (what I think is) the great joint task in moral education for philosophers, theologians, and psychologists to identify exemplars and position them and their virtues in the places they can best influence people—and to *be* the sorts of people worth imitating. Because I think one of the best ways to cultivate virtuous mimetic desire is through stories, let me illustrate by closing with the true story of one exemplar's influence on me.

Case Study: Gloria Lewis Vargas

Like many academics, I deal primarily with theories. I tend to hold practical truths at a distance, treating them as abstract objects of analysis rather than concrete processes to follow. (This tendency drives my engineer husband nuts. It would probably drive Aristotle nuts too—he taught that the "conclusion" of a practical argument is not an abstract statement but an action.) When I encounter good advice in a sermon, magazine article, or radio show, my first instinct isn't to take it but to think, "Yeah, people should do that"— and maybe later, if I'm especially reflective or lucky, it sinks in that *I'm* the one who should do that.

The thing about real people, though, is that they don't easily lend themselves to abstraction; they're undeniably concrete. Their stories tend to stick with an otherwise hopeless abstractionist like me, to soak in. And exemplars' stories might even have a fighting chance of getting me to *do* something—to emulate their protagonists in some small way. That didn't happen with regard to all of my exemplar interviewees, which probably says more about my intractability than their virtue. But it did happen with a few, including one who, although we still haven't met in person, has become a dear friend.

Gloria Lewis Vargas grew up in abject poverty in Barbados. (Decades after emigrating, she still speaks with a lovely Caribbean accent.) Although she loved her family and tight-knit community, she dreamed of living in the US— where, as she'd learned from watching a neighbor's tiny black-and-white TV, everyone lived in luxury. Surprisingly, as a young single mom, she received a marriage proposal from a US citizen. But instead of settling into her dream home and exploring her new environment in a fancy car, she waited alone all day in a cramped apartment to see whether her husband would come home— and when he did, he was often drunk, high, and/or abusive. And although her husband promised to change his ways if she had a baby with him, he didn't even show up for the birth.

Soon after that, Gloria gave up any hope of saving her marriage; instead, she focused on providing a safe environment for her two sons. She left her husband and took multiple low-wage jobs to make ends meet, eventually settling in Fort Lauderdale, Florida, and working as a waitress. She later married one of her customers—a younger man recently released from prison and struggling with anger issues. Shortly after that, her older son, who had moved back to Barbados to live with his grandparents, got into trouble and was imprisoned. (Although US prisons aren't nice places, Gloria tells me the ones in Barbados are much worse.)

This is where you'd expect Gloria's life story to spiral into something unimaginably awful—at least if this essay weren't about moral charisma. So how did she go from such a dire situation to being a recognized ethical rock star? Well, the way she tells it, when she was at her lowest point, a friend advised her to start watching Christian TV. She gave her heart to Jesus in the classic evangelical way, and her husband soon followed suit.

With considerable effort, they worked through his anger issues. With a lot of prayer (but no money for bail), her son was eventually released from prison and went on to become a responsible husband and father. And Gloria felt called to do more. As she says:

> I looked at all of my missteps, all that I've been through, at so many people around me in the same situation, and there was always this calling on my life that I had to do something to make a difference. I would stay up until two or three in the morning writing letters. I didn't know what I was supposed to do, but I had to do something. I wrote over one hundred letters to the media, to churches, to politicians, to public figures. Nobody would answer. I kept looking to people to make that move. I kept looking for the circumstances to line up in order for me to get to the next step. It still wasn't lining up.
>
> And then I told my husband, "We've got to go feed the homeless." And my husband kept saying, "We can't feed us; why do you want to feed the homeless?" I said, "You don't understand. I have to do this—this is not me. What is in me is stronger than me, and I can't get it to go away. I have to do this." And so, he said, "Okay, let's go."[50]

And so, just like that, they started feeding folks on the streets of Fort Lauderdale. They started with 20 meals one Sunday. That wasn't enough, so they brought 40 the next week. Then 60, then 80. As of the last time I asked her, they were bringing 200 meals, two days a week, cooked and packaged in their own kitchen by Gloria's family and a few volunteers. Fittingly, she calls her tiny organization Care in Action USA.

There are dozens of amazing stories I could tell you about Gloria. How she'll hand her last five dollars to anyone who seems to need it more than she does. How she freely gives out her cell number to random people on the street if they need someone to talk to. How she'll help people find a job—and then clothes (often from her own closet) to wear to work and a bicycle to get there. How she put up a family of six in a hotel for months while she raised money to get them permanent housing. How she "doesn't need sleep" and works around the clock to minister to people. How she refused to seek medical treatment for severe burns she suffered to her face and neck because her "brothers and sisters in the street" were expecting her.

Instead of telling all of those stories, though, let me tell you about Gloria's unique brand of moral charisma: her knack for getting people, from homeless gang members to hopeless academics, to stop and listen. As her son Cedric describes the phenomenon, "Mom, when you talk, people get stuck." Here's one example:

> Just recently I met a guy that was struggling. He was going to kill somebody, or somebody was going to kill him. I had stuff to do, but I

listened, and I said, "Stop." And he was a gang member, and he was like, "You don't understand." And I said, "Stop. Don't kill somebody if somebody is threatening you. You don't have to react. Is it worth your life? Is it worth going to prison? Do you want that on your head? Listen to me, you can't be responsible for what that person does, but you're responsible for your actions, and that's what God holds us accountable to. Go and give it to God and leave it right there."

And the guy actually listened to her! As he told her later, "When I was looking at you, I wanted to tell you to get out of my face and shut up. This little woman is telling me what to do? I was in gangs, and I have no problem picking up a gun, and this little woman is going to tell me how to live my life? But something about you kept me here, and I shut my mouth and I listened." True to form, she gave him her number; and when the rival gang approached, he called her. She told him again not to retaliate, even if they attacked. So, he sat silently as they stood over him. But no one attacked; after a while, they just walked away.

Reflecting on that very story, Gloria proceeded to get me "stuck" with a short rant on the dangers of overthinking:

[The gang member] says, "I heard about God, and people told me these things, but I *see* God through you and your husband and your son. You guys do what I see nobody do." I tell him, "It's not about us; it's about what we have in our heart."

Addressing me, she added:

We let our head control our heart. Instead of doing what your heart tells you to do, we let it go to our head, and then our head puts in all of these different reasons why we shouldn't do what the heart says. That last five dollars you got in your pocket that the homeless person is begging, your head is saying, "He's a drug addict. He's just going to take my money and go do drugs. I need my five dollars." You've got ten different reasons why you aren't supposed to give it to him. But you can't give me one reason that says, "He actually might be hungry. It is not my business; God is the judge. Let me just give him this five dollars. What he does is not about me. I'm going to do what my heart tells me to do, which is to give him that five dollars." And you know, this guy [I was telling you about], believe it or not, he was on the street, and then we had him in our backyard in a tent, and we've got him in a trailer home now. In less than two weeks.[51]

Gloria's comment keeps coming back to haunt me. As a philosopher, I'm pretty sold on the value of reason; I think using it is generally a good way to discern our ethical duties. But I can't deny the futility of *just* thinking about such things—practical truths are meant to be acted upon. And, as most of us have probably experienced, overthinking really *is* detrimental to the life of virtue. Surely, it's better to act on approximations than to think with precision but miss the opportunity to do something. (And after decades of habituation, Gloria's heart is probably a more reliable guide than my head anyway.)

Gloria gets my students "stuck" too—even a room full of undergraduate seniors taking their last required course, and even though she's exceptionally preachy, freely dishing out unsolicited advice and using "the Bible says" several times per paragraph. As one otherwise-cynical student reported, "Unlike anything else we've talked about in this [ethics] class, she actually makes me want to be a better person." She has the same effect on me.

So, back to the 90s, when we used to ask ourselves what Jesus would do: well, sometimes I really do find myself asking, "What would Gloria do?" Not that she's a better exemplar than Jesus, of course, but I often have a better guess as to how she'd act. For example, if there is someone begging just outside my nice conference hotel, I can be confident she'd give him a little food or money. If I'm busy but someone looks sad, I can be sure she'd stop and offer a listening ear.

Now, Gloria is the first to say that we're not all called to do exactly what she does. But we all can (and she thinks we all should) follow her lead in empathizing with and helping people instead of judging them, in being willing to sacrifice our trivial interests for the vital interests of others, and in treating everyone with love and dignity. Here's what she told my students in a recent honors seminar on moral heroes:

> We're all created different, and we all have something that God put in us that he needs in the world. It's gonna be very hard to do what I do, if you're trying to do something that you weren't created to do. You're gonna burn out … So, somebody might be a speaker, somebody might like to help people, somebody might like elderly people. You got to find what it is that's inside you that God put in there, and that's where you need to go.

That's advice even an academic might be able to take.[52]

Notes

1 Stalnaker (2006), 17.
2 Ibid., 17–18.
3 A personal note before I proceed; I'm not sure whether to label it a "disclaimer" or a "credential": In my own religious tradition (Catholicism), we take the connection between exemplars, imitation, and spiritual formation to be perfectly obvious. Imitation not only of Jesus Christ but also of admired saints whose particular *way* of following Jesus resonates with our own interests, personalities, and vocations is commonplace—you might even say it's how we've always done things. While that's served me well on a practical level (e.g., joining the lay Franciscans has helped me counter my tendencies toward pride and over-intellectualizing the spiritual life), it has made writing as a philosopher about such topics oddly difficult:

Not having a good feel for what seems obvious to those from other backgrounds, I'm left wondering whether I've pitched my explanations at too remedial a level or left gaps in them. Although I've done my best to avoid both infelicities, I apologize in advance for any instances that remain.

4 Ivanhoe (2000), ix–x.
5 Ibid., xiii.
6 For more on the "moral portraiture" of Confucius and other exemplars in the *Analects*, see Olberding (2011).
7 Confucius (2003), 2.1. Hereafter cited in-text.
8 *Junzi*, translated "gentleman" here, roughly means "virtuous person"; a "petty person" is a not-so-virtuous person.
9 Aristotle, Nicomachean Ethics, I.1.
10 Aristotle, (1994–2000), II.11.
11 Kristjánsson (2007), 105–06.
12 Ibid., 106.
13 Wolf (1982).
14 Carbonell (2009), 376.
15 Ibid., 380.
16 Zagzebski (2010); Zagzebski (2017).
17 Kidd (2019), 378.
18 Giebel (2021). Exemplars and their attractiveness can be found throughout the book; for my account of role modeling, both in general and in the life of a particular moral exemplar, see Chapter 11.
19 See, e.g., Mark 1:16–20 and 2:14.
20 "Charism" is the Greek word for "gift" used in the New Testament; these "charismatic gifts" are emphasized more in some Christian circles than others.
21 See, e.g., this news story from shortly after the film was released: https://www.wnd.com/2004/03/23966/.
22 Matthew 11:29, New American Bible (NAB).
23 von Balthasar (1982), 229.
24 For a helpful analysis comparing von Balthasar's approach with Confucianism, including an expansion of this point, see Harrison 2020).
25 Aristotle, *Poetics* IV (Internet Classics Archive).
26 See, e.g., Bandura, Ross, and Ross (1961).
27 See Vahedi (2020), 402.
28 Ibid., 403.
29 Colby and Damon (1992). The details of their selection process are in Chapter 2 and in Appendix A.
30 Damon and Colby (2015).
31 See, e.g., Walker and Frimer (2007).
32 Han, Kim, Jeong, and Cohen (2017).
33 Han and Dawson (2023).
34 See, e.g., Haidt (2000).
35 Kristjánsson (2006).
36 Colby and Damon (1992), 175, emphasis original.
37 Ibid., 177–78.
38 Noah Levinson, life story interview with the author. For more of Levinson's story, see Chapters 11 and 12 of *Ethical Excellence*.
39 Luke 24:13–35. Yes, his resurrected body probably looked different; and yes, people who die normally stay dead. But *still*.
40 See, e.g., Chartrand van Baaren (2009) and Leighton, Bird, Orsini, and Heyes (2010).
41 This progression, it seems to me, parallels those in other spheres of life. For example, as we progress in our careers, the people we once regarded with something like awe turn out to be ordinary colleagues, and the roles they fill turn out to be ones we're comfortable occupying.

42 I thank Tim O'Reilly for raising this question.
43 One might even claim a bit of philosophical support for this position of neutral-ity from the very theories of virtue ethics I've been using to support the special attractiveness of virtue: as I noted earlier, the Confucian word for moral charisma or "virtue," *dé*, can also refer to power or influence generally. And, though it's a bit old-fashioned, we can even use "virtue" in a similar way in English, as in the false statement, "I was able to finish my grading by virtue of my impressive time-management skills."
44 See, e.g., Girard (2004).
45 Wilson (2019).
46 As I wrote elsewhere, the higher good can be a tough sell in today's market: for example, a recent ethics student asked me with a touch of horror, "What would the world be like if we were all fully virtuous?" See Giebel (2022).
47 The apostle Paul seems to fall into this latter camp, saying in 1 Corinthians 3, though in another context, that one shouldn't worry about being "of Paul" or "of Apollo" or "of Cephas" but only of Christ.
48 By "Christian virtues," here I mean those virtues—like humility and kindness—that are extolled by Christianity. I'm not referring to infused/theological virtues, which aren't supposed to be "caught" by imitation at all. See Aquinas (1920), pt. I–II, q. 62.
49 See Pascal's famous "wager" in Section III of his *Pensees*. For a contemporary analysis and defense of the wager, see Rota (2016).
50 This quote also appears in (2021), 119.
51 Part of this quote also appears in (2022), 82–83.
52 I am grateful to Kendall Cotton Bronk, Stephen Davis, Thomas Jay Oord, Timo-thy Reilly, Brother John Baptist Santa Ana, James van Slyke, and Eric Yang for their insightful comments on a previous draft of this essay.

References

Aquinas, Thomas. 1920. *Summa Theologiae*, translated by Fathers of the English Dominican Province, pt. I–II, q. 62, https://www.newadvent.org/summa/2062.htm
Aristotle, *Nicomachean Ethics*, bk. I, chap. 1, translated by W. D. Ross, Internet Classics Archive, https://classics.mit.edu/Aristotle/nicomachaen.html.
Aristotle. 1994–2000. *Rhetoric*, bk. II, chap. 11, translated by W. Rhys Roberts, Internet Classics Archive, http://classics.mit.edu/Aristotle/rhetoric.html
Bandura, A., D. Ross, and S. A. Ross. 1961. "Transmission of Aggression through the Imitation of Aggressive Models." *Journal of Abnormal and Social Psychology* 63: 575–82.
Carbonell, Vanessa. 2009. "What Moral Saints Look Like." *Canadian Journal of Philosophy* 39, no. 3: 371–98.
Chartrand, T. L., and R. van Baaren. 2009. "Human Mimicry." *Advances in Experimental Social Psychology* 41: 219–74.
Damon, William and Anne Colby. 2015. *The Power of Ideals: The Real Story of Moral Choice*. New York, NY: Oxford University Press.
Colby, Anne, and William Damon. 1992. *Some Do Care: Contemporary Lives of Moral Commitment*. New York, NY: Free Press.
Confucius. 2003. *Analects, with Selections from Traditional Commentaries*, translated by Edward Slingerland. Indianapolis, IN: Hackett. 2.1.
Giebel, Heidi M. 2021. *Ethical Excellence: Philosophers, Psychologists, and Real-Life Exemplars Show Us How to Achieve It*. Washington DC: CUA Press.
Giebel, Heidi M. 2022. "Living Saints and Virtue Ethics: Is Being 'Too Good' Bad for Us?" *Logos* 25, no. 2: 72–92.
Girard, René. 2004. "Violence and Religion: Cause or Effect?" *The Hedgehog Review* 6, no. 1: 8–20.

Haidt, Jonathan. 2000. "The Positive Emotion of Elevation." *Prevention and Treatment* 3, no. 3: 1–5.

Han, Hyemin, and Kelsie J. Dawson. 2023. "Relatable and Attainable Moral Exemplars as Sources for Moral Elevation and Pleasantness." *Journal of Moral Education*. DOI: 10.1080/03057240.2023.2173158.

Han, Hyemin, Jeongmin Kim, Changwoo Jeong, and Geoffrey L. Cohen. 2017. "Attainable and Relevant Moral Exemplars Are More Effective than Extraordinary Exemplars in Promoting Voluntary Service Engagement." *Frontiers in Psychology* 8: 283.

Harrison, Victoria S. 2020. "Exemplar Reasoning as a Tool for Constructive Conversation between Confucians and Catholics." In *Confucianism and Catholicism: Reinvigorating the Dialogue*, edited by M. R. Slater, E. M. Cline, and P. J. Ivanhoe, 172–89, Notre Dame, IN: University of Notre Dame Press.

Ivanhoe, Philip J. 2000. *Confucian Moral Self-Cultivation*, ix–x, Indianapolis, IN: Hackett.

Kidd, Ian J. 2019. "Admiration, Attraction and the Aesthetics of Exemplarity." *Journal of Moral Education* 48, no. 3: 369–380.

Kristjánsson, Kristján. 2006. "Emulation and the Use of Role Models in Moral Education." *Journal of Moral Education* 35: 37–49.

Kristjánsson, Kristján. 2007. *Aristotle, Emotions, and Education*, 105–106, Hampshire, UK: Ashgate.

Leighton, J., G. Bird, C. Orsini, and C. M. Heyes. 2010. "Social Attitudes Modulate Automatic Imitation." *Journal of Experimental Social Psychology* 46: 905–10.

New American Bible (NAB), Revised Edition, edited and translated by the United States Conference of Catholic Bishops, 2019. https://www.usccb.org/offices/new-american-bible/books-bible.

Olberding, Amy. 2011. *Moral Exemplars in the Analects: The Good Person Is That.* New York: Routledge.

Rota, Michael. 2016. *Taking Pascal's Wager: Faith, Evidence, and the Abundant Life.* Downer's Grove, IL: IVP Academic.

Stalnaker, Aaron. 2006. *Overcoming Our Evil: Spiritual Exercises in Xunzi and Augustine.* Washington DC: Georgetown University Press.

Vahedi, Zahra. 2020. "Social Learning Theory/Social Cognitive Theory." In *The Wiley Encyclopedia of Personality and Individual Differences: Models and Theories*, vol. 1, edited by B. J. Carducci and C. S. Nave, 401–05, New York, NY: Wiley & Sons.

von Balthasar, Hans Urs. 1982. *The Glory of the Lord: A Theological Aesthetics*, vol. 1: *Seeing the Form*, Edinburgh: T. and T. Clark.

Walker, Lawrence J., and Jeremy A. Frimer. 2007. "Moral Personality of Brave and Caring Exemplars." *Journal of Personality and Social Psychology* 93, no. 5: 845–60.

Wilson, Jessica H. 2019. "The Unoriginal Augustine." *Notre Dame Church Life Journal*.

Wolf, Susan. 1982. "Moral Saints." *Journal of Philosophy* 79, no. 8: 419–39.

Zagzebski, Linda. 2010. "Exemplarist Virtue Theory." *Metaphilosophy* 41, no. 1–2: 41–57.

Zagzebski, Linda. 2017. *Exemplarist Moral Theory.* New York, NY: Oxford University Press.

2 Exemplar Communities and Moral Formation

Aaron D. Cobb

Introduction

Moral heroes capture our attention and admiration. Their lives display exceptional goodness—the kind of goodness many of us wish we could emulate. They are models of excellence in conduct and character, often displayed in the most difficult circumstances. They demonstrate extraordinary commitment in their response to concerns at the heart of virtue. Although reflection upon exemplars has an ancient pedigree, there has been a resurgence of scholarly interest in moral heroes in the disciplines of philosophy and psychology.[1] One noteworthy feature of these discussions is that they focus almost exclusively on the individual moral exemplar.[2] This individualistic understanding of exemplars, however valuable, is unnecessarily restrictive. Individuals are not the only subjects capable of moral excellence; there are morally exceptional social groups that deserve our attention and admiration.

In this chapter, I argue that studying exemplar communities can serve important pedagogical functions in the project of moral formation and character development. I illustrate these points through a consideration of the *L'Arche* communities, a network of over 140 homes dedicated to fostering relationships of mutual love and care between individuals with significant disabilities (core members) and their caregivers (assistants).[3] These communities seek to cultivate deep and abiding relationships within a common life where each person is committed to responding to others' vulnerabilities and needs.[4] I characterize their exemplarity as an expression of the virtue of hospitality.[5] This virtue involves a shared commitment to providing a space of *welcome and belonging* for individuals with profound disabilities—an ethos that stands in stark contrast to the indifference, disregard, exclusion, rejection, and hostility the disabled so often experience in contemporary society. Hospitable communities offer a portrait of how to address the substantive moral task of caring for those whose lives are marked by profound disability or impairment.[6]

The structure of the chapter is as follows. In part two, I provide a brief sketch of some of the pedagogical functions attributed to reflection upon the lives of exemplars. Then, I provide an extended discussion

DOI: 10.4324/9781032648392-4

of *L'Arche*, reflecting on the general structures of these communities. In part three, I develop a sketch of the virtue of hospitality and its opposing vices. Then, I consider how *L'Arche* communities exhibit this virtue through their shared lives together. Finally, in part four, I consider how appeals to *L'Arche* can serve important pedagogical functions in the formation of moral character.

L'Arche as an Exemplar Community

As a pedagogical tool, appeals to exemplars contribute to moral formation and character development in crucial ways.[7] Several recent scholars, including Michael Lamb, Jonathan Brant, and Edward Brooks, point to five characteristic functions of these appeals.[8] First, engagement with the lives of exemplars can motivate growth in virtue. They observe, "by embodying particular virtues, value, and ideals, exemplars offer role models to admire and emulate, which … can elevate our moral vision, increase our motivation, and inspire us to emulate the actions, attitudes, or character of those we admire" (2021, 88). Second, these appeals can provide action guidance by helping us to "imagine how an exemplary person *would* act in a similar situation, which can help us discern how we should act" (ibid.). Third, reflection on exemplars can deepen our understanding concerning the nature of the virtues, especially as they are realized in concrete circumstances. Fourth, exemplars show us that virtue is possible even when circumstances make its exercise exceptionally demanding. They note that their lives "supply moral reminders that make norms salient and offer concrete, living proof that abstract ideals or virtues are actually possible to embody or attain" (ibid.). Fifth, and finally, they contend that exemplars can help to train our capacities for moral perception and imagination, enabling us to see our situations in new ways and creatively think through how we might seek to realize virtue.

  In addition to these uses, appeals to exemplars can impress upon students a *rationale* for pursuing virtue. This is because the lives of exemplars often provide an attractive and inspiring portrait of a community's vision of what it means to live well. Rehearsing the stories of exemplars conveys an account of the intrinsic connections between living virtuously and living a fulfilling human life. Thus, the practice of appealing to exemplars can be a form of catechesis in what it means to flourish as a human.[9]

  The central aim of this chapter is to show that appeals to exemplar communities can serve similar pedagogical functions in motivating moral growth, deepening understanding of virtue, and helping to foster a sense of the connections between virtue and flourishing. To illustrate these claims, I focus on the *L'Arche* communities. Within these communities, the core members include individuals with a range of intellectual disabilities (often accompanied by physical impairments). In most cases, core members do not have family to assist in their care. Assistants commit to live communally with core members, cultivating relationships of mutual care and concern. Assistants provide care for the physical needs and impairments of core members; they receive care for their own emotional, psychological, and spiritual vulnerabilities.

Each local community is governed by the official *L'Arche* charter, which expresses its aim to "welcome people who have intellectual disabilities" in order to address the suffering caused by the inhospitality of the surrounding culture.[10] These homes seek to give those with intellectual disabilities "a valid place in society," a place where they "belong at the very heart of their communities" and can express their "particular gifts." As an orienting concern, *L'Arche* seeks to develop "covenantal relationships between people of differing intellectual capacity, social origin, religion and culture."[11] And through these relationships, they hope to be "a sign that a society to be truly human, must be founded on welcome and respect for the weak and downtrodden." When these communities fulfill their charter, they create space for the cultivation and maintenance of relationships characterized by deep, loving concern—relationships that both core members and their assistants experience as crucial to their own flourishing. *L'Arche* communities are committed to the dignity of each person in their community as well as the fundamental rights to life, care, shelter, education, and meaningful work. Assistants seek to address core members as companions and teachers in their own spiritual journeys and moral development.

The daily work and routines of each *L'Arche* community reflect the specific needs and concerns of those living together. Assistants work with core members to complete chores and tasks crucial to the function of the homes in which they live. They ensure that core members get to and from their various places of work, either within the home or the surrounding community. Each home is embedded within a local neighborhood so that those with disabilities are not isolated from society and invisible to those whose lives are not marked by the same kinds of impairments. Local *L'Arche* leadership seeks to ensure that assistants receive spiritual direction as well as the support of local volunteers and partners in their work. They work together, eat communally, and pray together.

Assistants come from a range of backgrounds. Their work is not lucrative. Generally, their compensation consists of shelter, food, and meager stipends. Assistants typically commit to living within a community for at least one year. This makes it more likely that they will be able to develop and foster stable and enduring relationships with core members. The sudden departure of an assistant can cause deep hurt to both core members and other assistants who have extended their trust and friendship. For individuals whose lives are often marked by rejection and social isolation, this kind of relational fracture can be very difficult to heal. Given this potential harm, a year-long commitment is important to the stability of the community. Some assistants live within these communities for many years beyond their initial commitment.

There is a body of research concerning *L'Arche* assistants, much of it focused on the ways these communities transform and shape individual character.[12] One of the key emphases in discussions of these communities is the extent to which assistants construe core members as their teachers and companions in personal development. Assistants often describe how core members help them to discover and address deep psychological and spiritual wounds that characterize their lives. In many ways, their psychological vulnerabilities mirror the physical vulnerabilities of the core members. Through the relationships and friendships that develop in these contexts, assistants and core members find resources to grow, heal, and deepen their love and concern for others.[13]

Although these homes are not able to provide care for many individuals, they offer distinct advantages in the intimacy of their care and the relationships formed among core members and assistants. They offer a portrait of a kind of care that can address the deep human needs within a community. They do not merely address pressing physical and biological frailties; they tend to human needs of belonging, friendship, and growth within the community. These homes bear witness to the value and gifts of those with intellectual disabilities and offer an ethos in which core members and their assistants can find deep personal fulfillment.

L'Arche and the Virtue of Hospitality

L'Arche communities are *hospitable communities*—they embody and express the virtue of hospitality.[14] Within traditions that recognize hospitality as a value, it has often been characterized in terms of its behavioral dimensions— that is, the activity of welcoming and providing for strangers who are in need. The term "strangers" is a term of art, referring to those who are vulnerable because of their lack of inclusion within and protection from a community. As a result of this exclusion, the stranger lacks both the resources sufficient to meet important needs and the standing to call upon the broader community for aid. The hospitable person makes the effort to welcome the stranger into a communal space to address their needs.

Although this behavioral description of hospitality is valuable, an analysis of a virtue of hospitality must do more than describe the characteristic activities of welcoming the stranger. As a virtue, hospitality is a disposition to fulfill the tasks of a *host*, but it involves more than this. There are affective, motivational, cognitive, and relational dimensions to the expression of the virtue of hospitality. It involves sensitivity and attentiveness to the vulnerabilities associated with estrangement. The hospitable person feels these needs as a summons he ought to address. This virtue transforms how a person perceives or construes those who are estranged from the community. They are not objects to be pitied; they are potential guests worthy of invitation, respect, care, and relationship. Additionally, in responding to the summons to host, the hospitable person opens himself to a relationship characterized by mutuality and reciprocity.[15] He is receptive to the gifts he receives in welcoming the guest.

It is instructive to contrast the virtue of hospitality with several opposing vices. As vices, these are patterns or habits of entrenched or dispositional inhospitality toward strangers.[16] Here, we might recognize two vices of deficiency: *hostility* and the inhospitality of *indifference*. *Hostility* involves an entrenched disposition to reject the stranger. The hostile person fails to see the stranger as a potential guest worthy of protection and care. He feels no attendant sense of responsibility to address their needs. Instead, he is disposed to keep the stranger outside. At the most extreme, he may even display a willingness to exercise violence against the stranger. He construes the stranger as an enemy. The inhospitality of *indifference* involves a lack of concern for strangers rather than an enmity toward them. Habitual or dispositional *indifference* involves a characteristic failure to perceive or be moved by the stranger's vulnerability. His needs fail to register as salient or worthy of regard. As a result, the indifferent person fails to respond; he has a settled habit of being unmoved by the need for welcome. His entrenched indifference to these needs results in a closed-off stance and an unwillingness to open himself to relationship with a stranger.

I've articulated a short profile of the virtue of hospitality and its opposing vices in terms of the individual person. But the purpose of this chapter is to look at exemplar communities and the ways they may collectively display the virtue of hospitality. For this reason, I need to augment this sketch to show how particular communities can manifest the virtue of hospitality. I propose that a hospitable community is one that devotes itself to a common project of hospitable welcome.[17] Participation in a common project characteristically involves shared attentiveness to the needs of strangers, a joint concern to address vulnerabilities rooted in their lack of standing, and coordinated activities aimed at receiving them into a common space where their needs can be met within the context of shared relationships. Participating in a common project of this sort is a commitment to a shared endeavor to welcome the guest fully into a community. The community opens itself to the guest because of a recognition of the individual's inherent value and need for care. A common project of this kind is more likely if enough members of the community care properly for this shared endeavor. When enough of the community commit to this project, they contribute to a common endeavor through integrated and coordinated efforts to address needs.[18]

The care *L'Arche* communities offer is a clear example of shared hospitable concern. The communal structure of these homes is a portrait of the kind of giving and receiving crucial to welcoming the stranger. The care they provide prioritizes the human needs of belonging and friendship for every individual within the community. These communities are dispositionally attuned to need, and they seek to find ways to ensure that they meet these needs together. Through their dedicated care for the needs of those with significant disabilities, assistants offer a portrait of what it means to attend to and care for the vulnerabilities of those with disabilities. And in the experience of friendship with core members, assistants receive love and care crucial to their own personal development. Communities characterized by hospitality tend to cultivate in their members a greater sensitivity to the scope and presence of need in their midst. In this way, they are likely to create dispositions for compassion and kindness in their members.

When one compares the ethos of the welcome and belonging characteristic of *L'Arche* to the kinds of treatment and reception individuals with physical and intellectual disabilities often experience in society at large, it brings the extraordinary hospitality of *L'Arche* into stark relief.[19] There are many communities that display open *hostility* toward the disabled. Their hostility disposes them to refuse care or to look for ways to immunize themselves from any sense of responsibility for tending to their needs. They actively seek to remove themselves from any context where they would be forced to share space or resources with those who are radically dependent. They look down upon those with disabilities as pitiable, construing their lives as deficient, lacking in value, and meaningless. Other communities may not be openly hostile, but they may be *indifferent* to the needs they perceive. They may recognize the profound needs and acknowledge the disabled as worthy recipients of care, but they fail to see themselves as summoned to welcome them, to tend to their needs, to share in relationship, and to be transformed by this encounter.

The Pedagogical Functions of Appeals to Exemplar Communities

We are now in a good position to consider whether appeals to communities like *L'Arche* can serve important pedagogical functions in character education. In what remains, I will focus on four potential uses of these appeals. First, studies of exemplar communities can draw attention to truths about the nature of the virtues as they are manifested within and through a community. In particular, communities like *L'Arche* offer a portrait of how we can better respond to substantive moral tasks associated with care for those with severe disabilities. This care goes beyond addressing physical needs. The welcome and belonging individuals experience in these communities involves attunement and responsiveness to both physical and social needs, especially common human needs of recognition, acknowledgment, love, belonging, and value within a community. Reflecting on the *hospitable community* also shows us how often our own communities fail to display the kinds of welcome we could provide. Reflecting on *L'Arche* can help us to see the subtle ways in which our communities display hostility, indifference, or disregard to those who are vulnerable because they are outside the protection of a community. As a result, we may come to appreciate how we might grow as a community through the expression of hospitable welcome.

Second, reflecting on normative dimensions of exemplary communities can help us to understand what it means to respond well to moral needs, especially those that can be addressed adequately only through the collective efforts of communities. One of the chief values of appealing to communal exemplars is to draw the student's attention to the ways communities address moral tasks together. Individually virtuous people often lack the capacity to address broad-scale needs. In cases where the needs outstrip the capacities of individuals, they can see clearly how social groups can work jointly to achieve great moral goods. Appeals to exemplar communities can move learners to recognize the need to act in concert with others to respond to moral needs effectively. Attending to the ways a community can address these kinds of needs as part of a shared endeavor can keep individuals from despairing the inability to address profound needs alone.

Third, studying exemplar communities can reveal traits crucial to promoting and maintaining flourishing within a community. Our study of the *hospitable community* offers important insights concerning human interdependence and its connection to our flourishing. *L'Arche* offers a portrait of the kinds of welcome and belonging that are the foundation for the development of communities that meet the basic need for deep and abiding relationships of mutual care and concern. And this form of community shows how individuals with a diverse range of abilities can cultivate relationships of trust, security, and belonging. Within the context of a common life together, both core members and assistants' needs—physical, emotional, and spiritual—receive the care and attention they deserve. And through these relationships, they can find deep meaning and significance.

Studying the exemplarity displayed by *L'Arche* communities also reveals to us the goods we might not otherwise be able to see. Close study of *L'Arche*, for instance, trains our focus on the goods of belonging and friendship between individuals with diverse mental abilities. The way assistants at *L'Arche* care for the physical needs of core members within their communities is only a small part of the exemplarity of this community. There is a deeper form of goodness these communities display—that is, the ways assistant and core members cultivate relationships of mutual love and concern is vital to their shared personal formation and flourishing. Reflecting on these communities enables us to see a good that we might have missed if it weren't for the presence of these exemplary communities.

Reflection upon exemplary communities can also reveal aspects of human fulfillment we may fail to recognize because they challenge prevailing conceptions of the components of human flourishing. The presence of individuals with significant cognitive impairments and profound needs may make life within these communities especially difficult. But these communities offer a compelling vision of the nature of fulfillment within community. The community itself offers a picture of the kinds of joy and beauty one can find in a culture that welcomes rather than isolates and institutionalizes those with significant cognitive disabilities. So, reflection on exemplar communities can challenge prevailing conceptions of the kinds of communal life that are genuinely fulfilling.

Fourth, and finally, appeals to social exemplars can inspire individual and collective development toward the ideals exhibited within these communities. Consider how our admiration for communities like *L'Arche* can induce within us a desire to cultivate the kinds of virtues we see manifested in their exemplary care. Our study of *L'Arche* can create a desire to become more like these groups. We see in these communities a pattern to which we could aspire in the life of our own communities. We feel drawn to cultivate communal ways of responding properly to the needs of others within our field of care and concern. And this may include individuals who are currently strangers to us—that is, individuals who are not bound to us by any personal bond. We see in *hospitable communities* a picture of the kinds of value one can promote by opening our community and our lives to friendship with vulnerable individuals. And the beauty of what we see instills within us the desire to become the kind of community that can reflect these kinds of commitments and concerns.

Our attraction to these communities may lead us to desire to emulate the qualities of these communities in our individual lives as well. The motivational connection between admiration and emulation in this context is more complicated than in the case of admiration for individual exemplars. To the extent that the community manifests a quality that has an individual analog, our admiration for the community may induce a deeper desire to inculcate this quality. So, for instance, if I admire the ways *L'Arche* expresses hospitality for those with profound disabilities, it can motivate me to seek to be a more hospitable person in my individual engagements with others.

But if the object of my admiration concerns a relational quality of the community—that is, a quality I cannot possess or manifest individually—then my desire to emulate the community must incorporate a desire for the types of relationships that make this community admirable. For example, I may admire a community like *L'Arche* because of the ways in which core members and their assistants cultivate spaces of belonging and welcome together. In this case, my admiration and respect can inspire me to seek out communities characterized by these traits or move me to call my own community toward a commitment to be more welcoming. Belonging to a community characterized by hospitable relations of this sort may become a focal object of my desire. Even if I cannot individually bring it about that I belong to a community of this kind, I can commit to the work of building a community characterized by this kind of commitment to others.

There is another element concerning the motivational power of these appeals to candidate exemplar communities worth noting in this context. Moral emotions like admiration and respect are socially embedded; a person's community shapes the qualities and persons she sees as admirable or worthy of respect. But more than this, these emotions are often experienced together. When a community experiences a collective admiration or respect for communal exemplars, they may deepen in their shared love of the goods manifested in these communities. For instance, as communities reflect together upon communities like *L'Arche*, they may experience a shared admiration and respect for the characteristic qualities of these spaces. And this shared experience may lead them to share in their desire to become a community that displays the same kinds of traits. These shared emotions can become the ground of a commitment to a good common project. A community may emulate these exemplars by seeking to make itself more welcoming to the needs of others in their midst. Admiration and respect may move the group toward a collective effort to become more like the community they admire. They may engage in practices oriented toward the goal of becoming more like exemplar communities.

In this chapter, I have argued that appeals to whole communities can serve several pedagogical functions in character education. Teachers can draw learners' attention to features of the community to teach them about the nature of the virtues as they are manifested within and through a community. As they reflect on the normative dimensions of these models, they may come to understand what it means to respond well to moral needs, especially those needs that can be addressed adequately through the collective efforts of communities. Studying candidate exemplar communities can reveal traits crucial to promoting and maintaining the flourishing of their own communities. Finally, educators can appeal to whole communities to move social groups to cultivate both individual and communally expressed virtues. As a means of eliciting moral emotions like admiration and respect, they can point to the ways communities respond to human needs, the ways members relate to each other, or how they attend to those outside their group. In reflection upon these communities, learners may experience elevating moral emotions not just for the individual members but also for the community itself. Good teachers can point to these communities as ideals for their own social lives. And together, they can seek to engage in social practices that resemble the activities of these communities in the hope that they might become *like them*.

Communities like *L'Arche* are uncommon; they manifest exceptional goodness in their activities, in the relations between core members and assistants, and in the ways in which they support, sustain, and extend the moral dimensions of their members' character. The community provides an ethos that enables its members to sustain, deepen, and persevere in their commitment to the good of the community and their shared projects. The community supports and extends the development of individual character traits relative to the needs they seek to address. Through appeals to exemplary communities like *L'Arche,* teachers can encourage moral formation and growth in both individual and communal character.[20]

Notes

1 For some representative discussions in philosophy, see Adams (1984); Carbonell (2009, 2012); Flescher (2003); Markovits (2012); Olberding (2012); Pybus (1982, 1986); Urmson (1958); Zagzebski (2010, 2013, 2015a, 2015b, and 2017); Vos (2018); and Wolf (1982). For some exemplar studies in psychology, see Bronk (2012); Bronk, King, and Matsuba (2013); Colby and Damon (1992, 1995); Damon and Colby (2013, 2015); Dunlop, Walker, and Matsuba (2012); Frimer *et al* (2011, 2012); Han *et al* (2017, 2022); Hart and Fegley (1995); Hart, Murzyn, and Archibald (2013); King, Oakes, and Furrow (2013); Matsuba (2002); Matsuba and Pratt (2013); Matsuba and Walker (2004, 2005); Peterson *et al* (2010);

Reimer *et al* (2012); van Slyke (2015); van Slyke *et al* (2012); Walker (1999, 2013); Walker and Frimer (2007, 2009); Walker, Frimer, and Dunlop (2010); Walker and Hennig (2004).

2 There are some notable exceptions to this individualistic focus in the philosophical literature: Blum (1988, 1994), Zagzebski (2017), and Hamilton (2019).

3 There is a body of literature testifying to researchers' admiration of these communities *as groups*. See, Dunne (1986); Brown and Reimer (2013); Greig (2015); Reimer (2008, 2009, 2013); and Thulberry and Thyer (2014).

4 For interesting research on *L'Arche* and spiritual formation, see Brown and Reimer (2013) and Reimer (2009). For discussion of the indispensable role of families and local communities, such as *L'Arche* in caring for those with disabilities, see Reinders (2000, 2008) and Greig (2015).

5 There is a small body of literature on the virtue of hospitality, much of it grounded in Jewish and Christian theological reflection. For extended discussion, see Bretherton (2006); Newman (2007); Oden (2001); Pohl (1999); and Reynolds (2008).

6 There is a case to make that hospitality is what MacIntyre (1999) would call a virtue of acknowledged dependence—that is, a disposition of attunement and care for human vulnerability and need. For further discussion, see Cobb (2019).

7 For further discussion of character education, see Watts and Kristjánsson (2022) and Porter (2016).

8 See Lamb, Brant, and Brooks (2021). In support of the use of exemplars in character formation, they point to the following studies: Algoe and Haidt (2009); Colby and Damon (1992); Colby *et al.* (2007); Cox (2010); Engelen *et al.* (2018); Han *et al.* (2017); Immordino-Yang and Sylvan (2010); Lockwood and Kunda (1997); Miller (2014, 2018); and Zagzebski (2017)

9 I would like to thank Nathan King for recommending that I stress this point explicitly.

10 See L'Arche Charter (2016)

11 *L'Arche* communities are intentionally formed religious communities, usually anchored by one faith tradition (e.g., Roman Catholicism). But they are open communities and accept both core members and assistants who profess alternative faith traditions or no religious beliefs whatsoever.

12 See Reimer (2008, 2009, 2013).

13 This sketch offers a brief portrait of an ideal local *L'Arche* community. Specific *L'Arche* homes may not approximate this ideal. There are cases where these communities fail to fulfill their charter, and, like all groups who live in close, intimate associations, each community experiences discord, hurt, and division. But in communities that are flourishing, there is forgiveness, reconciliation, and a celebration of the restoration of friendship.

14 In what follows, I draw from the analysis of the virtue of hospitality in Cobb (2019).

15 The behavioral expression of hospitality is often construed as a moral response to a tangible and temporally-bound need. See Wrobleski (2012) for further discussion. While I agree that the activity of welcoming and caring for the stranger's needs may have a temporal boundary, as a disposition, hospitality involves a reluctance to prescribe an endpoint of this sort. The hospitable person is open to providing protection and care for as long as the guest is in need.

16 In what follows, I focus on a range of vices one might call vices of deficiency. They manifest themselves in a habitual failure to welcome a stranger properly. This is, in part, because deficient forms of welcome are much more common than an indiscriminate or excessive expression of welcome. Nonetheless, it is worth noting that there could be instances of habitually *excessive* welcome. See Wrobleski (2012) for further discussions of the potential limitations that flow from the prudent exercise of hospitality. I should also note that there are counterfeit forms of

welcome that oppose the virtue of hospitality because they are actions rooted in self-rather than other-oriented concern.

17 On common projects, see Adams (2008).

18 It may be possible to participate individually in this effort without caring deeply or adequately about its goals. A person may be motivated by his identification with the community, by his care for other members of the community, or by his commitment to fulfilling a role well such that he is moved to participate in a common project even if he is not individually a hospitable person.

19 For a vivid depiction of the horrendous experience of social exclusion and abuse experienced by those with disabilities in institutions, see Blatt and Kaplan (1966). For a broad discussion of disability within the history of the United States, see Nielsen (2012).

20 Early work on this project was made possible through the support of a grant from The Beacon Project at Wake Forest University and the Templeton Religion Trust. The opinions expressed in this publication are those of the author and do not necessarily reflect the views of The Beacon Project, Wake Forest University, or the Templeton Religion Trust. I'm grateful to Craig Boyd, Nathan King, Judy Stewart, and Kevin Timpe for their helpful comments on early drafts of this project. The full development of this project was made possible through the support of Grant 62339 from the John Templeton Foundation. The opinions expressed in this publication are those of the author(s) and do not necessarily reflect the views of the John Templeton Foundation.

References

Adams, R. M. 1984. "Saints." *The Journal of Philosophy* 81(7), 392–401.

Adams, R. M. 2008. *A Theory of Virtue: Excellence in Being for the Good*. Oxford, UK: Clarendon Press.

Algoe, S. B., and Haidt, J. 2009. "Witnessing excellence in action: The 'other-praising' emotions of elevation, gratitude, and admiration." *The Journal of Positive Psychology* 4(2), 105–127.

Blatt, B. and Kaplan, F. 1966. *Christmas in Purgatory: A Photographic Essay on Mental Retardation*. Syracuse, NY: Human Policy Press.

Blum, L. A. 1988. "Moral exemplars: Reflections on Schindler, the Trocmes, and others." *Midwest Studies in Philosophy* 13(1), 196–221.

Blum, L. A. 1994. *Moral Perception and Particularity*. Cambridge, UK: Cambridge University Press.

Bretherton, L. 2006. *Hospitality as Holiness: Christian Witness amid Moral Diversity*. Farnham, UK: Ashgate Publishing Company.

Bronk, K. C. 2012. "The exemplar methodology: An approach to studying the leading edge of development." *Psychology of Well-Being: Theory, Research and Practice* 2(5), 1–10.

Bronk, K. C., King, P. E., and Matsuba, M. K. 2013. "An introduction to exemplar research: A definition, rationale, and conceptual issues." *New Directions for Child and Adolescent Development* 142, 1–13.

Brown, W.S. and Reimer, K. 2013. "Embodied cognition, character formation, and virtue." *Zygon* 48(3), 132–141.

Carbonell, V. 2009. "What moral saints look like." *Canadian Journal of Philosophy* 39(3), 371–398.

Carbonell, V. 2012. "The ratcheting-up effect." *Pacific Philosophical Quarterly* 93(2), 228–254.

Cobb, A. D. 2019. *A Virtue-Based Defense of Perinatal Hospice*. New York, NY: Routledge.

Colby, A. and Damon, W. 1992. *Some Do Care*. New York, NY: Free Press.

Colby, A. and Damon, W. 1995. "The development of extraordinary moral commitment." In Melanie Killen and Daniel Hart (Eds.), *Morality in Everyday Life: Developmental Perspectives* (pp. 342–370). Cambridge: Cambridge University Press.

Colby, A., Beaumont, E., Ehrlich, T., and Corngold, J. 2007. *Educating for Democracy: Preparing Undergraduates for Responsible Political Engagement*. San Francisco, CA: Jossey-Bass.

Cox, K. S. 2010. "Elevation predicts domain-specific volunteerism 3 months later." *The Journal of Positive Psychology* 5(5), 333–341.

Damon, W. and Colby, A. 2013. "Why a true account of human development requires exemplar research." *New Directions for Child and Adolescent Development* 142, 13–25.

Damon, W. and Colby, A. 2015. *The Power of Ideals: The Real Story of Moral Choice*. Oxford, UK: Oxford University Press.

Dunlop, W. L., Walker, L. J., and Matsuba, M. K. 2012. "The distinctive moral personality of care exemplars." *The Journal of Positive Psychology* 7, 131–143.

Dunne, J. 1986. "Sense of community in l'Arche and the writings of Jean Vanier." *Journal of Community Psychology* 14(1), 41–54.

Engelen, B., Thomas, A., Archer, A., and Van de Ven, N. 2018. "Exemplars and nudges: Combining two strategies for moral education." *Journal of Moral Education* 47(3), 346–365.

Flescher, A. 2003. *Heroes, Saints, and Ordinary Morality*. Washington, D.C.: Georgetown University Press.

Frimer, J. A., Walker, L. J., Dunlop, W. L., Lee, B. H., and Riches, A. 2011. "The integration of agency and communion in moral personality: Evidence of enlightened self-interest." *Journal of Personality and Social Psychology* 101, 149–163.

Frimer, J. A., Walker, L. J., Lee, B. H., Riches, A., and Dunlop, W. L. 2012. "Hierarchical integration of agency and communion: A study of influential moral figures." *Journal of Personality* 80, 1117–1145.

Greig, J. R. 2015. *Reconsidering Intellectual Disability: L'Arche, Medical Ethics, and Christian Friendship*. Washington, D.C.: Georgetown University Press.

Hamilton, B. 2019. "Navigating moral struggle: Toward a social model of moral exemplarity." *Journal of Religious Ethics* 47(3), 566–582.

Han, H., Kim, J., Jeong, C., and Cohen, G. L. 2017. "Attainable and relevant moral exemplars are more effective than extraordinary exemplars in promoting voluntary service engagement." *Frontiers in Psychology* 8, 283.

Han, H., Workman, C. I., May, J., Scholtens, P., Dawson, K. J., Glenn, A. L., and Meindl, P. (2022). "Which moral exemplars inspire prosociality?" *Philosophical Psychology* 35(7), 943–970.

Hart, D., and Fegley, S. 1995. "Prosocial behavior and caring in adolescence: Relations to self-understanding and social judgment." *Child Development* 66, 1346–1359.

Hart, D. A., Murzyn, T., and Archibald, L. 2013. "Informative and inspirational contributions of exemplar studies." *New Directions for Child and Adolescent Development* 142, 75–84.

Immordino-Yang, M. H., and Sylvan, L. 2010. "Admiration for virtue: Neuroscientific perspectives on a motivating emotion." *Contemporary Educational Psychology* 35(2), 110–115.

King, P.E., Oakes, R. A., and Furrow, J. 2013. "Cultural and contextual issues in exemplar research." *New Directions for Child and Adolescent Development* 142, 41–58.

L'Arche Charter. https://www.larcheusa.org/who-we-are/charter/ Accessed on 11/15/2016.

Lamb, M., Brant, J., and Brooks, E. 2021. "How is virtue cultivated? *Journal of Character Education* 17(1), 81–108.

Lockwood, P., and Kunda, Z. 1997. "Superstars and me: Predicting the impact of role models on the self." *Journal of Personality and Social Psychology* 73(1), 91–103.

MacIntyre, A. C. 1999. *Dependent Rational Animals: Why Human Beings Need the Virtues.* Chicago, IL: Open Court.

Markovits, J. 2012. "Saints, heroes, sages, and villains." *Philosophical Studies* 158(2), 289–311.

Matsuba, M. K. 2000. *Caring for Their Community: Study of Moral Exemplars in Transition to Adulthood.* University of British Columbia Dissertation.

Matsuba, M. K., and Pratt, M. W. 2013. "The making of an environmental activist: A developmental psychological perspective." *New Directions for Child and Adolescent Development* 142, 59–74.

Matsuba, M. K., and Walker, L. J. 2004. "Extraordinary moral commitment: Young adults involved in social organizations." *Journal of Personality* 72, 413–436.

Matsuba, M. K., and Walker, L. J. 2005. "Young adult moral exemplars: The making of self through stories." *Journal of Research on Adolescence* 15, 275–297.

Miller, C. B. 2014. *Character and Moral Psychology.* Oxford, UK: Oxford University Press.

Miller, C. B. 2018. *The Character Gap: How Good Are We?* Oxford, UK: Oxford University Press.

Newman, E. 2007. *Untamed Hospitality: Welcoming God and Other Strangers.* Grand Rapids, MI: Brazos Press.

Nielsen, K. E. 2012. *A Disability History of the United States.* Boston, MA: Beacon Press.

Oden, A. G. 2001. *And You Welcomed Me: A Sourcebook on Hospitality in Early Christianity.* Nashville, TN: Abingdon Press.

Olberding, A. 2012. *Moral Exemplars in the Analects: The Good Person Is That.* New York, NY: Routledge Press.

Peterson, G. R., Spezio, M., Slyke, J. A. V., Reimer, K., and Brown, W. 2010. "The rationality of ultimate concern: Moral exemplars, theological ethics, and the science of moral cognition." *Theology and Science* 8, 139–161.

Pohl, C. 1999. *Making Room: Recovering Hospitality as a Christian Tradition.* Grand Rapids, MI: Wm. B. Eerdmans Publishing Co.

Porter, S. L. 2016. "A therapeutic approach to intellectual virtue formation in the classroom. In J. Baehr (Ed.)," *Intellectual Virtues and Education: Essays in Applied Virtue Epistemology* (pp. 221–239). New York, NY: Routledge Press.

Pybus, E. M. 1982. "Saints and heroes." *Philosophy* 57(220), 193–199.

Pybus, E. M. 1986. "A plea for the supererogatory: A reply." *Philosophy* 61(238), 526–531.

Reimer, K. S. 2008. "Agape, brokenness, and theological realism in L'Arche." In C. A. Boyd (Ed.), *Visions of Agape: Problems and Possibilities in Human and Divine Love* (pp. 85–102). Burlington, VT: Ashgate Publishing.

Reimer, K. S. 2009. *Living l'Arche: Stories of Compassion, Love, and Disability.* London, UK: Bloomsbury.

Reimer, K. S. 2013. "Unexpected communion: Purpose, vocation, and developmental disability." *Perspectives on Science and Christian Faith* 65(3), 199–202.

Reimer, K. S., Spezio M. L., Brown W. S., Peterson G. R., Van Slyke J., and Monroe K. R.. 2012. "Virtuous courage: New methods for the interdisciplinary study of virtue." In K. R. Monroe (Ed.), *Science, Ethics, and Politics: Conversations and Investigations* (pp. 70–86). New York, NY: Routledge Press.

Reinders, H. S. 2000. *The Future of the Disabled in Liberal Society: An Ethical Analysis.* South Bend, IN: University of Notre Dame Press.

Reinders, H. S. 2008. *Receiving the Gift of Friendship: Profound Disability, Theological Anthropology, and Ethics.* Grand Rapids, MI: Wm. B. Eerdmans Publishing Company.

Reynolds, Thomas. 2008. *Vulnerable Communion: A Theology of Disability and Hospitality*. Grand Rapids, MI: Brazos Press.

Thulberry, S. C. and B. A. Thyer. 2014. "The l'Arche program for persons with disabilities." *Journal of Human Behavior in the Social Environment* 24(3), 348–357.

Urmson, J. O. 1958. "Saints and heroes." In A. I. Melden (Ed.), *Essays in Moral Philosophy* (196–216). Seattle, WA: University of Washington Press.

Van Slyke, J. 2015. "Understanding the moral dimension of spirituality: Insights from virtue ethics and moral exemplars." *Journal of Psychology and Christianity* 34, 205–215.

Van Slyke, J. A., Peterson, G., Brown, W. S., Reimer, K. S., and Spezio, M. L. (Eds.). 2012. *Theology and the Science of Moral Action: Virtue Ethics, Exemplarity, and Cognitive Neuroscience: Virtue Ethics, Exemplarity, and Cognitive Neuroscience*. New York, NY: Routledge.

Vos, P. H. 2018. "Learning from exemplars: Emulation, character formation and the complexities of ordinary life." *Journal of Beliefs & Values* 39(1), 17–28.

Walker, L. J. 1999. "The perceived personality of moral exemplars." *Journal of Moral Education* 28, 145–162.

Walker, L. J. 2013. "Exemplars' moral behavior is self-regarding." *New Directions for Child and Adolescent Development* 142, 27–40.

Walker, L. J., and Frimer, J. A. 2007. "Moral personality of brave and caring exemplars." *Journal of Personality and Social Psychology* 93, 845–860.

Walker, L. J., and Frimer, J. A. 2009. "Moral personality exemplified." In D. Narvaez and D. K. Lapsley (Eds.), *Personality, Identity, and Character: Explorations in Moral Psychology* (pp. 232–255). Cambridge: Cambridge University Press.

Walker, L. J., Frimer, J. A., and Dunlop, W. L. 2010. "Varieties of moral personality: Beyond the banality of heroism." *Journal of Personality* 78, 907–942.

Walker, L. J., and Hennig, K. H. 2004. "Differing conceptions of moral exemplarity: Just, brave, and caring." *Journal of Personality and Social Psychology* 86, 629–647.

Watts, P., and Kristjánsson, K. 2022. "Character education." In R. Curren (Ed.), *Handbook of Philosophy of Education* (pp. 172–184). New York, NY: Routledge.

Wolf, S. 1982. "Moral saints." *The Journal of Philosophy* 79(8), 419–439.

Wrobleski, J. 2012. *The Limits of Hospitality*. Collegeville, MN: Liturgical Press.

Zagzebski, L. 2010. "Exemplarist virtue theory." *Metaphilosophy* 41(1), 41–57.

Zagzebski, L. 2013. "Moral exemplars in theory and practice." *Theory and Research in Education* 11(2), 193–206.

Zagzebski, L. 2015a. "Admiration and the admirable." *Proceedings of the Aristotelian Society Supplementary Volume* 89(1), 205–221.

Zagzebski, L. 2015b. "Exemplarism and admiration." In C. Miller, R. M. Furr, A. Knobel, and W. Fleeson (Eds.), *Character: New Directions from Philosophy, Psychology, and Theology* (pp. 251–268). Oxford, UK: Oxford University Press.

Zagzebski, L. 2017. *Exemplarist Moral Theory*. Oxford, UK: Oxford University Press.

3 Imitating or Emulating?

How Exemplar Education Can Avoid Being Indoctrinating

Bart Engelen and Alfred Archer

Introduction

Recently there has been a renewed academic focus on and appreciation of the positive role that exemplars can play in moral education (Engelen et al. 2018; Kristjánsson 2006; Walker 2020; Zagzebski 2017). Exemplar education is often considered an effective and suitable way to inspire pupils to become better people instead of merely acquiring and refining knowledge and skills. It lets pupils engage with stories about activists like Martin Luther King or Malala Yousafzai, religious figures like Jesus or Buddha, people who showed courage in times of war or adversity, like the 13 Ukrainian border guards who told a Russian warship to go f*** itself, celebrities like Mr. Beast (whose online stunts include planting 25 million trees) or Emma Watson (an outspoken feminist), and philanthropists like MacKenzie Scott (who invests billions of dollars in nonprofits promoting racial equity, economic mobility, public health, and climate change) or Allan Saldanha (who, like others who took the 'Give What We Can' pledge, donates more than half of his income to effective charities).

The rationale behind employing such stories in education is to trigger emotional responses (admiration, inspiration, elevation, and guilt for not living up to similar standards) and more cognitive reflections (about moral duties and why to go beyond them) that help pupils figure out what morality requires from them, what exactly it means to be virtuous, and in what way they themselves can strive to lead better lives.

However, exemplar-based moral education—like other forms of character education—has also faced criticisms. In this chapter, we investigate one fundamental objection, namely that exemplar-based moral education is indoctrinating pupils as it imposes specific moral views on them. We aim to show how a specific, twofold approach to exemplar narratives can help avoid these worries.

In Section 2, we explain the objection and apply it to exemplar education. In Section 3, we detail a specific approach to exemplars, which arguably avoids this objection. In Section 4, we argue that this approach is still haunted by a related but distinct objection, according to which exemplar

DOI: 10.4324/9781032648392-5

education encourages an attitude of deference toward exemplars that is not conducive to the development of proper ethical reflection. In Section 5, we argue that a nuanced understanding of the distinction between imitation and emulating helps avoid that last objection. In Section 6, we argue why this approach aligns well with recent insights into the psychological and emotional mechanisms that play a key role here (admiration, inspiration, derogation, etc.). In Section 7, we conclude by formulating some practical advice for how to integrate moral exemplars in classroom settings without running the risk of imposing specific views of the good life on pupils.

Why Exemplar Education Arguably Constitutes Indoctrination

The main aim of character education—whether at a primary, secondary, or tertiary level—is to improve the characters of pupils, typically by encouraging them to develop moral habits, dispositions, and virtues, such as honesty, temperance, kindness, and (practical) wisdom. Educational tools like curricula, learning activities inside and outside the classroom, and teacher training are designed to facilitate pupils becoming better people (Lickona 1996).

For centuries now, character education has had both vocal proponents and staunch critics. Well-known objections—or "obstacles" as Berkowitz (1999) puts it—include widespread ambiguity and disagreement about what character is exactly, which values and virtues character education should promote, and what kind of educational activities are effective, systematic evidence of which is arguably lacking. In this chapter, we focus instead on the more fundamental and normative question of whether character education—more specifically, exemplar-based character education—is desirable, legitimate, and appropriate. The question here is simple: "should schools teach character?" (Berkowitz 1999, 6). The key objection in this respect is that character education is indoctrinating and thus illiberal.

Why would it constitute a case of indoctrination? Moral and character education, the argument goes, imposes specific substantive moral values and virtues on pupils and thus violates their freedom and autonomy, i.e., their right and capacity to develop their own views of the good life. While encouraging pupils to become "better people" seems uncontroversial, what that means varies both between and within cultures. Character education then faces a dilemma. Either it remains vague about what a good character is and thus what virtues it should promote (but then it stops being proper character education) or it specifies those in more detail, often in a (semi-)religious or (neo-)Aristotelian vein (but then it becomes indoctrinating).

What exactly characterizes indoctrination? According to Eamon Callan and Dylan Arena (2010, 105), it concerns a kind of "intellectual distortion" driven by "an ill-considered or overzealous concern to inculcate particular beliefs or values," in our case, moral values and beliefs concerning the good life and what morality requires. Instead of aiming for critical reflection, independence, intellectual humility, and open-mindedness, indoctrination is worrying as it produces—or aims to produce—a "close-mindedness that students are explicitly or implicitly taught to emulate" (Callan & Arena 2010, 116).

This is exactly what character education does, according to its critics. Lee Jerome and Ben Kisby (2019, 125–126), for example, criticize character education in Britain as "moralistic" and "inherently repressive," as it assumes that "the teacher possesses the 'correct' answers to various moral and political questions towards which they guide students," thus failing to promote genuine critical reflection and moral growth amongst pupils.

The objection that frames character education as indoctrination implies that it is illiberal and problematically perfectionist. After all, it inculcates specific views of the good in pupils and assumes there is a set of goods that everyone (or at least every pupil enrolled in this or that school) should strive for. According to anti-perfectionists, moral education is at odds with the kind of ethical independence that education in liberal societies should strive to develop. This does not naively assume that pupils are free from influence, as Ronald Dworkin (2011, 371) points out:

> We cannot escape the influence of our ethical environment: we are subject to the examples, exhortations, and celebrations of other people's ideas about how to live. But we must insist that that environment be created under the aegis of ethical independence: that it be created organically by the decisions of millions of people with the freedom to make their own choices, not through political majorities imposing their decisions on everyone.

Education should enable pupils to think for themselves and not instill the views of political majorities or of whatever the religious or non-religious ideologies are of, whatever powers that be. As Michel Croce (2019, 296) puts it, "indoctrinatory educational strategies should be avoided because they inhibit children's capacity for moral reflection and thereby deprive them of the necessary abilities to evaluate the goodness of their moral conduct" (and we personally think hardly anyone involved in moral or character education would disagree with this). In liberal and pluralist societies, critics argue, we should respect each person's own views on the good life, and education should try to stimulate pupils' reflective capacities to formulate, revise, and act on their own views, thus leading their lives according to their own lights, not the teachers'. The only virtues that education should promote are political ones, such as tolerance, mutual understanding, and autonomy, neither of which is to be understood as substantive views of the good life (Victoria Costa 2004). In liberal societies like ours, the argument goes, schools can and on most accounts should engage in civic or citizenship education, ensuring that pupils become good (i.e., independent) citizens, but should refrain from telling (or otherwise inculcating into) pupils what is right and wrong (Jerome & Kisby 2019, 115–118).

The objection to character education being an illiberal tool for indoctrination arguably also applies to exemplar education, in which moral exemplars—like those mentioned above—are selected as role models that pupils should admire and take as moral guides. Such an education arguably also imposes specific kinds of moral values and visions of the good life on pupils. After all, pupils are expected to (at least try to) act in ways that resemble the virtuous deeds and characteristics of the exemplars at hand. But why these exemplars, these deeds, and these characteristics (and not others)? What if pupils have good reasons for disagreeing with Jesus' teachings or with the teacher's view that a morally good person is committed to philanthropy? Perhaps it makes good sense to incorporate Martin Luther King and Malcolm X as exemplars in education if we want to turn pupils into social justice campaigners. However, that might not be the kind of life pupils themselves envision. Moreover, even if one succeeds in justifying the idea that social justice should matter for everyone, these two exemplars already offer quite different role models, embodying very different stances on the legitimacy of violence in protests and militancy. As such, picking one over the other will clearly push pupils in a certain direction, which can reasonably be labeled "imposing" or "indoctrinating."

Kristján Kristjánsson (2006, 408) sums up the objection against exemplar education as follows:

> The idea seems to be this: you present a model for emulation, somehow lure students into finding it attractive, and lo and behold, they will emulate it by latching on to it and copying it. But one can hardly avoid understanding this to be a description of emulation as mere *imitation*.

Again, this is hardly the kind of open-minded, critical, and autonomous reflection that character education (should) aim to encourage in pupils. While we return to this key distinction between emulation and imitation later on (Section 5), let us first describe an approach that arguably avoids this objection (Section 3) before discussing a further objection that can be raised against it (Section 4).

An Approach that Arguably Avoids Indoctrination

In this section, we detail a specific approach to exemplar education that can largely avoid worries about indoctrination and value imposition. The main gist of this is to have pupils pick *their own* exemplars. If pupils are asked and encouraged to think about whom they themselves admire, morally speaking, one obviously avoids the objection that teachers are imposing specific conceptions of the good, embodied by specific exemplars that they—or the educational system—(pre)selects. If there are pupils who do not admire Martin Luther King or Malala Yousafzai but rather think of Elon Musk or Jordan Peterson as moral exemplars, that is up to them. Instead of trying to instill that social justice warriors somehow *are* more admirable, this approach starts with what pupils themselves think and feel about particular people.

We implemented this strategy in a 4-year long research project called "What Would My Hero Do?" on exemplar narratives in a university setting.[1] At Tilburg University (The Netherlands), we developed a teaching module surrounding exemplar education that started out by asking around 1,000 students—both Dutch and international students, enrolled in Psychology or Business Economics Bachelor programs—whom they admired, morally speaking. The five most popular answers referred to people from their close surroundings, with the top five being mothers (clearly the most widely admired), specific friends, fathers, specific teachers, and grandfathers. Then came romantic partners, grandmas, and colleagues, but also historical and contemporary figures such as Aletta Jacobs (one of the first Dutch female physicians and very active in the women's movement), Bill Gates, Emma Watson, Jordan Peterson, and Michelle Obama. Just outside the top 10 came Jesus, Nelson Mandela, and David Attenborough.

After introducing what morality and ethics entail and why some well-known people—like Malala or Greta Thunberg—arguably qualify as moral exemplars, students were asked to identify, write about, and present their own moral exemplar, detailing who this person is and what makes them *morally* exemplary. Next, students were split up into two conditions. In the first, they were asked to *imagine* how their exemplar would act in a specific situation (e.g., when confronted by a sexist comment). In the second, they were asked to pick a situation in their personal life in which they were asked to try and *behave* like (they think) their exemplar would. While we found no systematically significant (condition, time, or interaction) effects of this intervention on emotional and psychological measures (like prosocialness, perspective taking, joy, compassion, etc.), anecdotal evidence from students' responses and writings suggests they found the exercises useful and inspiring, encouraging them to think differently and more thoroughly about situations they recognized as morally laden.

The key aspect of our approach then was to encourage students to pick *their own* exemplars, to explore what makes them admirable, and to think about what (they think) these exemplary people would do in specific situations. This arguably avoids charges of indoctrination and illiberal value imposition and encourages proper engagement with their exemplars.

Why Exemplar Education Arguably Promotes Moral Deference

That said, there is an additional objection to this approach, namely that it promotes an attitude of moral deference on the part of pupils, which is antithetical to the kind of open-minded, critical, and autonomous reflection that education should try to foster.

To see why the use of exemplars in moral education might be thought to promote moral deference, it is worth considering some of the ways in which exemplars have been claimed to have a useful role in moral education. Linda Zagzebski, for example, claims that admiration is useful in moral education because admiration, at least typically, involves a desire to emulate the person being admired. Emulation, according to Zagzebski (2017, 43), "is a form of imitation in which the emulated person is perceived as a model in some respect—a model of cooking, dancing, playing basketball, doing philosophy." In emulating someone, we attempt to be more like them in some specific respect. If I admire someone's ability as a cook, for example, I will take them as my model for cooking and try to cook in the way that they cook. The idea that moral exemplars serve as models to imitate has a long history. The Victorian author and reformist Samuel Smiles (1876, 82), for example, claimed that "Admiration of great men, living or dead, naturally evokes imitation of them in a greater or less degree." In the 13th century, the poet Thomasin von Zirclaere claimed that the way for a pupil to become virtuous was to "choose in his mind an excellent man and arrange his behavior according to that pattern" (cited in Jaeger 1994, 79–80). The idea here seems clear; we become better people by finding excellent people whose behavior we can copy. This idea was a clear source of inspiration for our second condition, which asked students to try and *behave* like their exemplar.

As we have argued, when pupils can pick their own moral exemplars, this goes some way to avoid the worry that educators are imposing their values on pupils. However, this approach still seems to be one in which pupils are not properly determining their moral values for themselves. As Bryan Warnick (2008, 16) has argued, one of the worries that has been raised against imitating exemplars as a path to moral virtue is that imitation seems to be "a form of enslavement" and that "if someone were truly free, he or she could not be simply copying another person." It is perhaps a peculiar form of enslavement in this case, in which the enslaved get to choose their own master. Nevertheless, the objection is clear: when someone is simply copying the actions of another, they are not acting freely, even if they choose who they would copy.

The reason for this comes from the fact that this form of action is heteronomous rather than autonomous; it is one in which a person gives control over their actions to another rather than making their own decisions about how to act (Warnick 2008, 21). As Jean Jacques Rousseau (1762/1979, 20; cited in Warnick 2008, 20) argued, imitation is fundamentally about being "transported out of ourselves" and taking on the role of another person. By imitating another person, we fail to make our own decisions about how we should act based on our own judgments about appropriate courses of conduct in particular situations. When pupils are encouraged to simply copy their exemplar and act in whatever way they think their exemplar would act in each situation, they are not being encouraged or enabled to explore their own moral commitments and form their own moral judgments. Likewise, encouraging people to find their "moral heroes," as we did, may implicitly be interpreted as an encouragement to find moral experts to defer to, rather than to figure out their own moral views and determine their own moral judgments.

There are two related further problems here. First, people who are motivated to perform moral actions in this way may perform the right actions but may fail to do so for the right reasons. For example, according to Immanuel Kant (1797/1983, 148), proper moral motivation involves a rational appreciation of what is morally required in the situation we are in. Someone who simply copies a moral exemplar is not motivated by this appreciation of the moral law but rather by other people's conduct (Warnick 2008, 21). While this is a distinctively Kantian account of moral motivation, it is a reasonable general moral view that people should be moved to perform an action by the considerations that make that action the right one to perform (Markovits 2010).[2] For example, if we find an injured person lying in the street, then the same reasons why helping that person would be the right thing to do should be the reasons why we are motivated to help that person. In this case, we might think the relevant reasons are reasons of care (they need help that we are able to give). Someone who helped the injured person in such a case because they had seen their moral exemplar perform similar actions in the past seems not to be motivated in the right kind of way. They should ideally be motivated out of a direct appreciation of the needs of the injured person, not from a desire to copy their exemplar. Copying one's moral exemplar, then, does not appear to be the right form of moral motivation for performing virtuous actions.

Second, by copying their moral exemplars, pupils likely overlook the many ways in which they are different from their exemplars. The first worry here is that moral exemplars likely have achieved a higher level of virtue than admiring pupils. As a result, emulation may constitute a dangerous form of what Bernard Williams calls "moral weightlifting" (1995, 190): trying to perform an action that is beyond one's moral capacities (Thomas et al. 2019). Consider a rather short-tempered, impatient man who admires the actions of a kind, compassionate, and patient person who works as a volunteer, caring for people with learning difficulties. If the impatient man tries to simply imitate his exemplar, he is likely to find himself failing. His inability to perform this work may have been easy to predict if, rather than trying to imitate his exemplar, he had instead thought to consider the various ways in which he is *not* like his exemplar.

The second, related worry here is that the admirer may have a distinctive set of potential talents that will be left unfulfilled if they simply try to imitate those they admire. Take the case of Friedrich Nietzsche, who admired Arthur Schopenhauer greatly but came to disagree strongly with Schopenhauer's philosophical views. The right response was not for Nietzsche to try to imitate Schopenhauer and become like him, but rather to try and develop his own potential. We don't, according to Nietzsche, develop our own unique talents by copying other people. Instead, we must find out our own unique talents and develop them (Nietzsche 1874/1997, 6.ii, 1.iii–iv; Robertson 2019, 101). By encouraging pupils to imitate their exemplars, then, exemplar education asks them to ignore their own unique talents and to develop talents that are not within their reach. To return to our previous example, the impatient man who is ill-suited to work as a caregiving volunteer may have exactly the right qualities to become a firefighter or a mountain rescuer. By attempting to imitate his moral exemplar, he would put himself on a course for moral failure and fail to cultivate his particular moral talents as a result.

In this section, we have argued that the kind of exemplar education that encourages pupils to imitate exemplars—even if these are identified by pupils—promotes an attitude of moral deference instead of one of critical and independent engagement. First, we have shown that imitating whom one admires is not necessarily conducive to genuinely virtuous action, i.e., doing the right thing for the right reasons. Second, we have shown that it may actually lead to not doing the right thing at all.

Emulating, Not Imitating Exemplars

However, these worries about the imitation of moral exemplars do not count conclusively against the use of moral exemplars in moral education. We can accept that there are problems with an approach to moral education that relies too heavily on imitation without thinking that this shows that an exemplar-based approach to moral education is misguided altogether.

To see why this is the case, we need to understand the difference between *imitation* and *emulation*. While imitation involves someone attempting to achieve the same goal as the person they are imitating by performing the same actions, emulation involves trying to achieve the same goal, though not necessarily by performing the same actions (Warnick 2008, 6). While imitating essentially involves copying or mimicking another person's actions, emulating can involve a broader attempt to find ways to succeed in similar (but not identical) ways.

This is important for exemplar education as an approach to exemplars that encourages pupils to emulate rather than simply imitate their exemplars, avoiding the worries we considered in the previous section. If pupils can be inspired to emulate their exemplars rather than imitate them, then they will be encouraged to consider what the valuable ends are that the exemplar is promoting and how they themselves can seek to achieve these same valuable ends. As Kristjánsson (2006, 41) has argued, the proper role of exemplars here is to "help you arrive at an articulate conception of what you value and want to strive towards." On this view, moral exemplars can help us determine for ourselves what our own moral ideals and values are and encourage us to find ways in which we too can embody these ideals.

Relatedly, one of us has argued that the motivational effects of admiring a moral exemplar are not limited to seeking to imitate or emulate the exemplar. Admiration for moral exemplars focuses our attention on the moral values or ideals that the exemplar embodies, and this is often accompanied by a desire to promote the value that we see in the exemplar (Archer 2019). However, there are ways of promoting this value that do not involve seeking to become an exemplar of that value, for instance, by supporting and encouraging those that do seek to become exemplars. We might also be inspired by our admiration for the exemplar to develop different virtues from those that they embody but that nevertheless will contribute to promoting the same valuable ends (Croce 2020).

To see the differences between these ways in which someone might be motivated by a moral exemplar, let us consider an example. When someone admires Greta Thunberg's environmental activism, their attention will be directed to the value of sustainability and the importance of finding ways to protect the environment. Recognizing this value could inspire someone to try to copy Thunberg by engaging in the same actions that she has performed, going on school strikes, engaging in social media activism, going on protests, and making speeches. This can be seen as a form of imitation, as it involves trying to achieve the same ends by performing the same kinds of actions. Alternatively, someone inspired by Thunberg can try to become a climate activist themselves, but not by performing the same actions. They may instead engage in more disruptive forms of civil disobedience, such as chaining themselves to the goalpost during a football match or gluing themselves to roads. This could be a form of emulation, as the aim is to embody the ideal of a climate activist, but not through performing the same acts that Thunberg performs. Finally, someone might be inspired by Thunberg's environmental commitments to seek to promote the value of sustainability without becoming an activist themselves. This could involve supporting activists through financial donations and voting for the green parties on election day. Or it could involve becoming a climate scientist or a rewilding officer. These forms of motivation may still arise from admiration for an exemplar but do not involve seeking to become an exemplar oneself.

What this means for exemplar-based education is that pupils should be encouraged to take a more nuanced approach to their exemplars, in which they are encouraged to emulate them in ways that do not merely involve imitation (Kristjánsson 2006; Moberg 2000) and also to think about how they can promote the values they admire in their exemplars in other ways (Archer 2019). Rather than encouraging pupils to simply imitate or copy their exemplar, pupils should instead (be encouraged to) investigate what makes their exemplar admirable and virtuous, what kind of moral ideals and virtues they embody, and which skills, attitudes, and knowledge they possess. In encouraging pupils to investigate these moral ideals and to seek to promote them, exemplar education can avoid the objection that it is encouraging the wrong kind of motivation for moral action. Moreover, by encouraging pupils not to simply mimic their moral exemplars but rather to take heed of the fact that they are not as exemplary as their exemplars and that they may possess talents that their exemplars do not, exemplar education can avoid the criticism that it is promoting the wrong kinds of actions.

The twofold approach that we developed to exemplar education encouraged pupils to take this kind of nuanced approach to their exemplars. Pupils were given a discussion exercise in which they were asked to identify the moral values that they think their exemplars embody. The aim here was to encourage pupils to focus not only on simply imitating exemplars but also to consider what makes them virtuous. In another exercise, we asked students to consider not only how their exemplar would act in a given situation, but also how the pupils themselves would act. This encouraged the students to think carefully about the differences between their own levels of moral virtue and those of their exemplars. One could also consider asking pupils to consider other ways in which they could promote the moral values that are promoted by their exemplars.

In summary, exemplar education need not encourage a problematic form of moral deference. A nuanced approach to exemplars can encourage pupils to think critically about how best to respond to exemplars in ways that go beyond simple mimicry. We have explained one way of doing this in our twofold approach to exemplar education.

Further Advantages of Our Approach to Exemplar Education

In this section, we identify three further advantages of the twofold approach to exemplar education that we have set out, in which pupils (1) get to choose their own moral exemplars and (2) are encouraged to investigate, explore, and engage with them instead of merely imitating those exemplars.

A first advantage is that it encourages pupils to focus on exemplars toward whom they actually have positive emotional responses. Research has shown that admiration and related positive emotions such as elevation and inspiration are key factors in triggering a desire to emulate and an (intrinsic) motivation to lead better lives (Algoe & Haidt 2009; Han & Dawson 2023; Immordino-Yang & Sylvan 2010; Kristjánsson 2017). As such, these positive emotions drive character growth, a complex process in which cognitive activities like reasoning and reflecting are arguably necessary but definitely not sufficient.[3] If we want pupils to become better people, getting them emotionally involved is necessary, and this is more likely to be successful when working with exemplars (that we can be sure) they admire, feel proud of, and are inspired by.

This ties into a well-known distinction between different categories of moral exemplars. While a "moral saint" is "a person whose every action is as morally good as possible, a person, that is, who is as morally worthy as can be" (Wolf 1982, 419), so someone excelling in and displaying all possible virtues, a "moral hero" is admirable for only one specific trait. Moral saints are arguably not ideal role models for how to lead a moral life, exactly because their moral perfection seems unattainable, not imitable, way too demanding, and therefore demotivating for ordinary chumps like you and me (see also Croce 2020). According to Linda Zagzebski (2017, 25), they might not even be particularly admirable in the first place. In contrast, less perfect moral heroes are, while still virtuous and admirable, much easier to relate to and more likely to trigger positive emotions (and less likely to trigger negative responses, see below).

This brings us to a second advantage. When free to pick their own exemplars, a lot of pupils spontaneously choose attainable and relatable exemplars. As mentioned, the most popular exemplars in our own study were (grand)parents (26% of students chose relatives), friends, and teachers (18% chose nonrelatives close to themselves). In contrast to seemingly flawless exemplars—typical "moral celebrities" that figure in quite conventional stories—moms, dads, and friends are more accessible and attainable for pupils and, hence, more effective *as exemplars*. As Rebecca Stangl (2020) argues in her book "Neither Heroes nor Saints," people can be genuinely good (what she calls "ordinarily virtuous") without being perfect ("extraordinarily virtuous"). Imperfect but virtuous exemplars are psychologically closer to ourselves—at least to those of us who are not perfect moral saints ourselves—and thus much easier to relate to. This has also been confirmed in a study about exemplar stories in a classroom setting (Han et al. 2017), where so-called "close-other exemplars," like parents and friends, were shown to more effectively promote moral elevation and prosocial behavior than historic figures and extraordinary exemplars do. Again, the former was shown to be perceived as more attainable and more relatable.

Experimental research confirms that (perceived) relatability (understood as exemplars with similar sociocultural backgrounds than pupils) and—to a lesser extent—attainability (understood as the extent to which pupils deem exemplars "emulatable") are key factors in exemplar stories effectively motivating pupils (Han et al. 2022). Stories were shown to have a bigger positive impact on pupils when the exemplar was made more relatable, for example by adding that they had the same national and cultural background as pupils (Han & Dawson 2023; Han et al. 2022). Now, instead of having to tweak and rewrite narratives about prepicked exemplars in attempts to make them as relatable as possible, which has obvious downsides and constraints, letting pupils pick themselves automatically leads to them engaging with whomever they find relatable and attainable.[4]

An interesting factor here is gender, another factor that can make an exemplar more relatable. In our own study, no less than 90% of male participants picked a male exemplar and 55% of female participants picked a female exemplar, which in part can be explained by systemic and structural factors that lead to more men ending up in visible positions (of power and esteem, for example) that are deemed "exemplary." Again, instead of trying to tailor exemplar stories to heterogeneous student populations, giving pupils control over those stories quasi-automatically increases relatability.

This also reveals an obvious risk with letting students pick their own exemplars, namely that a trade-off between relatability and diversity can arise. If most of the selected exemplars closely resemble the characteristics of pupils, they will lack diversity in homogeneous school populations. This can reinforce existing inequities in positions of status and the attention given to people in those positions (by society at large, the media, history textbooks, etc.). When structural factors influence the opportunities for members of different groups to occupy places where they can grasp the public's attention, the number of well-known and relatable exemplars that are available to people from different groups inevitably varies. When historically, a disproportionate amount of attention goes to men and/or white people, other groups will have fewer relatable exemplars available to them.

While this is a real worry, as the above-mentioned difference between male and female participants also suggests, we were pleasantly surprised by the diversity of public figures that students picked as exemplars. These ranged from Dutch influencers (like Diede Joosten), sports people (like paralympic athlete Bibian Mentel), and historical figures (like Anne Frank) to a wide variety—in gender, race, ethnicity, background, expertise, domain, etc.—of exemplary people from all over the world (like German student and anti-nazi activist Sophie Schnoll, Desmond Tutu, Bulgarian philanthropist Dobri Dobrev, and Vasily Arkhipov, the Soviet K-19 officer who prevented a nuclear torpedo launch).

A third advantage of this approach is that, by focusing on emulation rather than imitation, it encourages pupils to acquire and refine the skills needed to identify how they can develop their own moral capabilities, thereby avoiding the dangers of narratives about exemplars, which trigger backlash rather than admiration. An important risk involved in exemplar education is that stories of moral exemplars can trigger "do-gooder derogation," a phenomenon in which people respond to the good deeds of others with resentment and hostility rather than admiration (Minson & Monin 2012). In some cases, this may lead people to be *less* motivated to develop their own virtues than they were before encountering the stories of moral exemplars (Monin et al. 2008). This phenomenon appears to be more likely to occur when pupils take the behavior of the exemplars to pose an implicit challenge to pupils' views of themselves as morally good people and respond to this in a defensive way (Han et al. 2017; Minson & Monin 2012; Monin et al. 2008).

Encouraging pupils to pick their own exemplars seems to be an effective way of avoiding do-gooder derogation. When pupils pick their own exemplars, they are unlikely to pick people that they feel threatened by. Instead, we can expect them to pick exemplars who they actually admire and feel inspired by. In our own study, asking pupils to pick their own exemplar seemed to have exactly this effect, with pupils reporting positive emotions (such as admiration, adoration, awe, pride, and joy) much more frequently than negative emotions such as envy (only 2% of participants) and shame (only 1%). This suggests, then, that our twofold approach is an effective strategy for avoiding the risks of do-gooder derogation.

Conclusion

In this chapter, we have discussed how programs and teachers involved in character education can make fruitful use of moral exemplars without being charged with indoctrination. If the main worries lie with those programs and teachers preselecting moral exemplars and encouraging pupils to imitate their exemplary actions, we have argued that those worries can be avoided by having pupils—instead of teachers—pick their own exemplars and encourage pupils to emulate—rather than imitate—them or to consider other ways in which they might promote the values embodied by their exemplars. This twofold approach avoids the indoctrination objection, as pupils select their own exemplars rather than having moral values imposed upon them. It also avoids the moral deference objection, as pupils are encouraged to think critically about the values embodied by their exemplars and how they can promote those values in their own lives.

In addition to avoiding these two major worries with exemplar education, our twofold approach also makes it more likely that pupils will actually feel admiration and other positive emotional responses toward their exemplars and thus avoid potential reactance and do-gooder derogation. Evidence suggests that most pupils pick exemplars that they not only look up to but also can relate to and are motivated to emulate. If those involved in exemplar education then encourage pupils to actually and critically engage with their exemplars, for example, by having them think about what it is they find admirable in them—their values, their commitments, specific aspects of their character, and so on—it can play a key role in stimulating the kind of active, non-deferential attitudes that spur genuine moral growth.

Our discussion in this chapter then highlights the importance of careful attention to the details of the specific ways in which exemplars are used in the classroom for both the theory and practice of exemplar education. Theoretically, we need to pay close attention to these details, as important ethical objections will apply for some uses of exemplars in education but not for others. Practically, we need to pay attention to these details in order to use exemplars in actual classroom settings in ways that are both effective and morally justified.

Acknowledgments

This research was funded by the John Templeton Foundation as part of the project "Exemplar Interventions to Develop Character" (grant ID 61514), which was hosted at Wake Forest University and led by Eranda Jayawickreme and Michael Lamb. The views expressed in this publication are those of the authors and do not necessarily reflect the views of Wake Forest University or the John Templeton Foundation. We want to thank the other researchers in our project, namely Anne Reitz, Jelle Sijtsema, Joanne Chung, Theo Klimstra (Theo also helped with some of the analyses detailed in the chapter), and, in particular, Renée Zonneveld, who has been key in making the entire research project succeed.

Statement of ethics

The study "What Would My Hero Do" received ethical clearance from the Research Ethics and Data Management Committee of Tilburg School of Humanities and Digital Sciences (identification code: REDC #2020/006).

Notes

1 This work was supported by the John Templeton Foundation under Grant 61514 ("Exemplar Interventions to Develop Character"). We are also grateful to Wake Forest University for support of this research.
2 Like Kant, Aristotle stresses the ethical importance of the right kinds of motivations and attitudes. We should not only do the right thing but also do so "at the right time, with the right motive, and in the right way" (Aristotle, Nicomachean Ethics II.9, 1108b). Virtuous people (1) know that they are performing virtuous actions; (2) decide on those themselves; and (3) use their rational capacities to figure out which moral principles are relevant and how to apply them to their situation (Khan 2005, 42).
3 See Gunnar Jorgensen (2006) for a nuanced account of the views on moral development and moral reasoning—and the role that reason and emotion play in these—espoused by Lawrence Kohlberg and his supposed biggest critic, Carol Gilligan.
4 One can only assume that the 49% of students in our own study who picked famous and historical figures and the 6% who picked religious and fictional figures find those relatable and manage to distill something attainable from them. Popular "celebrity exemplars" were, for example, Diede Joosten, a young Dutch influencer and entrepreneur who aims to inspire and support women to maintain a (physically and psychologically) healthy lifestyle, and Jameela Jamil, a British actress (known for example from 'The Good Place') and activist who is critical of media industry standards and unhealthy body images and often speaks from personal experiences, for example with eating disorders. Those who do pick celebrities thus hardly ever pick moral saints, but rather opt for flawed exemplars (and anecdotal evidence suggests they often do so because exemplars recognize those flaws explicitly).

References

Algoe, S. B., & Haidt, J. 2009. "Witnessing excellence in action: The 'other-praising' emotions of elevation, gratitude, and admiration." *The Journal of Positive Psychology, 4*, 105–127.

Archer, A. 2019. "Admiration and motivation." *Emotion Review, 11*, 140–150.

Aristotle. 1908 [350 B.C.E.]. *Nicomachean Ethics*. Translated by W. D. Ross. Online: http://classics.mit.edu/Aristotle/nicomachaen.html.

Berkowitz, M. W. 1999. "Obstacles to teacher training in character education." *Action in Teacher Education, 20*(4), 1–10.

Callan, E., & Arena, D. 2010. "Indoctrination." In: Harvey Siegel (ed.), *The Oxford Handbook of Philosophy of Education*. Oxford, UK: Oxford University Press, 104–121.

Croce, M. 2019. "Exemplarism in moral education: Problems with applicability and indoctrination." *Journal of Moral Education, 48*(3), 291–302.

Croce, M. 2020. "Moral exemplars in education: A liberal account." *Ethics and Education, 15*(2), 186–199.

Dworkin, R. 2011. *Justice for Hedgehogs.* Cambridge, MA: Harvard University Press.

Engelen, B., Thomas, A., Archer, A., & van de Ven, N. 2018. "Exemplars and nudges: Combining two strategies for moral education." *Journal of Moral Education, 47*(3), 346–365.

Han, H., & Dawson, K. J. 2023. "Relatable and attainable moral exemplars as sources for moral elevation and pleasantness." *Journal of Moral Education, 53*(1), 14–30. https://doi.org/10.1080/03057240.2023.2173158.

Han, H., Kim, J., Jeong, C., & Cohen, G. L. 2017. "Attainable and relevant moral exemplars are more effective than extraordinary exemplars in promoting voluntary service engagement." *Frontiers in Psychology, 8*, 283.

Han, H., Workman, C. I., May, J., Scholtens, P., Dawson, K. J., Glenn, A. L., & Meindl, P. 2022. "Which moral exemplars inspire prosociality?" *Philosophical Psychology, 35*(7), 943–970.

Immordino-Yang, M. H., & Sylvan, L. 2010. "Admiration for virtue: Neuroscientific perspectives on a motivating emotion." *Contemporary Educational Psychology, 35*, 110–115.

Jaeger, C. S. 1994. *The Envy of Angels: Cathedral Schools and Social Ideals in Medieval Europe, 950–1200.* Pennsylvania, PA: University of Pennsylvania Press.

Jerome, L., & Kisby, B. 2019. *The Rise of Character Education in Britain: Heroes, Dragons and the Myths of Character.* Cham: Palgrave MacMillan.

Jorgensen, G. 2006. "Kohlberg and Gilligan: Duet or duel?" *Journal of Moral Education, 35*(2), 179–196.

Kant, I. 1797/1983. "Metaphysical principles of virtue." Translated by: J. W. Ellington. In: *Immanuel Kant: Ethical Philosophy.* Indianapolis, IN: Hackett Publishing Company.

Khan, C.-A. B. 2005. "Aristotle's moral expert: The Phronimos." In: L. Rasmussen (ed.), *Ethics Expertise: History, Contemporary Perspectives, and Applications.* Dordrecht: Springer, 39–54.

Kristjánsson, K. 2006. "Emulation and the use of role models in moral education." *Journal of Moral Education, 35*, 37–49.

Kristjánsson, K. 2017. "Emotions targeting moral exemplarity: Making sense of the logical geography of admiration, emulation and elevation." *Theory and Research in Education, 15*(1), 20–37.

Lickona, T. 1996. "Eleven principles of effective character education." *Journal of Moral Education, 25*(1), 93–100.

Markovits, J. 2010. "Acting for the right reasons." *The Philosophical Review, 119*(2), 201–224.

Minson, J. A., & Monin, B. 2012. "Do-gooder derogation: Disparaging morally motivated minorities to defuse anticipated reproach." *Social Psychological and Personality Science, 3*, 200–207.

Moberg, D. 2000. "Role models and moral exemplars: How do employees acquire virtues by observing others?" *Business Ethics Quarterly, 10*, 675–696.

Monin, B., Sawyer, P. J., & Marquez, M. J. 2008. "The rejection of moral rebels: Resenting those who do the right thing." *Journal of Personality and Social Psychology, 95*(1), 76–93.

Nietzsche, F. 1874/1997. "Schopenhauer as educator." In: D. Breazeale (ed.) and translated by R. J. Hollingdale, *Untimely Meditations.* Cambridge: Cambridge University Press.

Robertson, S. 2019. "Nietzsche on admiration and admirableness." In: A. Archer & A. Grahle (eds.), *The Moral Psychology of Admiration*. London: Rowman & Littlefield, 95–109.

Rousseau, J. J. 1762/1979. *Emile: Or, on Education*. Translated by: A. Bloom. New York, NY: Basic Books.

Smiles, S. 1876. *Character*. London, UK: John Murray.

Stangl, R. 2020. *Neither Heroes Nor Saints: Ordinary Virtue, Extraordinary Virtue, and Self-Cultivation*. Oxford, UK: Oxford University Press.

Thomas, A., Archer, A., & Engelen B. 2019. "How admiring moral exemplars can ruin your life: The case of Conrad's 'Lord Jim.'" In: A. Archer & A. Grahle (eds.), *The Moral Psychology of Admiration*. London, UK: Rowman & Littlefield, 233–248.

Victoria Costa, M. 2004. "Rawlsian civic education: Political not minimal." *Journal of Applied Philosophy*, 21, 1–14.

Walker, L. J. 2020. "The character of character: The 2019 Kohlberg memorial lecture." *Journal of Moral Education*, 49(4), 381–395.

Warnick, B. R. 2008. *Imitation and Education: A Philosophical Inquiry into Learning by Example*. New York, NY: State University of New York Press.

Williams, B. 1995. "Replies." In: J. E. J. Altham & Ross Harrison (eds.), *World, Mind, and Ethics: Essays on the Ethical Philosophy of Bernard Williams*. Cambridge: Cambridge University Press, 185–224.

Wolf, S. 1982. "Moral saints." *The Journal of Philosophy*, 79(8), 419–439.

Zagzebski, L. T. 2017. *Exemplarist Moral Theory*. Oxford, UK: Oxford University Press.

4 Model Exemplars

Eric Yang

Introduction

Many of us want to become morally better people (or so I would hope). We may also think of ourselves as being fairly decent at picking out morally good people, i.e., exemplars that we admire or want to imitate. If asked to provide some candidate exemplars, several of us would likely name real people, such as Josephine Bhakita or Confucius. Some may name fictional characters, such as Lucy Pevensie or Samwise Gamgee. We also typically include people who are not well known, such as family members or close friends.

According to an exemplarist moral theory, good people are the foundation of our moral understanding. We come to know what good character traits are or what right conduct (in a particular circumstance) is based on our knowledge of exemplars. As evident from the examples given, we often take real individuals to play the role of such exemplars.

There are, however, a couple of problems with including real people as exemplars. First, while we may know quite a bit about some of our exemplars, we may not know enough about them to know how to imitate them in certain circumstances, especially in situations that are quite unlike the ones that the exemplar may have faced. Let us call this the *"Ignorance Problem."* Secondly, there have been many occasions where someone has selected an exemplar only later to find out that this person is morally vicious or has engaged in morally reprehensible behavior. It was not too long ago that many people would have identified Mahatma Gandhi or Jean Vanier as exemplars. In light of recent information and evidence about their behavior, their status as exemplars have been revoked or at least rendered suspect by many people. Let us call this the *"Bad Exemplars Problem."*

In this chapter, I begin by laying out a version of exemplarism, and I develop the *Ignorance Problem* and the *Bad Exemplars Problem* in greater detail. Rather than giving exemplarism up, I offer a solution to these problems by presenting a view that advocates construing exemplars as models of real (or fictional) people. One understanding of models, as employed in some domains such as the sciences, is to take them as intentionally distorted representations of some portion of reality. Models are simplifications and

DOI: 10.4324/9781032648392-6

idealizations, and so models are different from the things they represent. According to my view, exemplars are (or should be) models of people in this sense. My aim is to motivate this view by showing that a model-theoretic approach to exemplarism avoids both the *Ignorance Problem* and the *Bad Exemplars Problem*.

Exemplarism and Admiration for Real People

Exemplarism treats good people as fundamental in moral theorizing. Right or wrong actions, good or bad motives, and virtues or vices are analyzed in terms of exemplars. For example, an action is morally right in a particular circumstance just in case a good person would take that action to be most favored by the balance of reasons in that circumstance, and a virtuous trait is one we admire in a good person (Zagzebski 2010, 54).

An exemplar can be identified without providing any necessary or sufficient conditions for what makes someone a good person, or even without providing any particular description that a good person must satisfy. To defend this claim, Linda Zagzebski utilizes the theory of direct reference as developed by Putnam (1979) and Kripke (1980), according to which natural kinds can be denoted through some initial dubbing or some other reference-fixing act such as pointing and using a demonstrative indexical. We can pick out water by pointing to it and saying, "that is water." And we do not have to know that the thing we are pointing to is comprised of H_2O or that it is colorless, odorless, potable, etc.

Similarly, Zagzebski avers that we can do the same with exemplars. We can point to someone and say, "Good persons are persons like that" (Zagzebski 2017, 15). Moreover, we do not randomly point at just anyone when we say that. What enables us to pick out exemplars is the emotion of admiration. We admire good people because they are "imitably attractive" (ibid., 43). Admiration is a fallible guide, and so we can be mistaken about who we pick out as being a good person. So our identification of exemplars is revisable (ibid., 16). However, we do not have to take our emotions of admiration at face value. After careful reflection, we may discover that someone we admire is not worthy of being so. Even though we may make mistakes about those we identify as exemplars, our admiration may be justified when it survives conscientious reflection (ibid., 50).

Merely listing facts about someone may neither lead to admiration of that individual nor help us realize they are a good person. We may admire people that we observe, but we can also admire someone when we learn about them through stories. We can acquire relevant data concerning characters in narratives, by which we may come to admire that figure. While I cannot now observe Confucius, I can glean data about Confucius when reading the stories or mini-vignettes in which he is involved in the *Analects*, whereby he is presented as "the most complete and compelling exemplar" (Olberding 2012, 105). Since we may identify exemplars through narratives, it may not matter to our moral development whether the story is fictional or nonfictional, and hence we can take real or fictional characters as exemplars since we can admire them and find them worth imitating (Zagzebski 2010, 51). By reading stories about Josephine Bhakita, I find myself admiring her and wanting to imitate her in order to inculcate her character traits. It is thus easy to suppose that my exemplar is Bhakita. However, when we take real people as our exemplars, we run into some trouble.

Ignorance and Bad Exemplars

The *Ignorance Problem* for exemplarism may be construed as a specific version of the action-guidance problem for virtue ethics. As the latter problem goes, some normative theories, such as deontological ethics and utilitarianism, are able to offer specific prescriptions of moral behavior in particular situations. Is the act non-universalizable or does it treat someone else as a mere means? If yes, then don't do it (says the Kantian). Would the action lead to a consequence that would increase the total aggregate of happiness? If yes, then do it (says the utilitarian). However, the virtue ethicist encourages us to cultivate virtuous character traits such as courage, prudence, temperance, and the like. And we are supposed to act in some circumstance in the way that a virtuous agent would act in that very circumstance. But we do not always know how a virtuous agent would act in some circumstances, and sometimes virtuous agents can act in competing or conflicting ways in a particular circumstance.

Exemplarism appears to have an advantage over bare-bones virtue ethics insofar as we can identify specific exemplars and specific qualities and traits of those exemplars. Whereas I may not know whether the generic "virtuous agent" would or would not push a person of sufficient mass and density off the bridge to stop an oncoming train that would kill several people, I can say with a lot more confidence that Martin Luther King Jr. would not have done so. However, my knowledge of many exemplars will be considerably limited, and so situations may arise where one does not know exactly how to imitate that person.

One way of imitating someone is to observe directly what they are doing and to copy it as closely as one can, yet many exemplars are not directly observable. Another way is to learn about their personality and character from narratives, especially for exemplars that are no longer living or are not within the observable vicinity. But if we are going to imitate an exemplar, then we need to be able to situate them in our context, facing a circumstance that is pressing to us. To do so, we need to be able to ascertain the truth-value of various counterfactuals relevant to understanding the character of the exemplar.

So begin with a subjunctive conditional schema:

1 If S were in circumstance C, then S would perform action A in C.

Since I regard Bhakita as my exemplar, I should plug "Bhakita" in for S, and I should substitute a particular circumstance I face in for C. One regular situation I face is being in a classroom teaching a course entitled "Philosophy and Science Fiction" to students at Santa Clara University. So I can fill in the schema as follows:

2   If Bhakita were teaching a course entitled "Philosophy and Science Fiction" to students at Santa Clara University, then Bhakita would perform_____when teaching a course entitled "Philosophy and Science Fiction" to students at Santa Clara University.

I still cannot assess the truth value of (2) because the schema in (1) has not been completely filled. But how do I fill in the blank in (2) given what I know of Bhakita? Despite the several narratives I have read of her life, I have no idea how to fill it in, let alone for many other potential candidates for the substitution of S.

Now perhaps the blank in (2) cannot be filled in if the action is too narrowly described (e.g., "Bhakita would teach a section on time travel…"), but we may be able to fill it out at a more coarse-grained level. We can say that she would be compassionate and empathetic (especially for struggling students) in that environment. The problem, however, is that real people are complex. Many times, our expectations or predictions of how someone will behave are mistaken, and this may be the case not only when someone is acting out of character but also because we may not understand or appreciate the full depth of their character. People's personalities and character traits may be more nuanced and subtle than we realize, and so people may be acting in character and yet in unpredictable or unexpected ways due to our limited understanding of their character. The lack of knowledge of that nuance may lead us to fill in the blank incorrectly. Moreover, if we fill in the blank in a way that is too coarse-grained, then the counterfactual may be trivial or unhelpful for imitation (e.g., "Bhakita would act in a way that a good person does"). Our ignorance of real people, then, leads us either to fail to fill in the blank, to fill in the blank incorrectly, or to fill in the blank in a trivial way that is unhelpful for the practice of imitation. So goes the *Ignorance Problem*.

Yet there is another worry for exemplarism: the *Bad Exemplars Problem*. Good people are picked out by reflective admiration, i.e., admiring someone who is regarded as admirable after conscientious reflection. But as noted above, this method is fallible, and so we may still select a bad exemplar through this procedure. We need not completely reject a procedural method merely because it is fallible. However, there are some reasons to be worried about admiration. We are naturally drawn to some individuals, even at a young age, where certain types of people become attractive to us. The admiration of someone may be so strong that an open-minded or critical stance will not be psychologically possible for some people. Some cult leaders have been extremely charismatic, to the point that even after their misdeeds or secret lives have been revealed, their followers continue to defend them and seek to be like them or follow in their paths. To be sure, this need not give us reason to reject reflective admiration entirely as a helpful heuristic in selecting exemplars. But the problem remains that such a heuristic may permit too many bad people to be regarded as exemplars.

Bad people may be regarded as exemplars because of hidden or unknown facts about them. Some people lead secret lives, as has been revealed about some people who would have been regarded as exemplars prior to the discovery of their secrets. Now exemplarism takes exemplars as that which grounds other moral concepts. And we use those exemplars to plug in for the subject of the relevant counterfactuals. But if we are plugging in the actual person in the counterfactual judgment, then it may turn out that many of our counterfactual judgments about that person are false if we have selected a bad person as an exemplar.

For example, suppose I take someone named "Pretendsy" to be an exemplar because he appears to be generous and compassionate even though he leads a double life and engages in morally reprehensible behavior in secret, including embezzling. In aiming to imitate Pretendsy, suppose I form the judgment that if Pretendsy were in my shoes, then Pretendsy would give a sizeable amount of my income away to charitable organizations. However, taking a possible world semantics for counterfactuals, the nearest possible world (or nearby possible worlds) is one where Pretendsy is only pretending to give money away while being engaged in embezzlement and profiteering. If Pretendsy is my exemplar, then my counterfactual judgment is false, since I would not thereby be imitating Pretendsy, since giving my money away is not what Pretendsy would do if he were in my circumstance.

Reflective admiration as a tool to pick out exemplars cannot account for those who lead secret lives engaging in morally reprehensible behavior. This prevents genuine imitation, at least of the sort that seeks to be more than mere copying behavior but also aims at cultivating relevantly similar motives or character traits of the exemplar. So if we take a bad person as our exemplar, many of our counterfactual judgments involving them turn out to be false (since we are mistaken about what that person would do in the circumstance we are considering). But we might instead take the construct of who we thought the bad person was as our exemplar. In that case, our counterfactual judgments turn out to be true. However, the real person no longer counts as the exemplar. Perhaps this is the direction we should be pursuing.

Model Exemplars

Exemplars are, in a sense, models or paradigmatic examples of a good person. But there is another sense of "model" that I want to bring to bear on this issue, in particular an understanding of models that come from the sciences. In this sense, models are simplified and typically idealized representations of some target object (Potochnik 2017). For example, a map is a model of some geographical location. Some models may be abstractions of the target domain, as a map may leave out many of the features of some particular region, depending on what the purpose of the model is. If the map is trying to show how drivers should navigate various freeways in some cities, many of the topological boundaries and ecological features may be left out, focusing solely on the structures of the freeway. Moreover, some models may not be abstractions but rather deliberate distortions of the represented target, where such distortions are ineliminable or beneficial given the purpose of the model (Batterman 2002; Rice 2019).

In the sciences, models are not typically measured by their accuracy as a representation. Rather, models are evaluated based on whether they are *adequate for a purpose*. A two-dimensional map may not be as accurate of a representation as a three-dimensional model of some geographical location, but a two-dimensional map may be adequate for the purpose of helping a driver navigate around the city. Some models may be deliberately distorted such that we might even regard them as false models of some target reality, and yet such models may be useful in arriving at more plausible theories or explanations about some object or target domain (cf. Bokulich 2009, 2011, 2016; Elgin 2009).

Epistemologically, distorted models, while involving some falsehoods, may yield epistemic goods such as understanding. One way of analyzing understanding is to construe it as a non-propositional cognitive grasp of the structure of some domain (Zagzebski 2001). For example, someone can understand how the scenes of a narrative fit together or how a musical composition thematically hangs together. Someone may read a book many times, grasping each individual sentence, but perhaps after reading it for the umpteenth time, they declare, "Now I get it!" when they comprehend the structural framework that enhances their appreciation of the narrative as an aesthetically sophisticated piece of literature (this happened to me after reading Jane Austen's works over and over again). In the sciences, the falsity of posited physical laws (e.g., the ideal gas law) can make understanding the behavior of some physical phenomena more tractable, allowing for greater explanatory and even predictive power (Elgin 2006). Much more can be said about models and the epistemic and scientific benefits of distorted models, including false models. But what has been said about models should be adequate to offer a modification to exemplarism.

The view I propose is as follows:

Model Exemplarism: all of our immediate exemplars are (or should be construed as) models of real or fictional people.

A few remarks on *Model Exemplarism*. Many people ordinarily state a real person as an exemplar, e.g., Jesus, Confucius, Bhakita, etc. A view may be regarded as counterintuitive if it takes people as being mistaken about whom they identify as their exemplars. So I do want to grant that Confucius can be regarded as someone's exemplar, but only indirectly. What *Model Exemplarism* denies is that Confucius (the real person) is someone's immediate exemplar. To be an immediate exemplar is to be a substitution candidate in counterfactual judgments such as (1) when one employs such judgments for the aim of imitation. So Confucius can be an indirect exemplar for someone by virtue of someone having a model that represents Confucius as their immediate exemplar. Moreover, a model of a real person can help attain an understanding of that person's character, even if that model involves distortions or some false propositions concerning the real person (just as a biography of a person can capture the authentic personality of a historical person even if there are hyperbolic or false statements made about that person).

Now Xunzi may believe that the real Confucius is his immediate exemplar. However, when he is trying to imitate Confucius, he will have to fill in the blank of (1). But the subject of (1) should be Xunzi's conceptual model of Confucius. After all, Xunzi does not grasp the entirety of Confucius' psychology let alone the nuance and complexity of anybody's psychological profile. Models are distinct from the target reality they represent. So Xunzi's model of Confucius is distinct from the real Confucius. Now Xunzi may think his concept of Confucius is identical to Confucius, but this would be mistaken, for he may believe that Confucius would act in a certain way in a certain circumstance when the real Confucius would have perhaps acted in a different way. In virtue of Xunzi's model of Confucius being a representation of the real Confucius, we can admit that Confucius is one of Xunzi's (indirect) exemplars. However, the immediate exemplar for Xunzi is the model of Confucius that Xunzi has in mind, for it is that model that Xunzi will use to plug in for the subject in the relevant counterfactual judgments.

Someone may resist and insist that the real person is their immediate exemplar. If they do so, then the *Ignorance Problem* and the *Bad Exemplars Problem* can be raised again to show why that will not work. And so for such individuals, we can take *Model Exemplarism* to be a normative thesis such that we ought to take our models of (real or fictional) people as our immediate exemplars.[1]

As has already been stated, the primary advantage of *Model Exemplarism* is that it provides a way of answering the *Ignorance Problem* and the *Bad Exemplars Problem*. The *Ignorance Problem* arose because we often know too little to make reliable counterfactual judgments involving real people. But a model of a real person is a simplified conceptual representation. My simplified understanding of Bhakita and her character allows me to plug that conceptual model into a counterfactual schema such as (1). Given the model of Bhakita, I may take it that in my SCU class, she would ensure that I allot time for those students who are likely reticent to speak up given their social location to be able to give voice in the discussion. Would the real Bhakita do that? I believe so, but I'm not sure. But I don't have to be sure. My model of Bhakita would do that, and so now I have some guidance regarding how to act in a particular circumstance. Of course, my conceptual model of Bhakita can be refined as I learn more about the real

Bhakita through biographical narratives, just as models can undergo revision given their relationship to the extant data as well as to the acquisition of new data.[2]

Model Exemplarism also has the resources to avoid the *Bad Exemplars Problem.* We might and sometimes do make false judgments about who a good person is, especially since they may be living a secret life that involves morally reprehensible behavior, or they may have begun as morally good people but later became morally vicious. But if real people need not be the exemplars we use as the immediate object of our imitation, then we can avoid imitating morally bad people as well as ensure that our counterfactual judgments regarding our exemplar are true. For we may be imitating a model of a morally vicious person, where the model itself would count as morally good or virtuous given the qualities and traits that belong to the model. The vicious or bad traits of the real person need not be attributed to the model—indeed, they will not be attributed to the model in those cases where we do not know that the person is living a secret life. Models are not identical to the target reality they represent; the model of a bad person is not identical to that bad person. But it is possible for the model not to be bad even when the person the model is representing is in fact bad since it is an abstraction or distortion of the target object. Models do not include all the features of the target reality. The model may also be picked out in the way that exemplarism standardly prescribes, viz., reflective admiration. We may find the conceptual model of some individual admirable even under conscientious reflection.

Now suppose the real person that the conceptual model is representing is hiding morally pernicious behavior. That does not prevent the model from counting as admirable, even if the real person is not admirable. So even if Pretendsy is morally bad or morally vicious, the model of Pretendsy I have developed based on my knowledge of him may be a legitimate immediate exemplar worthy of imitation, for that model is not identical to the real Pretendsy. As long as we do not conflate or confuse the model of the person with the real person (e.g., assuming that the real person perfectly satisfies the description of the model), the *Bad Exemplars Problem* is avoided.

Model Exemplarism can even explain why it is that people who are trying to imitate the same exemplar sometimes make different judgments about what they should do or what their exemplar would do in a particular circumstance. Two people may both take Martin Luther King Jr. as an exemplar, but both may prescribe different courses of action in a particular situation, where one person believes King would act in one way and the other person believes that King would act in an incompatible way. What would explain this deviation is that both have different models of the same person, and their distinct conceptual models account for their differences in judgment and prescription. Both models may count as immediate exemplars, and depending on how one handles moral dilemmas, one may suppose that both actions are morally permissible (cf. Hursthouse 1998).

Conclusion

In order to avoid the *Ignorance Problem* and the *Bad Exemplars Problem*, I recommend that exemplarists embrace *Model Exemplarism*. It may seem surprising to treat all of our immediate exemplars as models, but it seems that many of us already do so without explicitly acknowledging that the person we are actually imitating is the conceptual model we possess of some person (whether real or fictional). There is a sense in which we can still say we are imitating a real person, but we imitate them indirectly by imitating our model of that person. Yet for those still insisting that they are directly imitating a real person, the *Ignorance Problem* and the *Bad Exemplars Problem* should have them reconsider who their immediate exemplar really is. Exemplars are models in the imitative sense. I hope to have shown that exemplarists should also regard exemplars as models in the representational sense.[3]

Notes

1 Our model of a fictional person is also not identical to the fictional person it represents (granting that fictional objects exist), since there may be a mismatch between what the model would do and what the fictional person would do, which perhaps is determined by what the author(s) would claim the fictional person would do in such a circumstance (and if fictional objects do not exist, there can still be a mismatch between the model and what the author claims the fictional person would do in such a circumstance).
2 There is a complicated relationship between models and data, and naïve approaches that take there to be unfiltered data from which models are to be construed should be rejected in favor of approaches that take seriously a model-data symbiosis (cf. Bokulich 2020, 2021; Parker 2020).
3 Many thanks to Meilin Chinn, Kimberly Dill, Erick Ramirez, Pilar Lopez Cantero, and Brother John Baptist Santa Ana for helpful feedback. I am also grateful to the SET Foundations and its director, Meghan Page, for their support of my research on the use of models in the sciences.

References

Batterman, Robert. 2002. *The Devil in the Details: Asymptotic Reasoning in Explanation, Reduction, and Emergence*. Oxford: Oxford University Press.
Bokulich, Alisa. 2009. "Explanatory fictions." In *Fictions in Science: Philosophical Essays on Modeling and Idealization*, edited by M. Saurez, New York, NY: Routledge.
Bokulich, Alisa. 2011. "How scientific models can explain." *Synthese* 180: 33–45.
Bokulich, Alisa. 2016. "Fiction as a vehicle for truth: Moving beyond the notice conception." *The Monist* 99: 260–279.
Bokulich, Alisa. 2020. "Towards a taxonomy of the model-ladenness of data." *Philosophy of Science* 87: 793–806.
Bokulich, Alisa. 2021. "Using models to correct data: Paleodiversity and the fossil record." *Synthese* 198: 5919–5940.
Elgin, Catherine. 2006. "From knowledge to understanding." In *Epistemology Futures*, edited by S. Hetherington, Oxford: Oxford University Press.

Elgin, Catherine. 2009. "Exemplification, idealization, and understanding." In *Fictions in Science: Philosophical Essays on Modeling and Idealization*, edited by M. Saurez, New York, NY: Routledge.

Hursthouse, Rosalind. 1998. "Normative virtue ethics." In *How Should One Live? Essays on the Virtues*, edited by R. Crisp, Oxford: Oxford University Press.

Kripke, Saul. 1980. *Naming and Necessity*. Oxford: Blackwell.

Olberding, Amy. 2012. *Moral Exemplars in the Analects: The Good Person Is That*. New York, NY: Routledge.

Parker, Wendy. 2020. "Local model-data symbiosis in meteorology and climate science." *Philosophy of Science* 87: 807–818.

Potochnik, Angela. 2017. *Idealization and the Aims of Science*. Chicago, IL: University of Chicago Press.

Putnam, Hilary. 1979. "The meaning of 'meaning'." In *Mind, Language, and Reality*. Cambridge: Cambridge University Press.

Rice, Collin. 2019. "Models don't decompose that way: A holistic view of idealized models." *The British Journal for the Philosophy of Science* 70: 179–208.

Zagzebski, Linda. 2001. "Recovering understanding." In *Knowledge, Truth, and Duty: Essays on Epistemic Justification, Responsibility, and Virtue*, edited by M. Steup, Oxford: Oxford University Press.

Zagzebski, Linda. 2010. "Exemplarist virtue theory." *Metaphilosophy* 41: 41–57.

Zagzebski, Linda. 2017. *Exemplarist Moral Theory*. Oxford: Oxford University Press.

5 Admiration and its Companion Emotions

Sabrina B. Little

Introduction

Admiration is an emotion that appreciably perceives an excellent other and inclines an agent to imitate the perceived good. As such, admiration functions as a kind of "bootstrapping" emotion in the moral life. That is, admiration construes the perceived good as one that the agent can acquire, and it initiates the process of virtue acquisition through imitation. For Christians, this emotion is vital because of the injunction to imitate Jesus Christ (1 Peter 2:21, Philippians 2:3-8, John 13:12-15, John 13:34, John 15:9-11, 1 Corinthians 11:1, 1 John 2:6, Ephesians 4:32, Colossians 3:13). However, a common assumption of the faith is that agents do not become excellent by their own efforts. Christians participate in their own sanctification (2 Peter 1:5, Romans 13:14, Colossians 3:9-12, Ephesians 4:22-24), or spiritual maturation, with the understanding that their virtue is not acquired on their own, but freely received (Ephesians 2:8-9, 2 Peter 1:3, 2 Corinthians 12:9-10, 1 Corinthians 15:10, Titus 2:11-14).

With these things in mind, this chapter examines the role admiration plays in Christian spiritual formation, as well as its limitations. It assesses additional emotions of the spiritual life—awe, contrition, and gratitude—which both constrain and assist admiration in various ways. For example, awe is sometimes a more salient emotion than admiration, such as in worship. Also, gratitude assists a learner in recognizing the role divine assistance plays in a learner's advancement toward virtue.

This chapter has three parts. (1) It first defines admiration, drawing on the work of philosophers Linda Zagzebski and Kristján Kristjánsson and psychologists Sara Algoe and Jonathan Haidt, among others. This section also examines the potential value of the emotion for Christian spiritual formation. (2) Next, the chapter assesses limitations of admiration unique to the context of spiritual development. For example, Soren Kierkegaard critiques the emotion's attraction to a kind of "loftiness" unsuitable for the imitation of Christ. Kierkegaard's critique is addressed here. (3) The chapter concludes by evaluating additional emotions, namely contrition, gratitude,

DOI: 10.4324/9781032648392-7

and awe. These emotions support admiration so that it can play a productive role in Christian spiritual formation.

Why the emotional architecture of the spiritual life matters is that emotions are concern-based construals of the world around us (Roberts 2003, 66–69). They reflect our understanding of an object or subject—in this case, God. In this chapter, I argue that, to experience admiration exclusively, or even primarily, toward a trinitarian God is to misconstrue God's nature in unhelpful ways and to undermine our spiritual formation.

Admiration

We experience admiration broadly toward any number of good things. For example, in "On Horsemanship," Xenophon describes purchasing an "admirable" horse (2008, IV). We may also admire a sunset or a stunning peacock.

In this section, we will focus on the admiration we experience that is directed at persons. It should be noted that the excellences that characterize those we admire are wide-ranging rather than strictly moral. We can admire people for their non-personality traits, like red-headedness or height; non-normative personality traits, such as soft-spokenness or introversion; and character traits, such as honesty or wisdom.

Admiration is an emotion that appreciably perceives an excellent other, which may incline one to imitate the excellence observed (Roberts & Spezio 2019; Zagzebski 2015, 205). Alongside gratitude and awe, admiration is a member of a class of emotions that Algoe and Haidt have called the "other-praising" emotions (2009). These are positive-valence emotions[1] that mediate our responses to excellent people, which vary both in what they construe in the encounter with an excellent other and in the responses they elicit.

For example, gratitude perceives itself to be the beneficiary of another's kindness, and it disposes a person to repay the benefactor (Algoe & Haidt 2009; Onu et al. 2016). Awe perceives an excellence that far exceeds its own. This emotion disposes an agent to pause or to be arrested from movement. Awe often provokes contemplation, and sometimes submission (Keltner & Haidt 2003; Onu et al. 2016).

There is some debate about the form that admiration's action potential takes. For example, Mark Schroeder writes that admiration's characteristic motivation is to "emulate the people you admire, insofar as you are able" (2010, 42). Likewise, Linda Zagzebski writes that those we admire are "imitably attractive" to us (Zagzebski 2013, 2015). She describes how "the feeling of admiration is a kind of attraction that carries with it the impetus to imitate" (2010, 54). Both Schroeder and Zagzebski centrally define admiration in terms of this action potential—the disposition to imitate.

Robert Roberts and Michael Spezio agree that admiration motivates emulation, at least when it comes to morally excellent people (2019). Unlike when we admire an outstanding hockey player or business leader, whom we may admire for reasons of skill or talent, *moral* admiration characteristically bears a drive to be likewise excellent. In part, this is because moral traits are open to us to acquire. But it is also the case that "the moral is an arena to which we are all called" (2019, 100). Moral virtue is normative; we understand ourselves as having a responsibility to change our characters. However, Roberts and Spezio also note that whether we are motivated to imitate an admired person's moral excellences may depend on the depth of the admirer's *understanding* of the admired traits, such as that they are bound by the same moral norms. An admirer may lack this understanding. So, admirers may not be motivated to imitate the admired excellence, though they ought.

By contrast, Alfred Archer argues that approval, rather than imitation, is the motivation of our admiration and that imitation only sometimes results from our approval. We are motivated to "promote the value that is judged to be present in the object of admiration," or to affirm the excellence observed (2018, 140). Archer makes this case on the grounds that admiration is so widely felt—toward sunsets and peacocks, as well as to non-acquired qualities of persons, such as hair color and height (ibid., 142–3). The motivation to emulate is only relevant for acquired traits (ibid., 143). For example, I cannot emulate another's tallness (accidental trait), but I can emulate his or her perseverance (acquired trait). In cases of acquired human excellences, I may be inclined to emulate, but for most instances of admiration, this inclination is not relevant. Moreover, when I *am* inclined to emulate, this inclination is an expression of a more fundamental motivation—to promote the value judged to be present in the admired object.

As Archer himself points out, the debate about admiration's central motivation is won and lost in the definitions, or in where lines are drawn in the conceptual geography among moral emotions (ibid.). For example, a theorist may contend that admiration is only relevant toward human excellences. I might say that I admire a sunset, but this is a misuse of the term. Really, I *appreciate* a sunset or feel some other neighboring emotion. Zagzebski delimits admiration in this way. She restricts admiration to human excellences and—more narrowly—to *acquired* human excellences, on the basis that it feels different to encounter someone who has worked to achieve some excellence versus a person who just happens to be excellent by nature (2017, 39). Naturally, then, for Zagzebski, emulation follows from one's admiration. On accounts that see admiration as having broader relevance (such as to sunsets and non-acquired traits), a motivation like value promotion is more fitting.

In addition to value promotion and emulation (Onu et al. 2016; Schindler et al. 2015, 220), the psychology literature names several other actions potentially elicited by the emotion—self-improvement (Algoe & Haidt 2009), praising the admired person to others (Algoe & Haidt 2009), and feeling energized (Immordino-Yang & Sylvan 2010; Onu et al. 2016, 220; Smith 2000).

This debate about the motivational role of admiration is important because discerning with greater specificity the actions elicited by the emotion will give us more clarity about the probable impact of admiration on spiritual development.

Admiration's Role in Moral Development

Admiration has two kinds of impacts on the moral life—epistemic and motivational.

To admire is to appreciably perceive another's excellence, so admiration's epistemic—or knowledge-assisting—role is to gain clarity about what is choice-worthy or excellent. This is an important emotion for correcting an asymmetry that often results in how we otherwise encounter the *moral*. Often in moral learning, we are presented with ought-*nots* and are cautioned about what not to do. But admiration does the opposite—it provides us with a vision of what to *do* or to *be* instead.

For virtue development, acquiring a vision of which actions are choice-worthy or excellent is valuable for two reasons. First, it is unclear, upon first learning about a virtue (e.g., honesty), what being excellent in this respect involves. For example, honesty in a courtroom requires different conventions of speech and standards of precision than honesty among good friends or honesty on one's taxes. There is a good deal of practical wisdom required to act in terms of a virtue across situations. An exemplar, or someone we admire, can model how to act in terms of the virtue in particular situations.

Second, in admiring others, we do not view a virtue with indifference. We *appreciably* perceive it or see it *as good*. Learning about virtue by way of an exemplar assists a learner in identifying traits under the aspect of goodness. This epistemic role is so robust that Linda Zagzebski (2017) and Michael Slote (2021) describe agent-based accounts of ethics in which virtues are *grounded* in exemplars, or in the people we admire. For Zagzebski, we can use our admiration to both identify and distinguish among various virtues. Regardless of whether exemplars are sufficient for this purpose, or whether we need an additional way to identify virtues (e.g., an account of flourishing), it is certainly true that exemplars are a significant means by which we learn about excellence.

The motivational role of admiration follows from its epistemic role. In perceiving a virtue as good, or as desirable, we are inclined toward virtue ourselves.

Admiration fills a lacuna in the process of character development. Aristotle describes moral virtues as being acquired by doing, or by repeated practice—an assumption most virtue theorists still maintain. Learners are not blank slates; they have natural dispositions in place that may incline them to perform actions that compete with virtuous practice (Jimenez 2020: 185–6). So how does the process of virtue acquisition begin? This is a problem of initiation—how to motivate an agent to dishabituate, endorse, or redirect natural tendencies and to habituate good ones in their place. Admiration, as an emotion that motivates good action, can initiate this process and fill this lacuna. It can provoke us to practice the virtues.

Earlier, I introduced a debate about the particulars of admiration's action potential—or about the actions or tendencies reliably elicited by admiration.

Identifying the particular actions elicited by admiration clarifies the role admiration can play in our moral development. If admiration reliably (or even sometimes) inclines us to emulate the good observed, this directly answers the problem of initiation in virtue acquisition. It means admiration offers practice in good actions—the kind of practice that forms virtues. If, instead, admiration prompts "value promotion" or praising an admired person, these tendencies may indirectly set us up for virtuous practice or incline us toward virtue in other ways. For example, I may praise the excellences of an admired person. This can contribute to my community becoming more hospitable or sensitive to virtue. Alternatively, my admiration may incline me to do good actions in ways irrelevant to the virtue observed. Or maybe I will be more likely to develop virtue in a remote future, removed from my experience of admiration here.

Admiration's Role in Spiritual Development

In broad strokes, admiration's role in Christian spiritual development is continuous with general moral development: the emotion offers information about the good life and potentially initiates the process of virtue acquisition. However, there are at least three important differences.

First, in the case of secular (e.g., Aristotelian) virtue versus Christian virtue, there is a different objective, or goal, in one's formation as a person. For example, Aristotle orders virtue to our greatest good, which he describes as a kind of flourishing suited to our human nature. For Thomas Aquinas, our greatest good is the beatific vision or communion with God. The significance of this different end is that the virtues that constitute the good life will vary. Aquinas adds three virtues—faith, hope, and love—which are absent on Aristotle's account because they facilitate relationship with God.

Second, admiration may incline us to imitate another person's traits and actions and even (what we perceive to be) their motivations for good actions, but imitation is an incomplete means for becoming likewise excellent in one of the ways most salient to spiritual development—the transformation of one's beliefs.

An example is this: a Christian friend, Kate, is generous with her time. I admire Kate for this, and I imitate her in this respect, spending more time volunteering, for example. I may even imitate what I perceive as Kate's motivation for being generous with her time—love of others. However, I cannot imitate the *beliefs* Kate has, which ground her desire to be as excellent as she is. Kate's actions and virtues supervene on her conviction that Jesus is her savior. Becoming like Kate with respect to these grounding beliefs requires that I assent to the set of beliefs that Kate has. Perhaps imitating Kate's actions and motivations makes it more likely that I eventually assent to these beliefs too, but the formation of beliefs is not part of my imitation (Zagzebski 2017, 146–7). Assent is a separate task from imitation.

In the specific case of the imitation of Christ, I may admire Christ and be inclined to imitate him—showing preference to the poor, speaking difficult truths, and so forth. My imitation of these actions can occur without assent-ing to any claims, such as that he is the Messiah or that God is sovereign. In situations in which people imitate Christ in this way—as an exemplar of good actions, yet do not assent to his beliefs—they regard Christ as a moral teacher, or as a role model.

Considering that Jesus claims of himself *not* to be a teacher but God Incarnate, then to admire Jesus as a teacher seems an odd posture to have toward him. First, admiring a person who makes such audacious claims about himself—while not accepting these claims—is strange. If Jesus says he is God and someone does not accept that he is God, then, at the very least, these claims should give the non-believing admirer some pause about the sort of person he or she is admiring. Second, it seems possible that we and others may benefit, in a common grace way, from the imitation of Christ's good features apart from these beliefs. For example, communities benefit when someone advocates for the oppressed, on whatever grounds they do so. However, our concern in this essay is *spiritual development*—or communion with God—and this will be impeded by unbelief. If Jesus is God, and we admire Jesus in a generic way apart from the claims he makes about himself, this practice certainly does not advance the relationship. Ad-miring Jesus as a normal person seems not to be constructive for spiritual development when spiritual development is defined as drawing closer in relationship with God. The difference of belief is central to the relationship; it concerns one party's identity.

A final difference between virtue formation in general and Christian spir-itual development in particular is perhaps the most significant. It is the process of virtue acquisition. Earlier, I alluded to a lacuna in the process of Aristotelian virtue development, described as the problem of beginnings: given that vir-tues are acquired by practice, how is virtue acquisition initiated, such that we are inclined to practice virtues before we desire them? An answer I supplied, drawing on Aristotle, is the emulation of excellent others (*Rhetoric* 1388a28-1388b). We see excellent people and are drawn to be likewise excellent.

A similar puzzle arises in the Christian context: apart from Christ, people are described as having hardness of heart, being blind and deaf to sins, and as scoffers (Ephesians 4:17-19; 2 Corinthians 4:4, Matthew 13:13; 2 Peter 3:3). These metaphors gesture at poor epistemic and motivational standing—both being unable to see God and not desiring God either. So, in spiritual forma-tion, there is also a problem of beginnings—of what motivates us to pursue God in the first place.

On this locus sit several theological debates regarding how much agency we have in our salvation and in our being made righteous. Some of these debates concern the degree to which a person has free will to choose God, whether God's choice undermines our own choice, whether both parties have agency in the divine-human relationship, how Jesus' actions as propitiation for our sins impact our spiritual state, whether all people or a select few are chosen, whether God is the first actor in our salvation (and what this first action amounts to), and so forth. I am not going to take any positions here. Instead, I will offer a clarification and a conditional:

Virtues are typically understood to be a kind of personal achievement— "something with which you can be credited as having had some hand in the production of it"—rather than qualities possessed by nature or habituated in us apart from our own choosing (Roberts 1988, 142). *If* spiritual development is not primarily, or even largely, the product of our own choosing in this ordinary sense of achievement, *then* there are repercussions for the role admiration can play in spiritual development.

Assuming the antecedent is true—that a nontrivial part of our spiritual development is non-acquired (e.g., gifted to us; chosen for us)—then admiration's role in spiritual development becomes more modest. Earlier, I described Linda Zagzebski's account of admiration's construal. She writes that those we admire are "imitably attractive" to us (Zagzebski 2013, 2015). She describes how "the feeling of admiration is a kind of attraction that carries with it the impetus to imitate" (2010, 54). Assuming the antecedent is true, we might wonder how *imitable* the excellences we admire in a Christian, or in Christ, really are. We might also wonder whether it is presumptuous to perceive them as such.

For example, Aquinas describes two sets of virtues—acquired and infused. Acquired virtues, such as fortitude and temperance, are imitable; we can acquire them by way of intentional practice. He also names faith, hope, and charity as infused or gifted. We cannot acquire these virtues independently of the saving work of Christ. Moreover, these excellences transform the character of the acquired virtues too. For example, if I love others (charity— infused) as I ought, then I will be more inclined to take fitting risks (fortitude—acquired). Admiration, in perceiving excellences *as* imitable, is only correct for the acquired set, and even acquired virtues are only somewhat imitable, apart from the transforming influence of faith, hope, and love. If I perceive all of these goods to be open to me by ordinary means, then I am wrong about my status before God, and about my ability to become like Christ, apart from Christ himself.

This kind of error happens in non-theological situations too. Maybe I am 5'4" and dispositionally timid, yet I am certain I can play basketball like LeBron James. Indeed, some of his excellences are open to me, such as his determination and kindness, which we see on display in his many charitable endeavors. I cannot emulate his wingspan, height, or ability to dunk. To perceive these excellences as imitable would be to misunderstand (a) who I am, (b) who he is, and (c) which excellences are open to me. Likewise, to assume I can put on Christ's excellences—or to place myself on equal standing with God through my own efforts—is to be mistaken about (a) who I am, (b) who Christ is, and (c) which excellences are open to me apart from Christ's actions on my behalf.

Second, assuming the antecedent is true—that a nontrivial part of our spiritual development is non-acquired (gifted to us, chosen for us, etc.)—then there are emotions that are often more salient than admiration is in spiritual development—namely awe, contrition, and gratitude. I address these emotions in the section on auxiliary emotions of spiritual development.

The Limitations of Admiration

There are many ways in which admiration can go awry. In the same way that other emotions can be directed at the wrong objects or be outsized (e.g., feeling angry at a tree's root that I carelessly trip over, or feeling angrier than the disobedience of a child warrants), admiration can err. An example is that I might admire the wrong people, such as a charismatic yet corrupt preacher or a sanctimonious parishioner. Other times, I may admire the wrong qualities in the right people—such as the hubris of an otherwise admirable missionary. Each of these instances of admiration is likely to impede, rather than foster, one's spiritual development.

Additionally, even when I admire fitting traits in fitting people, I may not always admire these traits in suitable ways. For example, I may become transfixed by the excellences of another and develop a preoccupation with this person, or I may demonstrate affiliative behavior toward this person rather than doing something more productive, such as attempting to acquire the admired excellence myself. An example is emulating the hairstyle of an excellent Bible study leader. This emulation is not, strictly speaking, bad or harmful, but emulating the accidental features of an excellent person will not advance my spiritual formation.

For these reasons—that our admiration is often poorly directed and otherwise immature—philosopher Linda Zagzebski calls for "reflective admiration" of one's exemplars (2013, 193). Critically reflecting on the objects of our admiration mitigates the potential for error. For example, it makes us less likely to unreflectively conform to any charismatic person we happen to encounter (Kristjánsson 2006, 37–49).

The Loftiness Concern

In "How Admiring Moral Exemplars Can Ruin Your Life," Alfred Archer, Bart Engelen, and Alan Thomas name a more significant error of admiration. They describe how admiration can set one up for "a distinctive kind of moral error"—one may not realize the ways in which he or she is not an exemplar (2019, 233–248). That is, by holding an exemplar in mind, we begin to think of ourselves in terms of the excellences the exemplar possesses, but we do not actually have these excellences ourselves. The risk of committing such an error is that our admiration, in this case, makes us *less* amenable to improvement. We perceive ourselves as already good.

There is a Christian-specific version of this worry, which appears in many of the short stories of Flannery O'Connor. She depicts a kind of loftiness or conceit in the Christian life. For example, in "Revelation," wealthy southerner, Ruby Turpin, delivers a memorable prayer in which she thanks Jesus for making her wealthy, non-ugly, and not "trash" (1965, 203). To Mrs. Turpin, being a Christian, or Christlike, is socially elevating. It involves growing in status over others.

Soren Kierkegaard describes the same phenomenon in *Practice in Christianity*. He critiques Christians for their "loftiness"—"that an individual human being speaks or acts as if he were God" (1991, 94). Furthermore, Kierkegaard seems to think that this loftiness is, if not the consequence of, certainly sustained by, one's *admiration* of Christ. He writes, "An imitator is or strives to be what he admires, and an admirer keeps himself personally detached [and] does not discover that what is admired involves a claim upon him to be or at least to strive to be what is admired" (1991, 241).

Kierkegaard has two worries about admiration. First, *mere* admiration—pleasant or favorable feelings toward Jesus, unaccompanied by imitative action—is not productive for spiritual formation. But the situation is more pernicious than being non-productive. Admiration can involve a kind of "delusion" (ibid., 246). Admirers may comfort themselves with their positive feelings toward Jesus, assuring themselves of a salvation they do not have.

Second, Kierkegaard points out that what the imitation of Christ requires is exceedingly difficult. It involves requirements to "die to the world, to surrender the earthly...self-denial," and so forth, as Jesus himself did (ibid., 252). These imitative actions *oppose* loftiness and conceit. So, admiration of Christ—genuine admiration of Christ, which Kierkegaard just calls "imitation"—should involve these things (ibid.). Placed in the context of our earlier discussion about the various kinds of motivations that follow from one's admiration (e.g., imitation, value promotion, praise, etc.), for Kierkegaard, the only fitting response to Jesus is to imitate him.

For the loftiness concern of admiration, I argue in the final section of the chapter that, alongside Zagzebski's prescription of reflective admiration, the presence of certain emotions can play a role in constraining admiration toward its proper objects.

Limited Construal Concern

Earlier I noted that emotions have cognitive content. While we often think of emotions in terms of the subjective feelings and the physiological states they dispose in us, emotions are also construals or representations of the world around us. For example, anger (rightly or wrongly) perceives an injustice. Admiration perceives another as *good*.

The cognitive content of admiration is what makes it an important epistemic tool in the moral life—one that can teach us what a good life, or a life in communion with God, can look like. Earlier in this section, I raised several ways in which admiration's construal can be faulty—such as when we admire the wrong people. Even when admiration has high coverage reliability—consistently directing our attention toward those who warrant our admiration—the scope of the emotion is too narrow to suffice for spiritual development.

Stated differently, admiration may pick out admirable traits and actions, and incline us to imitate them. Even so, to experience admiration exclusively, or even primarily, toward a trinitarian God would be to misconstrue God's nature in unhelpful ways, and thereby to undermine our spiritual formation. In the final section, I clarify what I mean here, naming a set of emotions that are sometimes more salient in assisting a learner in drawing closer to God.

Auxiliary Emotions of Spiritual Development

Often in the Bible, when people encounter *God*, they fall to their faces, sometimes in worship (Genesis 17:3, Numbers 20:6, Joshua 5:14-15, Daniel 8:17, Matthew 17:6, Acts 9:4). This seems a proper response to God's holiness—a mix of awe and holy terror. For example, God promises Abram that he will be a father of many nations. When God appears, Abram falls on his face and listens from a prostrate position on the ground (Genesis 17:3).

In encountering *Jesus*, these moments of collapse also occur (John 18:4-6, Luke 8:28, Revelation 1:13-18); however, they are rarer. Instead, we often see admiration and imitation directed at the person of Jesus (Luke 7:37, John 13:12-15). Moreover, Jesus instructs his disciples to love one another, to take up their cross, or to imitate his own actions (John 13:34, Matthew 16:24). This response seems suitable since Jesus appears in human form. We can imitate him.

Lastly, when confronted with the *Holy Spirit*, people tend to respond in gratitude or with joy (Ephesians 5:18-20, 2 Thessalonians 2:13, Luke 1:41-5, Luke 1:67-8, Acts 13:52). These responses—thanksgiving and praise—seem fitting for the person of the Trinity described as a "Helper" (John 14:15-18, Romans 8:26-7). We are beneficiaries of the Holy Spirit's assistance. Beyond the Holy Spirit, gratitude is a suitable emotion in spiritual development more generally, to the extent that our spiritual standing is received,[2] rather than an achievement of our own.

There are at least three separate emotional responses here to the persons of the Trinity, each with different construals and different action-potentials. In the first case, we see awe—the emotion that perceives holiness, transcendence, or an excellence that far exceeds one's own. This emotion disposes an agent to be stunned to passivity or arrested from movement (Keltner & Haidt 2003; Onu et al. 2016). It inclines Abram to fall on his face before God.

In the second case, we see movement instead of passivity—imitating and actively working to be like Christ. In the third case, we have gratitude. Gratitude is an emotion that perceives itself to be the beneficiary of another's kindness, and it disposes a person to repay the benefactor (Algoe & Haidt 2009; Onu et al. 2016) or to praise them, expressing thanks (Berger 1975, 42; Manela 2022, 1155).

The oddity of a Trinitarian God is that all three persons are one. Yet, we seem to respond in different ways to the different persons. Moreover, while all of these responses are fitting, we cannot experience them all at the same time. For example, we cannot imitate and arrest our movement at once.

I do not imagine there is some analytic principle for determining when, or how frequently, we ought to experience each of these emotions in the Christian life. It does seem that failing to experience any of these emotions might be a problem. It might mean distancing oneself from aspects of the Trinity, such as the holiness of the Godhead or the guidance of the Holy Spirit. This is because of the important epistemic role that our emotions play. They are a means by which certain features of the world are made salient to us. For example, in experiencing anger, I construe something worthy of ire or perhaps unjust. When I experience love, I see someone or something as loveable. In failing to experience an emotion such as awe, this can mean we fail to recognize something important about God—holiness. If the objective of spiritual development is growing in relationship with God, then all of these emotions are important because they are instructive about who God is.

Other Candidates

There may be additional emotions, alongside awe and gratitude, which also aid or constrain admiration. One example is contrition—a kind of sorrow for one's shortcomings. Other examples are ameliorative prosocial emotions such as regret or remorse. The virtue of humility supervenes on emotions such as these—emotions that position us to be aware of personal deficiencies and to say we are sorry. Humility is critical for constraining admiration since it answers the loftiness critique. The humble admirer knows he is not yet excellent. He does not, in Kierkegaard's words, "[speak] or [act] as if he were God" (1991, 94). Therefore, he is more likely to perform imitative actions to become more Christlike.

Other important emotions—for their constraining impact on admiration—include fear (namely well-ordered fear, as in fortitude, such that one takes fitting risks) and love (specifically self-love, such that one is motivated to improve one's spiritual state). The virtue of magnanimity supervenes on emotions such as these—emotions that position us to aspire to spiritual goods. The magnanimous (or great-souled) Christian is more likely than the pusillanimous (or weak-souled) Christian to experience admiration when she ought.

For example, perhaps I encounter a missionary who is exemplary in her service. I may experience awe toward this person, considering her wholly "other" because of the ways she exceeds me. Realistically, I ought to experience admiration toward this person, who is similarly positioned to me—as a human person my own age who attends my church—and I should take advantage of the fact that she is modeling how to be likewise excellent. The magnanimous Christian will be more inclined to correctly detect when excellences are open to her and imitable than will the pusillanimous Christian, who is so meek and self-doubting she assumes she cannot improve in the given respect.

Conclusion

Admiration is an emotion that appreciably perceives an excellent other. It is a critical emotion in spiritual development for both drawing our attention to excellences of the Christian life and motivating us to acquire them. But it is also an emotion that can easily misdirect our spiritual formation. Moreover, misdirection aside, it is insufficient as an emotional response to a Trinitarian God.

In this chapter, I examined the strengths and limitations of admiration for Christian spiritual formation. Furthermore, whereas Zagzebski calls for "reflective admiration" of one's exemplars—using critical reason to refine the objects of our admiration—I argued for a set of emotions that do similar work. Awe, gratitude, and contrition, among other emotions, constrain and support our admiration of Christ and of others, so that this admiration can be productive for spiritual development.

Notes

1 Aristotle defines emulation as "distress at the apparent presence among others like him by nature, of things honored and possible for a person to acquire… [accompanied by] an effort to attain good things for himself" (Aristotle 2007, 146 (1388a29–38)). Philosopher Linda Zagzebski argues that emulation is an instance of, or a close relative of, admiration (Zagzebski 2015, 214). If emulation is an instance of admiration, this is a possible exception to the exclusively positive valence of the "other-praising" emotions. Although, Kristjánsson points out that, while emulation involves distress, it is not strictly negative valence because it also involves "pleasure at the presence of 'the honored thing'" (2017, 24).

2 Or cooperatively received. Again, this is the locus of many debates regarding human freedom and divine action. If, to any extent, our virtue is received, we should experience gratitude.

References

Algoe, Sara B., & Haidt, Jonathan. 2009. "Witnessing excellence in action: The 'other-praising' emotions of elevation, gratitude, and admiration." *Journal of Positive Psychology*, 4, 105–127.

Archer, A. 2018. "Admiration and motivation." *Emotion Review*, 11(2), 140–150.

Archer, A., Engelen, B., & Alan Thomas, A. 2019. "How admiring moral exemplars can ruin your life: The case of Conrad's 'Lord jim.'" In: Alfred Archer & Andre Grahle (eds.), *The Moral Psychology of Admiration*. New York, NY: Rowman & Littlefield, 233–248.

Berger, Fred. 1975. "Gratitude." *Ethics*, 85, 298–309.

Immordino-Yang, M. E. & Sylvan, L. 2010. "Admiration for virtue: Neuroscientific perspectives on a motivating emotion." *Contemporary Educational Psychology*, 35, 110–115.

Jimenez, M. 2020. *Aristotle on Shame and Learning to be Good*. Oxford: Oxford University Press.

Keltner, D., & Haidt, J. 2003. "Approaching awe, a moral, spiritual, and aesthetic emotion." *Cognition & Emotion*, 17(2), 297–314.

Kierkegaard, S. 1991. *Practice in Christianity*. Translated by H. Hong. Princeton, NJ: Princeton University Press.

Kristjánsson, K. 2006. "Emulation and the Use of Role Models in Moral Education." *Journal of Moral Education* 35(1): 37–49.

Kristjánsson, Kristján. 2017. "Emotions targeting moral exemplarity: Making sense of the logical geography of admiration, emulation, and elevation." *Theory and Research in Education*, 15(1), 20–37.

Manela, A. 2022. "Can you be grateful to a benefactor whose existence you doubt?" *Religions*, 13(12), 1155.

O'Connor, F. 1965. "Revelation." In: *Everything That Rises Must Converge*. New York, NY: Farrar, Straus and Giroux.

Onu, D., Kessler, T., & Smith, J. R. 2016. "Admiration: A conceptual review." *Emotion Review*, 8(3), 218–230.

Roberts, R. 1988. "Humor and the virtues." *Inquiry* 31(2): 127–149.

Roberts, R. 2003. *Emotions: An Aid in Moral Psychology*. New York, NY: Cambridge University Press.

Roberts, R., & Spezio, M. 2019. "Admiring moral exemplars: Sketch of an ethical sub-discipline." In: Nancy Snow & Darcia Narvaez (eds.), *Self, Motivation, and Virtue: Innovative Interdisciplinary Research*. Abingdon: Routledge, 85–108.

Schindler, I., Paech, J., & Löwenbrück, F. 2015. "Linking admiration and adoration to self-expansion: Different ways to enhance one's potential." *Cognition and Emotion*, 29(2), 292–310.

Schroeder, M. 2010. *Value and the Wrong Kind of Reason*. Oxford, UK: Oxford University Press.

Slote, M. 2021. Agent-based virtue ethics. In Halbig, C.m Timmermann, F. (eds). *Handbuch Tugend und Tugendethik*. Springer VS, Wiesbaden, 363–372.

Smith, R.H. 2000. Assimilative and contrastive emotional reactions to upward and downward social comparisons. In Suls J.M., Miller R.L. (Eds.) *Handbook of Social Comparison: Theory and Research*, 173–200.

The Holy Bible. New Revised Standard Version with Apocrypha. 2006. Edited by B.M. Metzger, Translated by NRSV Bible Translation Committee. Oxford, UK: Oxford University Press.

Xenophon. 2008. *On Horsemanship*. Translated by H. G. Dakyns. Chapel Hill, NC: The Project Gutenberg.

Zagzebski, L. 2010. "Exemplarist Virtue Theory." *Metaphilosophy*, 41(1/2), 41–57.

Zagzebski, L. 2013. "Moral exemplars in theory and practice." *Theory and Research in Education*, 11(2), 193–206.

Zagzebski, L. 2015. "Admiration and the admirable." *Proceedings of the Aristotelian Society*, 89, 205–221.

Zagzebski, L. 2017. *Exemplarist Moral Theory*. Oxford, UK: Oxford University Press.

Part II

Psychological Inquiry into Exemplars and Imitation

6   The Role of Empathy in the Appraisal Processes of Holocaust Rescuers

James A. Van Slyke

Introduction

During the holocaust, moral exemplars performed many courageous actions to help save Jews from the genocidal regime of the Nazis. In a context where so many persons acted morally reprehensibly or just indifferently, holocaust rescuers are a paradigmatic case of moral heroism. Understanding the psychology of holocaust rescuers and moral exemplars more generally can help illuminate the various factors that contribute to morally praiseworthy behavior.

This chapter will focus on one aspect of the psychology of moral exemplars, empathy. I will argue that empathic appraisal played a unique role in the moral schemas of rescuers as they saved Jews during the holocaust. As Otto Springer famously stated, "The hand of compassion was faster than the calculus of reason." Empathic appraisals of the inherent worth of Jewish persons were a key ingredient in the moral psychology of Holocaust rescuers. These appraisals were part of the moral schemas of the rescuers, causing them to feel they had no choice but to take action on behalf of the victims of the holocaust and attempt to save them.

To make this case, I will start with a description of appraisals at work in sensorimotor systems and then move to a discussion of emotions more generally and an appraisal framework for emotions. Then, I will describe the components of empathy and its importance for pro-social behavior. However, empathy has received some criticism for not being a basic ingredient of morally praiseworthy behavior. Although I agree that parts of the critique are warranted, the type of empathic appraisals that are a part of the moral psychology of holocaust rescuers are unique and vital to their rescuing behavior. Finally, I'll describe the moral psychology of holocaust rescuers and the importance of empathic appraisals.

I will make a case that the defining feature of holocaust rescuers was an empathic emotional appraisal of the intrinsic worth of Jewish persons, which necessitated action from the rescuers on behalf of the Jewish person in danger. This appraisal wasn't straightforwardly cognitive but required an emotional appraisal that played a unique role in the decision-making process of

DOI: 10.4324/9781032648392-9

the rescuers. As Monroe (2012) has noted, they did not feel that they had a choice in this situation; they had to act. Empathic appraisals are the types of processes that can accomplish this task.

Motor Systems as Appraisal Processes

To understand how empathic appraisal systems work, it is helpful to start with a somewhat simpler example of sensorimotor systems and movement as appraisals. Sensorimotor systems are various parts of the body and brain that enable movement in a variety of different contexts. One of the first principles of sensorimotor function is that "motor output is guided by sensory input" (Pinel & Barnes 2017, 197). In terms of appraisals, various sensory systems are constantly making appraisals (mostly unconscious) of the current environment to determine the next motor movement. This could be due to factors such as gradient, texture of the surface, or unevenness. These appraisals are *recurrent* in that each appraisal affects the next one, and motor output is continually adjusted based on changes occurring in the environment. For example, as you begin to walk up a hill, the sensorimotor system adjusts the output of your muscles to compensate for more load as you begin to walk up something with a higher gradient.

The sensorimotor system is hierarchically organized between higher-level association areas, premotor, and motor areas of the neocortex, and lower-level areas of the spinal cord and motor units of the muscles (Pinel & Barnes 2017). Each area of the sensorimotor system is specialized to serve a particular function. Motor units adjust tension in the muscles, while association areas take in information from sensory systems and adjacent areas of the brain to plan and execute motor output. Motor functions recruit various areas of the brain and body to execute motor functions, but those areas are also implicated in other types of functions besides motor output. So, the role of a brain area is determined not by the anatomical area, but by the current role it serves in accomplishing some function. Each area plays a unique role in the appraisal and associated motor output.

A considerable amount of these appraisal processes occur at the unconscious level, in that as persons are walking or running, their sensorimotor systems are unconsciously making adjustments based on the recurrent feedback received from the environment. When persons are walking down a very well-known path, like walking home from a frequently visited park, most of the appraisal process is unconscious and persons are often free to let their minds wander to other topics. This illustrates another aspect of sensorimotor function. As learning occurs, more of the motor actions are accomplished by lower levels in the hierarchy. This is true for many systems in the brain and body. As various motor functions are learned and refined, less and less conscious attention is needed to accomplish the same task. Various aspects of motor activity become automatic and need less conscious attention to be directed toward them in order to accomplish the goals of the activity.

Thus, a few factors should stand out as defining characteristics of appraisals.

1 Appraisals are recurrent feedback systems that continually take in information from the environment.
2 Appraisals are dependent on various areas of the brain and body that each serve a specialized function in the appraisal process.
3 Appraisal does not occur in a particular part of the brain but is distributed in various areas based on the current function.
4 The role of conscious attention will fluctuate based on previous learning and frequency of particular activities, with well-known activities requiring less and less conscious attention.

In terms of rescuers, empathy appraisal systems are continually taking in social information about current relationships with others. Various areas of the brain and body play a unique role in how persons process empathic information relevant to current relationships. Thus, there is not one area in the brain where empathy occurs, though there are certain areas that are specialized for particular functions. Empathic appraisal varies in terms of the role of consciousness when making the appraisals. Practiced empathic appraisal processes require less conscious effort over time in the sense that empathy becomes more habitual as it becomes associated with particular relationships or views of persons. To understand how emphatic appraisals work, it's important to first understand how emotion works more generally to illuminate the unique role of empathic appraisal among rescuers.

Defining Emotion

In psychology, emotion has been notoriously difficult to define. The classic dilemma has been whether our conscious experience of feelings is the interpretation of unconscious emotional processes (Pinel & Barnes 2017). If a fearful object such as a bear is perceived, emotional processes produce perspiration, increased heart rate, and other types of physiological reactions that occur unconsciously prior to our conscious perception of being in a state of fear because of the bear. This could be considered an adaptive response from an evolutionary perspective. If a predator is encountered in the wild, the body needs to be immediately ready for action, and consciousness is too slow to enable a quick response. According to the Canon-Bard theory, both the feeling of emotion and the accompanying physiological response co-occur when something fearful is encountered in the environment. Contemporary biopsychosocial definitions of emotion see these processes as mutually influencing each other, depending on the situation (Pinel & Barnes 2017).

Dimensions of Emotion

An important first distinction to make when defining emotion is to differentiate emotions from feelings. Feelings are the conscious experiences we often associate with particular emotional states (Adolphs & Anderson 2018). In contrast, emotions are the various autonomic, physiological, and brain processes that may or may not be conscious and typically occur prior to the conscious state associated with feelings. Adolphs and Anderson (2018) functionally define emotions as more complex than simple types of reflexes, but not as complex as more controlled cognitive processes. Reflexes are too rigid and only linked to specific stimuli to be a good model for emotion. Emotions can be learned and are generalizable to other relevant situations. However, emotions are still not the same as cognitive states that involve planning and goals, though they are indispensable to and actively influence these states. Current context plays an important role here as well, since emotions can at times play the leading role in certain cognitions or actions. For example, when someone is angry, mourning the loss of a friend, or engaged in a passionate embrace with a loved one, emotion tends to play the leading role.

Adolphs and Anderson (2018) offer several helpful dimensions of emotion to help distinguish emotional states from other functional states of the brain and body. A two-dimensional model of emotion based on level of arousal and pleasantness vs. unpleasantness provides insights into some of the basic functions of emotion. Emotions may involve high levels of arousal (fear) or lower levels of arousal (feeling sleepy). Emotions may be highly pleasant (happiness) or more distressing (anger). This may be related to basic categories of approach (smells that lead an animal to food) or avoidance (smells that indicate contaminated water).

Emotions are scalable in that the arousal states associated with them scale upward based on a potential threat or arousal associated with movement toward someone you love. Emotions can persist even after the emotionally arousing event has ended, which helps to facilitate learning and integrating different types of information associated with the context that elicited the emotion. Emotions are also generalizable, so once an emotion is associated with some type of environmental cue, that learning can be applied to novel contexts and experiences. Each of these elements plays an important role in the appraisal of different situations. Persons, contexts, or other perceived phenomena can be appraised as either pleasant or unpleasant, with lower or higher arousal, and generalized to different contexts.

Emotion as a Component of the Appraisal Process

Emotional appraisals increase the efficacy of adaptive responses to different aspects of the environment that are relevant to the well-being of the organism (Moors et al. 2013). Well-being here includes survival and reproduction but also goes beyond that definition to include other forms of human flourishing associated with various emergent forms of human culture. With human emotional responses, there is an increase in behavioral adaptability and physiological complexity associated with these types of appraisal systems used for a variety of different functions.

Appraisals are composed of a number of different components that inform the appraisal, including environmental evaluations, motivations, potential actions, somatic and physiological responses, and subjective feelings (Moors et al. 2013). Emotions serve as a type of signal in the appraisal process to alert or mark certain features of the environment as "goal relevant, goal congruent/incongruent, positive/negative, novel and/or urgent" (Moors & Scherer 2013, 140). Appraisals occur at both the conscious and unconscious levels and can operate automatically depending on the stimulus and the context. Subjective feelings are the parts of appraisals closest to conscious awareness and may be reflections on past appraisals, while goal states, positive and negative valences, and urgency may often be active more at the unconscious level.

So, an emotional state of fear would alert the organism to potential danger, while an emotional state of sexual arousal would help to elicit a mating response. An emotional response is one factor that influences the appraisal of the current situation and helps to elicit a proper action response. The idea of appraisal is helpful here because cognition and emotion are not necessarily at odds with one another. Instead, emotion provides one type of appraisal of the current situation that can be integrated with other forms of cognition to produce adaptive behavior. Emotion may sometimes automatically elicit a response (jumping in fear during a horror movie), may provide signals that influence a response (empathizing with a child when they've scrapped their knee), or may be overridden to accomplish a task (getting up to speak in front of a group of strangers).

Emotion and Adaptive Response

Recent evidence in cognitive neuroscience demonstrates two important findings:

1 Emotion is an important component of adaptive actions, not a detriment to them.
2 Emotional or cognitive contributions to adaptive actions are not easily distinguishable, neither in the brain nor in their role in an adaptive response.

The importance of emotional appraisal is demonstrated by several studies that were prompted by a re-examination of the famous case of Phineas Gage (Damasio et al. 1994). Gage was a construction foreman on a railroad who experienced a terrible accident when a large metal tamping rod he was using exploded upward out of the top of his head, damaging his prefrontal cortex. Amazingly, he never lost consciousness and at first seemed fairly stable despite his dramatic injury. However, what was soon apparent to his friends and family was that Gage was "no longer Gage." There was a radical change in his personality that was puzzling for those who knew him. Gage was not able to hold his job as a foreman, made several poor decisions regarding both his finances and family, and ended up in a sideshow at a local carnival until his death 11 years later due to seizures.

It was later determined that one of the primary areas damaged in the accident was the ventromedial prefrontal cortex, which was implicated as an important area of the brain for integrating aspects of emotional appraisals with decision-making. One patient who had similar brain damage to Gage and a similar profile of lacking the ability to make adaptive decisions was known as Elliott and was studied by Damasio and his colleagues (Damasio 1994). When Elliott was exposed to emotionally charged stimuli (e.g., a collapsed building from earthquakes, burning buildings, severe physical injuries, or potential flood victims), he reported that his emotions about these kinds of stimuli had changed; although these images were used to evoke strong feelings, he no longer had any reaction to them, either positive or negative (Damasio 1994).

Elliot also performed poorly on a test constructed by Damasio and his colleagues, the Iowa Gambling Task (Bechara et al. 1997). Participants would start with a set monetary amount (e.g., $1000) and would begin picking from various decks of cards. Each card had various payouts (+ $100) or takeaways (−$75) that were randomly placed in each of the four decks. What the participants didn't know was that two of the four decks had significantly larger payouts, but also takeaways, which made those decks more risky when trying to collect money in the game.

Bechara and colleagues (1997) noticed an intriguing pattern when comparing control participants to persons with damage to the frontal cortex, specifically the ventral medial prefrontal cortex (VMPFC). When control participants were picking from the more risky decks, they would develop a mini-emotional autonomic response to choosing from those decks, measured by a skin conductance response (SCR). SCRs would occur prior to the controls having a conscious conception of those decks being more risky, yet the autonomic responses would guide their behavior on the task, in a sense, before they had a fully formed abstract understanding of the contingencies of the game. However, persons with damage to the VMPFC did not have this same autonomic response to the game, and their performance on the task was diminished.

This experiment illustrates a few things discussed about emotional appraisals thus far. First, these emotional processes seem to be working at a level somewhere between reflexes and controlled cognitive processes. Contingencies of the game are learned at an unconscious level, and those appraisals are fed into the more controlled cognitive systems to influence decision-making. Secondly, the emotional appraisals seem to be marking certain decks as negative or more risky, so they seem to be providing information about a particular emotional valence (positive or negative) about different aspects of the game.

This experiment, along with others, indicates that emotional appraisals play a unique role in decision-making, at least at times outside of conscious awareness. Damasio refers to this as "somatic markers," which function as a type of emotional signal that actively influences decision-making. It focuses attention on the negative outcome to which a given action may lead and functions as a type of automated alarm signal that says, "Beware of danger ahead if you choose the option which leads to this outcome. The signal may lead you to reject, immediately, the negative course of action and thus make you choose among other alternatives." (Damasio 1994, 173).

Research in cognitive neuroscience indicates that these forms of emotional appraisal are necessary for effective decision-making and that the absence of these appraisals is a severe detriment to adaptive behavior. To an extent, this is not necessarily news; psychology has often recognized the importance of emotional, motivational, and arousal systems for proper human functioning. As far back as the early 1900s, the Yerkes-Dodson law set out the parameters of human performance based on the amount of emotion (in their terms arousal) necessary for optimal performance (Yerkes & Dodson 1908). This was indicated by a graphical curvilinear relationship in the form of an upside-down U shape; the lowest levels of performance were associated with either too little or too much arousal, but somewhere in the middle was the area of optimal arousal necessary for performance.

Research on patients like Elliott indicates a unique role for emotional appraisals in decision-making. In their case, the absence of autonomic input caused a severe deficit in their ability to make decisions related to moral issues, including family, money, and work. This research demonstrates that the input of emotional appraisals often works at the unconscious level, but still has a tremendous effect on decision-making. Thus, autonomic somatic markers act as an emotional signal in the appraisal process and play an important role in social cognition and behavior, including morality.

Defining Empathy

Empathy is an important emotional process for many different forms of social interaction and communication because it is the way in which we understand the emotional state of another person. At its most basic level, empathy is the perception of the emotional state of another person, which at least partially activates the emotional state of the observer in a similar way (Singer & Lamm 2009). So, part of the perceptual process of understanding the feelings of another is that those same feelings are felt and understood by the observer. According to Decety and Cowell, empathy has three primary components:

1 Affective sharing—the natural way humans are aroused by the emotional state of others, which is most similar to emotional contagion.
2 Empathetic concern—motivation to care for another
3 Perspective taking—putting yourself in the mind of another (2015, 3)

Empathy and Pro-sociality

Several studies show a link between empathy and various forms of pro-social behavior. When participants viewed a person being excluded by two others, it activated areas of the brain associated with both affective sharing (among highly empathic persons) and perspective taking and increased the likelihood of pro-social behavior toward the excluded individual (Masten et al. 2011). Among children aged 5–6, those in the empathy induction condition (viewing a girl who had lost her dog) were more likely to act pro-socially (shared more stickers with others) in comparison to controls (Williams et al. 2014). Pro-social behavior was highly correlated with the emotional ratings of the young girl, who was worried about her dog. Activation of a prominent area of the brain related to empathic mentalizing (dorsomedial prefrontal cortex) predicted monetary donations and time spent helping others (Waytz 2012).

Individuals who experienced higher levels of positive affect, associated with viewing pictures of the orphans they were meant to help, donated more money to them (Genevsky et al. 2013). Activation of the nucleus accumbens (NAcc), which has been associated with pro-social behavior, predicted pro-social giving in a crowdfunding choice task more accurately than self-reports (Genevsky et al. 2017). Autonomic empathic responses to viewing others in pain were predictive for being willing to take on the pain yourself to prevent others from experiencing the same pain (Hein et al. 2011).

Another component of empathy, compassion, which is often defined as empathic concern directed at another person, has also demonstrated evidence of promoting different types of pro-social behavior. Participation in short-term compassion training increased helping behavior in a pro-social game (Leiberg et al. 2011). Compassion training, which consisted of a contemplative technique that attempts to cultivate feelings of benevolence and friendliness while in a state of quiet concentration, decreased feelings associated with empathic distress (which often decreases pro-social behavior) and strengthened emotional resilience (Klimecki et al. 2014). Persons who had engaged in long-term meditation training related to compassion were less likely to punish others when they were victims of fairness violations, and they were more likely to compensate victims (McCall et al. 2014).

Against Empathy

Although there are several studies that seem to demonstrate a link between empathy and various sorts of pro-social actions, Bloom has made a case *against empathy*, arguing that an empathic response in terms of sharing or mirroring the emotional experience of another person is not a feature of exemplary moral action (Bloom 2017). One of the case examples he uses is the reaction to the Sandy Hook elementary school shootings. When this event occurred, many people empathized with the lives of the children who had witnessed these atrocities and sent stuffed animals to try and soothe their grief, which would seem like a natural and good response. However, most of these stuffed animals ended up unseen and unused in a warehouse because there were just too many of them (Brown 2012). Bloom's point is that although the initial empathetic response *feels* morally right, it doesn't necessarily lead to effective moral action.

As a second example, the news often focuses on stories that are empathetically engaging but not necessarily reflective of the severity of different issues going on in the world. The news media paid a considerable amount of attention to a young woman, Gabby Petito, who was lost but ended up being murdered by her abusive boyfriend (Weitzman & Narvaez 2022). The story is truly horrific and sad for her and for her family and friends, but should this story get more attention than droughts, famines, and wars going on throughout the world where thousands of more lives are at stake? Also, is the empathy driven by real moral concern or because the woman is young, attractive, and white? This woman was not the only murder that occurred in the US in the same time period, but we often seem empathetically drawn to certain types of stories.

Empathy and Non-moral Behavior

Bloom identifies several problems with empathy as a shared emotional response. For example, persons are more likely to unfairly move a young girl up a waiting list for treatment when asked to empathize with her (Batson et al. 1995). When persons are shown the picture of an individual child in need of life-saving money, they are more likely to help in comparison to being asked to help a group of eight individual children in the same situation (Kogut & Ritov 2005). Empathy seems to also be subject to in-group biases. When participants viewed someone receiving the same shock they had experienced, they felt more empathy when the person was described as a fan of their soccer team than when the person was described as a fan of a rival soccer team (Hein et al. 2010).

Empathy can sometimes lead us to make unsound judgments regarding different social policies (Bloom 2018). Empathy tends to be individually focused, so even if a furlough policy for inmates leads to an overall drop in crime if one person is assaulted because of the program, the weight falls more in favor of the individual person assaulted than the overall good the program could have brought to the community. Or if a vaccine is found to cause adverse side effects in a small number of children, this is sometimes given more weight than the much larger proportion of persons it helps. Empathy can also cause us to arbitrarily take sides against someone who is no better or worse than another. In one experiment, persons were told about a financially needy student who had entered a competition for a cash prize. When participants were motivated to feel sympathy for this student, they were more likely to administer higher levels of hot sauce to the student competitors, though they had not done anything deserving of this kind of punishment (Buffone & Poulin 2014). Evoking this type of empathy is often seen in politics, where persons are asked to empathize with a person who was attacked by an immigrant. Although the vast majority of immigrants would never be involved in a violent encounter, the empathizing with the victim moves the needle toward a more anti-immigrant stance.

Too Much Empathy and Burnout

Besides cases where empathy is biased. There are also cases where persons can experience *too much* empathy, which can lead to emotional flooding. Persons can sometimes become overwhelmed with particular emotions, and the activation of those emotions can become more *repulsive* than motivating for certain kinds of behavior. One theory about this process is that when the personal distress of empathizing with someone meets a certain threshold, persons attend to their own feelings of distress rather than using the distress of others as motivation for moral action (Eisenberg & Fabes 1990). One study showed that persons will help others until it begins to take on a personal cost (Lockwood et al. 2017).

An excessive amount of empathy may also lead to different forms of burnout. For example, there has been a large increase in nurses who have recently left the field of medical care, which primarily seems to be related to the spike of treatment needed during the COVID-19 pandemic (Mandowara & Leo 2023). Part of recent decreases in nurses seems to be related to psychological factors involving burnout. Among three different categories of burnout (emotional exhaustion, depersonalization, and personal accomplishment), emotional exhaustion was the highest reported symptom based on a meta-analysis of several different studies accessing risk factors during the COVID-19 pandemic (Galanis et al. 2021). A US sample of critical care nurses found that 84% of the nurses surveyed experienced moderate levels of burnout during the pandemic as well as moderate levels of moral distress (Guttormson et al. 2022). Many nurses experience compassion fatigue, which is the emotional, physical, and spiritual exhaustion associated with observing and feeling the problems and suffering of others. This is slightly different from burnout, which is caused by feelings of apathy and hopelessness that decrease performance on job tasks (Hunsaker et al. 2015).

Issues with the Critique of Empathy

A few issues stand out in the critique of empathy. First, there is a broader issue in the study of morality more generally, especially in the neurosciences. If you are studying the way that the average person processes moral information, are you really studying morality? This is sometimes referred to as cognitive averaging or not screening persons in terms of their abilities for the target of investigation (Peterson et al. 2010). It would seem that you need to study persons who are experts in morality or moral exemplars to understand how they process empathetic information, not just the average person. Spezio (2015) uses the example of studying a non-fluent person as opposed to a fluent person in Spanish. The non-fluent person will still process the Spanish language, and different areas of their brain will show activations using fMRI, but you aren't really studying fluent Spanish, you are studying something else. To understand the role of empathy in moral action, it would require studying empathy as a part of the moral psychology of moral exemplars, not necessarily the average person.

A related issue here is maturity. Persons do not process emotional information in the same way when they are younger as they do when they are older. Developmentally, as persons mature, they learn to metabolize different forms of emotion from others. For example, a parent is able to metabolize and name the emotions of their young children and reflect them back to their children in a digested way that is not only overwhelming for them but also teaching them about the relevance of their emotions and how they can regulate their emotions themselves. What's important here is that this is not an exact mirroring or mimicking of emotions, but it probably would not be said that parents are not feeling the emotions of their children either. What is occurring, when things go well, is a modulation of the emotions the parents are feeling and sharing with their children. It's this modulation that requires a certain level of expertise, which is not *merely* empathizing or sharing the emotions of others, but empathizing in a particular way.

As another example, think of a therapist working with a client who was dealing with grief over the loss of a loved one in therapy and had broken down and was crying uncontrollably. It would not be in the client's best interest for the therapist to break down as well, but this doesn't mean that the therapist wouldn't be feeling what the client was feeling at some level. Understanding the feelings involved with grief involves sharing those feelings while not getting overwhelmed by them, but this is not just a purely cognitive exercise, where you know cognitively how they feel. I would argue that you feel what they feel in some way. This is often why we seek out persons who have similar experiences as our own. Their ability to share in our emotional experience and talk about it from their perspective is part of what is able to soothe our own pain. Here again, though, it's not just anyone who has experienced something similar to ourselves, but someone who has the ability to metabolize our emotions and the wisdom to know how to deal with modulating our own emotions.

What Bloom and others get right is that *merely* empathizing with the emotions of another person is not sufficient to lead to moral action. Empathy must be properly attuned to the needs of the individual at that time, and the person must have sufficient experience and wisdom when dealing with their own emotions to take on the emotions of the other. Certainly, burnout and other types of emotional fatigue are negatively related to certain types of helping behavior, but the issue here is not that sharing the emotions of others will necessarily lead to burnout. Burnout is caused when there is emotional overload and not paying proper attention to one's own emotional state or not recognizing the need to seek out help and support from others. I would still argue that some amount of emotion sharing, in this case empathic appraisals, is required for certain types of morally exemplary behavior, though the proper exercise of empathic appraisals may require a certain level of expertise.

Holocaust Rescuer Stories

Monroe (2004, 2012) had the unique opportunity to interview several rescuers who saved Jewish persons during the Nazi Holocaust during World War II. Rescuers like Otto, who was ethnically German but saved 100 Jewish persons before ending up in a concentration camp; or John, who was a Dutchman on the Gestapo's most wanted list but managed to organize an escape route for Jewish persons to Switzerland and Spain. Irene was a Polish nurse who hid 18 Jews in the house of a German major who had forced her into slave labor. Each of the rescuers did extraordinary acts of moral courage that easily placed them in the category of moral exemplars.

Over several years, Monroe (2012) developed a theory of moral choice based on her interviews with moral exemplars as well as bystanders and even Nazis that actually *deemphasized* the role of conscious choice, at least as it is traditionally understood. Based on the moral exemplars she interviewed, they did not feel like they had a choice but were compelled to help the Jews in their relational orbit. Here is an exchange between Monroe and John, one of the rescuers.

Monroe: "You used the phrase, "You had to do it." Most people didn't do it, though. How did you feel you had to do it, when other people did not?"

John: "I had to do what everyone should do (John shrugged). I do it."

Monroe: But why did you have to do it?

John: "Because I have to help those in need, and when people need help, then you have to do it."

(Monroe 2004, 111)

Most of the moral exemplars answered in a similar fashion, emphasizing that they didn't feel like they had a choice. They were compelled to do something about the lives of the Jewish persons whom they knew were in grave danger. Interestingly, the rescuers were not the only persons who felt they did not have a choice. Bystanders expressed a similar understanding of a lack of choice in the situation but, in contrast to the moral exemplars, did nothing.

Here is one exchange with a bystander, who was referred to as Beatrix and was a cousin to one of the moral exemplars interviewed by Monroe.

Q. Did you know about the concentration camps during the war?

Yes.

Q. Did you know that the Jews were being gassed?

Yes. I can't tell you who told this, but my husband heard a lot when he worked in the hospitals.

Q. How did you react?

You couldn't do anything.

Q. There was nothing you could do?

No. No. … You could not do anything

(Monroe 2012, 92)

This sets up a very strong contrast between persons with familial relations, expressing the inability to make a choice, and acting in morally divergent ways.

Monroe's theory

Ethical Perspective

Monroe developed a theory of moral psychology that is in contrast to the rational choice theories that were so prevalent in her early studies of politics and economics (Monroe 2012). Monroe's model of moral psychology assumes that all persons have an ethical framework that is developed over time based on a number of different influences that are unique to the individual. The ethical framework provides a type of scaffolding for future moral cognition and subsequent moral action. A primary component of the ethical framework is a concept of the self and their relationship to other persons. This ethical perspective provides a model for seeing the world in a particular way and the role of the self in relationship to different persons. As different potential moral situations arise, it provides a menu of different moral actions. The ethical framework is very similar to the psychological concept of schemas, or more appropriately, in this case, moral schemas.

Development of Moral Schemas and Moral Salience

In general, psychology defines schemas as cognitive structures that contain general knowledge and expectations about a variety of different domains taken from our past experiences with objects, persons, and situations.

Schemas often work at the unconscious level, providing basic information and routine actions associated with specific situations. For example, most persons have a particular schema for what to do in a restaurant (this is also referred to as a script). In a classic psychological experiment, Bower, Black, and Turner (1979) found 73% agreement among participants on the order in which persons should order food at a restaurant (i.e., sit down, look at menu, eat, pay bill, leave). These actions are not consciously recalled each time a person enters a restaurant, but rather they become part of the unconscious expectations that persons use when going to restaurants without even being aware of them.

Moral schemas are similar to the general schemas we use every day, except that they involve different social relationships and obligations. Moral judgment development involves transformations in how an individual construes obligation to others. With greater social experience (especially experiences that increase perspective taking), an individual's sense of moral obligation expands, moving from concern for self, to concern for known others, and to concern for the welfare of strangers (Narvaez & Lapsley 2010).

In the case of holocaust rescuers, their moral schemas involve certain obligations and values that view another person as important in a morally relevant situation. During the holocaust, rescuers saw themselves in a particular relational stance toward the Jews, in which they felt obligated to help them. Overall, rescuers tended to view life as sacred and saw all persons as part of a common universal humanity. Rescuers did not make strong in-group vs. out-group distinctions and were open to the points of view of other persons. This was not the result of a conscious choice but was based on their moral schemas, creating a tight coupling between perception and action.

Ethical acts emanate not so much from conscious choice but rather from deep-seated instincts, predispositions, and habitual patterns of behavior that are related to our central identity (Monroe 2012). As moral schemas and ethical perspectives develop over time, they become more and more a part of a person's moral identity. As this moral identity becomes solidified over time, it increases the consistency and reliability of the moral actions of exemplars. In fact, several studies demonstrate a relationship between moral identity and different forms of moral action. Persons who consider their morality closely aligned with their identity have a more expansive moral concern for outgroups and more favorable attitudes toward providing aid to outgroups (Reed & Aquino 2003). Characteristics associated with binding persons together in groups and consequently viewing out-groups more negatively can be overcome among persons with a strong moral identity (Smith et al. 2014). More explicit moral traits are associated with humanitarian experts in contrast to novice both for their own self-understanding and their expectations regarding romantic partners (Reimer et al. 2011). Moral identity among rescuers sets the menu of possible moral actions, and for them the only option was to do something to help the Jewish persons in need.

According to Monroe, one of the primary aspects of rescuer schemas was the moral salience of the other.

> Moral salience is the feeling that causes another's suffering to be experienced as relevant for the agent, thus creating an emotional drive that compels the agent to help or to turn away and do nothing
> (Monroe 2012, 256).

For rescuers, the moral salience of the persecuted Jews created a context in which their suffering was morally relevant to them and required action. For rescuers, the only items on the menu of possible moral actions were to act in response to the needs of the Jews who were being persecuted. Their actions were more related to unconscious and habitual aspects of their identity than conscious choice.

Bringing It All Together

To understand the role of empathetic appraisals in Monroe's account, it's important to note several things. First, any account of moral action will include both cognitive and emotional elements. Moral schemas, moral identity, and a conception of the other involve important cognitive features in order to represent that type of information. The important point here is that the empathic appraisal played a unique role in the process of moral action formation and execution. Empathy did not work against cognition, but in concert with it to produce the type of exemplary behavior seen in the holocaust rescuers. However, several factors point to the important role of empathic appraisals in their actions.

The first factor is time. The decisions to help rescue Jews during the holocaust were made too quickly to be simply a rational calculus. They required some type of motivational component that was emotional in character. Emotions function at a level between reflexes and more deliberative cognitive functions, which allows them to process information faster. This faster processing is part of the reason that holocaust rescuers did not struggle before engaging in rescuing behavior. They did not engage in deliberation over what to do because the empathic appraisals of the inherent worth of the Jewish persons caused them to need to help regardless of the potential consequences.

The second factor is moral salience. The empathic appraisal is what provides the perception that the lives of the Jews who are being persecuted are of moral relevance to the rescuer, and the empathic concern is part of the motivational structure for the rescuer that prompts them to act. Certainly, the cognitive perception of a universal humanity is also part of the motivating structure, but absent the empathic motivation, the rescuers would not be motivated to help. The empathic appraisal provides a type of motivation that cognition and rational deliberation alone cannot provide in order to prompt moral action. It seems highly unlikely that the moral psychology of rescuers would be *non*-empathetic. Thinking about what the Nazis were doing to the Jews at that time would induce some type of emotional state, and I would argue that the emotional state it induces would be a primary factor in determining moral action or non-action.

It is important to note that bystanders during the holocaust also did not feel as if they had a choice during the holocaust. Their response was often, "there was nothing I could do." I would argue that they also had an emotional appraisal of the situation, but it was not an empathic one. Their emotional appraisal was more fear-based and related to self-preservation than empathy, thus their belief that there was nothing they could do. The appraisal of fear and self-preservation confirmed their perception that there was nothing they could do, and they acted accordingly. The differences in emotional appraisal can help explain the fact that persons can cognitively perceive the situation similarly yet act very differently. However, it remains an open question whether they did perceive the situation differently or whether the differences in appraisal cause differences in perceptions, although there was obviously an overlap in many of the elements of the perception.

One open question that will require more experimentation and thought is understanding the difference between the empathy shown by holocaust rescuers and the type of empathy demonstrated by Bloom and others that led to immoral action or just non-action. One possibility is that there is virtuous empathy and non-virtuous empathy. There is the type of emotional connection and identification that leads to moral action and courage, and there is the type of emotional imitation and contagion that leads to emotional flooding and flight from the situation. Empathy can sometimes lead us to see the other as ourselves and motivate us to act on their behalf, and empathy can sometimes activate in-group biases and motivate us to act against those perceived to be different.

One way to think about this difference is emotional reactions persons may have while watching a movie. Sometimes, when watching a movie, we identify with or share the emotional states of the characters in a movie, and it makes us uncomfortable when someone is in an embarrassing situation in a romantic comedy or in a state of fear as in a horror movie. This can cause the type of feeling that makes us want to escape or want to move away from the situation. But other types of movies can enlighten us about the plight of racial minorities or other types of injustices, and we can see those persons as ourselves, which can motivate us to take moral action and fight against injustice. For example, the movie "Just Mercy" describes the plight of a black man who is wrongly accused of murder, and the identification and empathy that the viewer experiences when watching the movie can motivate them to act against other types of injustices.

The differences may also simply be a difference in emotional maturity or moral development. Emotional contagion is an instinctual process and part of the natural way that human beings begin to understand their emotions.

From babies that begin to cry simply from hearing other babies cry to adults who are moved to cry by simply observing someone else crying, emotional contagion and mimicry are natural states. The maturity comes about from the calibration of these emotions and the understanding of their meaning. It is also important to differentiate one's own emotions from the emotions of other. It does seem that the fusion of emotions between the self and the other is one of the problematic aspects of emotional contagion or immature empathy, whereas mature empathy involves feeling the feelings of others or identifying with them at some level, while also maintaining some understanding of the distinction between self and other.

Conclusion

Emotion is an important part of the moral psychology of holocaust rescuers. Specifically, empathetic appraisals of the moral salience and inherent worth of Jews during the holocaust played a unique role in resecuring behaviors of these particular moral exemplars. More work needs to be done in neuroscience, moral psychology, and psychology more broadly to understand the nuances of empathic processes and the differences between the sharing of emotions that are problematic vs. the ones adaptive for moral action. Most likely, individual differences in the moral psychologies of moral exemplars will be identified that may vary based on context, time period, and the moral exemplar themselves. So not all morally exemplary behavior may be dependent upon empathetic appraisals, but I would argue that a significant proportion of morally exemplary behavior is dependent on at least some form of virtuous or mature empathic concern, and understanding this development will increase our understanding of both moral exemplarity and morality more generally.

References

Adolphs, R., & Anderson, D. J. 2018. *The neuroscience of emotion: A new synthesis.* Princeton, NJ: Princeton University Press.

Batson, C. D., Klein, T. R., Highberger, L., & Shaw, L. L. 1995. "Immorality from empathy-induced altruism: When compassion and justice conflict." *Journal of Personality and Social Psychology, 68,* 1042–1054.

Bechara, A., Damasio, H., Damasio, A. R., & Tranel, D. 1997. "Deciding advantageously before knowing the advantageous strategy." *Science, 275,* 1293–1295. https://doi.org/10.1126/science.275.5304.1293

Bloom, P. 2017. "Empathy and its discontents." *Trends in Cognitive Sciences, 21*(1), 24–31. https://doi.org/10.1016/j.tics.2016.11.004

Bloom, P. 2018. *Against empathy: The case for rational compassion.* New York, NY: Ecco Press.

Bower, G. H., Black, J. B., & Turner, T. J. 1979. *Scripts in Memory for Text.* Cognitive Psychology *11*.2.

Brown, K. V. 2012. "Teddy bears and toys inundate Newtown." *Connecticut Post.* December 27, 2012. https://www.ctpost.com/local/article/Teddy-bears-and-toys-inundate-Newtown-4150578.php

Buffone, A. E. K., & Poulin, M. J. 2014. "Empathy, target distress, and neurohormone genes interact to predict aggression for others–even without provocation." *Personality and Social Psychology Bulletin*, 40(11), 1406–1422. https://doi.org/10.1177/0146167214549320

Damasio, A. 1994. *Descartes' error: Emotion, reason, and the human brain.* New York, NY: Quill.

Damasio, H., Grabowski, T., Frank, R., Galaburda, A. M., & Damasio, A. 1994. "The return of Phineas Gage: Clues about the brain from the skull of a famous patient." *Science*, 264(5162), 1102–1105.

Decety, J., & Cowell, J. M. 2015. "Empathy, justice, and moral behavior." *AJOB Neuroscience*, 6(3), 3–14. https://doi.org/10.1080/21507740.2015.1047055

Eisenberg, N., & Fabes, R. A. 1990. "Empathy: Conceptualization, measurement, and relation to prosocial behavior." *Motivation and Emotion*, 14(2), 131–149. https://doi.org/10.1007/bf00991640

Galanis, P., Vraka, I., Fragkou, D., Bilali, A., & Kaitelidou, D. 2021. "Nurses' burnout and associated risk factors during the COVID-19 pandemic: A systematic review and meta-analysis." *Journal of Advanced Nursing*, 77(8), 3286–3302. https://doi.org/10.1111/jan.14839

Genevsky, A., Västfjäll, D., Slovic, P., & Knutson, B. 2013. "Neural underpinnings of the identifiable victim effect: Affect shifts preferences for giving." *The Journal of Neuroscience*, 33(43), 17188–17196. https://doi.org/10.1523/jneurosci.2348-13.2013

Genevsky, A., Yoon, C., & Knutson, B. 2017. "When brain beats behavior: Neuroforecasting crowdfunding outcomes." *The Journal of Neuroscience*, 37(36), 8625–8634. https://doi.org/10.1523/jneurosci.1633-16.2017

Guttormson, J. L., Calkins, K., McAndrew, N., Fitzgerald, J., Losurdo, H., & Loonsfoot, D. 2022. "Critical care nurse burnout, moral distress, and mental health during the COVID-19 pandemic: A United States survey." *Heart & Lung*, 55, 127–133. https://doi.org/10.1016/j.hrtlng.2022.04.015

Hein, G., Lamm, C., Brodbeck, C., & Singer, T. 2011. "Skin conductance response to the pain of others predicts later costly helping." *PLoS One*, 6(8), e22759. https://doi.org/10.1371/journal.pone.0022759.t001

Hein, G., Silani, G., Preuschoff, K., Batson, C. D., & Singer, T. 2010. "Neural responses to ingroup and outgroup members' suffering predict individual differences in costly helping." *Neuron*, 68(1), 149–160. https://doi.org/10.1016/j.neuron.2010.09.003

Hunsaker, S., Chen, H., Maughan, D., & Heaston, S. 2015. "Factors that influence the development of compassion fatigue, burnout, and compassion satisfaction in emergency department nurses." *Journal of Nursing Scholarship*, 47(2), 186–194. https://doi.org/10.1111/jnu.12122

Klimecki, O. M., Leiberg, S., Ricard, M., & Singer, T. 2014. "Differential pattern of functional brain plasticity after compassion and empathy training." *Social Cognitive and Affective Neuroscience*, 9(6), 873–879. https://doi.org/10.1093/scan/nst060

Kogut, T., & Ritov, I. 2005. "The singularity effect of identified victims in separate and joint evaluations." *Organizational Behavior and Human Decision Processes*, 97, 106–116.

Leiberg, S., Klimecki, O., & Singer, T. 2011. "Short-term compassion training increases prosocial behavior in a newly developed prosocial game." *PLoS One*, 6(3), e17798. https://doi.org/10.1371/journal.pone.0017798.t002

Lockwood, P. L., Hamonet, M., Zhang, S. H., Ratnavel, A., Salmony, F. U., Husain, M., & Apps, M. A. J. 2017. "Prosocial apathy for helping others when effort is required." *Nature Human Behaviour*, 1(7), 0131. https://doi.org/10.1038/s41562-017-0131

Mandowara, K., & Leo, L. 2023. "One-third of US nurses plan to quit profession, survey shows." *Reuters*, May 1, 2023. https://www.reuters.com/world/us/one-third-us-nurses-plan-quit-profession-report-2023-05-01/

Masten, C. L., Morelli, S. A., & Eisenberger, N. I. 2011. "An fMRI investigation of empathy for 'social pain' and subsequent prosocial behavior." *NeuroImage, 55*(1), 381–388. https://doi.org/10.1016/j.neuroimage.2010.11.060

McCall, C., Steinbeis, N., Ricard, M., & Singer, T. 2014. "Compassion meditators show less anger, less punishment, and more compensation of victims in response to fairness violations." *Frontiers in Behavioral Neuroscience, 8*, 424. https://doi.org/10.3389/fnbeh.2014.00424

Monroe, K. 2004. *The hand of compassion: Portraits of moral choice during the holocaust.* Princeton, NJ: Princeton University Press.

Monroe, K. 2012. *Ethics in an age of terror and genocide: Identity and moral choice.* Princeton, NJ: Princeton University Press.

Moors, A., & Scherer, K. R. 2013. "The role of appraisal in emotion." In M. D. Robinson, E. Watkins, & E. Harmon-Jones (Eds.), *Handbook of cognition and emotion* (pp. 135–155). New York, NY: The Guilford Press.

Moors, A., Ellsworth, P. C., Scherer, K. R., & Frijda, N. H. 2013. "Appraisal theories of emotion: State of the art and future development." *Emotion Review, 5*(2), 119–124. https://doi.org/10.1177/1754073912468165

Narvaez, D., & Lapsley, D. K. 2010. *Moral identity, moral functioning, and the development of moral character.* Cambridge: Academic Press. https://doi.org/10.1016/s0079-7421(08)00408-8

Peterson, G. R., Slyke, J. A., Spezio, M., Brown, W. S., & Reimer, K. S. 2010. "The rationality of ultimate concern: Moral exemplars, *theological ethics, and the science of moral cognition.*" *Theology and Science, 8*(2), 139–161. https://doi.org/10.1080/14746701003675520

Pinel, J., & Barnes, S. 2017. *Biopsychology* (10th ed.). Saddle River, NJ: Pearson.

Reed, A. I., & Aquino, K. F. 2003. "Moral identity and the expanding circle of moral regard toward out-groups." *Journal of Personality and Social Psychology, 84*(6), 1270–1286. https://doi.org/10.1037/0022-3514.84.6.1270

Reimer, K. S., Young, C., Birath, B., Spezio, M. L., Peterson, G., Slyke, J. A. V., & Brown, W. S. 2011. "Maturity is explicit: Self-importance of traits in humanitarian moral identity." *The Journal of Positive Psychology, 7*(1), 36–44. https://doi.org/10.1080/17439760.2011.626789

Singer, T., & Lamm, C. 2009. "The social neuroscience of empathy." *Annals of the New York Academy of Sciences, 1156*(1), 81–96. https://doi.org/10.1111/j.1749-6632.2009.04418.x

Smith, I. H., Aquino, K., Koleva, S., & Graham, J. 2014. "The moral ties that bind … even to out-groups: The interactive effect of moral identity and the binding moral foundations." *Psychological Science, 25*(8), 1554–1562. https://doi.org/10.1177/0956797614534450

Spezio, M. 2015. "Embodied cognition and loving character." *Philosophy, Theology and the Sciences, 2*(1), 25. https://doi.org/10.1628/219597715x14268452692906

Waytz, A. 2012. "Response of dorsomedial prefrontal cortex predicts altruistic behavior." *The Journal of Neuroscience, 32*(22), 7646–7650.

Weitzman, T., & Narvaez, C. 2022. "Gabby Petito case: A timeline of her disappearance and homicide." *CBS News*, November 17, 2022. https://www.cbsnews.com/news/gabby-petito-brian-laundrie-timeline/

Williams, A., O'Driscoll, K., & Moore, C. 2014. "The influence of empathic concern on prosocial behavior in children." *Frontiers in Psychology, 5*, 425. https://doi.org/10.3389/fpsyg.2014.00425

Yerkes, R. M., & Dodson, J. D. 1908. "The relation of strength of stimulus to rapidity of habit-formation." *Journal of Comparative Neurology and Psychology, 18*(5), 459–482.

7 Families with Exemplary Commitments to Shared Purpose

An Exemplar Study

Kendall Cotton Bronk

Since the year 2000, research on the individual pursuit of purpose has exploded. A Psych Info search reveals that only about a thousand studies were published on individual purpose in all the years prior to 2000, but nearly 10,000 have been published in the two decades since. One reason for the remarkable growth in research on purpose has to do with perhaps the most consistent finding to emerge from this line of inquiry: purpose is a critical component of well-being (Bronk 2013; Bronk et al. 2023). Leading a life of purpose has been linked to a broad range of positive developmental outcomes, including higher rates of life satisfaction (Bronk et al. 2009), greater longevity (Hill & Turiano 2014), more high-quality social relationships (Steptoe & Fancourt 2019), and even to higher incomes and greater net worth (Hill et al. 2016).

Individuals who pursue a purpose in life are actively engaged in advancing a personally meaningful cause because doing so enables them to contribute to the world beyond themselves (Damon et al. 2003). Individuals find purpose in caring for their families, serving their communities, protecting the environment, enacting their religious beliefs, advancing social and political change, creating novel kinds of art, and pursuing careers that enable them to have an impact on the broader world (Damon 2008). Consequently, in addition to benefiting the individuals who pursue purposes, the construct is also associated with societal benefits (Bronk 2013; Damon et al. 2003).

Given that the individual pursuit of purpose has been established as such an important factor in individual and societal thriving, attention has turned to collective purposes. Collective purposes, at least in theory, have the potential to benefit both the groups that pursue them and the people and causes in the broader world that groups find purpose in serving (Bronk et al. under review). In fact, given the collective effort behind advancing purposeful aims in the broader world, collective purposes have the potential to benefit the broader world in even more significant ways than individual purposes do.

However, despite their promise, relatively little is known about what collective purposes entail. Only a handful of studies on the topic have been conducted. Within this budding area of study and practice, practitioners have explored and encouraged shared purposes among educators

DOI: 10.4324/9781032648392-10

(Hudson 2022), in business organizations (Quinn & Thakor 2018), and in religious settings (Holland 2022). Less empirical research has examined shared family purposes.

Since all people are members of families and family functioning is key to individual well-being (Lavee et al. 1987; Pederson & Revenson 2005), looking at family purposes—as one instance of collective purpose—represents a worthwhile aim. To that end, my colleagues and I conducted a four-year study of family purpose that relied on exemplars of the construct. We sought to understand what highly developed forms of family purpose look like as a means of better understanding what family purposes entail, how they develop, and how they might be cultivated. The present chapter outlines how the exemplar method was applied and the kinds of findings it generated in the study of family purpose. In so doing, this chapter sheds light on the role exemplar research can play in psychological investigations.

Family Purpose Study

Members of our research team came from the United States and Europe. The project team leads included Principal Investigator Kendall Cotton Bronk, Professor of Psychology at the Claremont Graduate University, Co-Principal Investigator Tarek el Sehity, Researcher and Lecturer at Sigmund Freud University in Vienna, and advisors, William Damon, Professor of Education at Stanford University and Heinrich Liechtenstein, Professor of Managerial Science and Applied Economics at IESE in Barcelona. Generously funded by two grants from the John Templeton Foundation, the project lasted four years, from 2019–2022. During that time, we proposed a working definition of family purpose and designed and executed the first empirical investigation of the construct.

Family Purpose Defined

Before we launched our study of family purpose, we needed a definition of the construct to guide our work. We read the small body of research on the topic, conferred with relevant researchers and practitioners, conducted pilot interviews, and built on our understanding of individual purpose. With this background knowledge, we proposed that extended families who use their shared resources to collectively address meaningful issues in the broader world would likely be guided by a shared family purpose. More formally, we proposed that a family purpose refers to *an active and sustained commitment shared among multigenerational family members for the way they want to use the family's collective resources to contribute to the broader world* (Bronk 2022). Five dimensions of this definition are important to highlight. First, the pursuit of family purpose represents a *long-term intention*. Although a family's purpose is likely to evolve over time, it manifests as a thread of consistent focus and vision that extends across time and generations. Second, a family purpose is *meaningful* to members of the family. In fact, it is so important to family members that they actively engage in making progress toward it. A family purpose is an *ongoing, lived commitment* rather than something family members merely contemplate or discuss. Third, a family's purpose is reflected in its history, present activities, and intentions for the future. This means that a family's purpose is more than an aspirational vision; rather, it is *consistent with the family's actions in the past, in the present, and in its forward-looking aims.* Fourth, a family purpose is shared by members of the intergenerational family network. This does not mean that every family member necessarily supports the purpose—in large extended families with 100 or more members, this would be unlikely—but it does mean that *most members recognize the aim as significant and meaningful to the family.* Finally, a family purpose is *oriented toward a cause beyond the family.* Working together toward a meaningful aim in service of people or causes outside the family provides inspiration and motivation.

Family Purpose Study Design

Our investigation of family purpose relied on qualitative methods since the topic was novel and the theory available to guide our investigation was limited (Creswell & Poth 2018). We created a semi-structured clinical-style interview protocol that featured questions, some of which were inspired by the Family Circumplex Model (Michael-Tsabari & Lavee 2012; Olson 2011), about family communication and culture, shared family values and goals, and religious and spiritual beliefs.

Family Purpose Sample

To maximize our chances of finding families with purpose and to build on literature suggesting that family purposes likely convey special benefits to families with shared enterprises (Jaffe 2020; Ward 1997), we recruited a sample of families with a variety of shared enterprises (e.g., nonprofit organizations, family businesses, etc.). The limited research on family purpose suggests that families with shared enterprises often reference the value they place on shared commitments and purposes that enhance the long-term stability and positive social impact of their businesses or other enterprises (e.g., Jaffe 2020). Some shared enterprises, such as nonprofit organizations and family foundations, are themselves purpose-driven (Quinn & Thakor 2018), and families with for-profit businesses have many opportunities to significantly influence the broader world (Schervish 2005). Identifying a shared purpose may provide families with shared enterprises with a reason to stay close (Jaffe & Lane 2004), and shared purposes, adopted by successive generations, may be fundamental to the overall success of multigenerational family enterprises (EY 2020; Jaffe 2020). Because families with shared enterprises are well positioned to benefit from family purposes, we limited our sample to those families.

An exemplar sample. To gain an understanding of the full scope of family purpose, we sought to identify a sample of families that demonstrated highly developed forms of family purpose. Although we did not explicitly set out to secure an exemplar sample, we ultimately followed the steps associated with exemplar research. Exemplars, or highly developed examples of some dimension of human development, have been used by scholars and practitioners as sources of inspiration and guidance for thousands of years (Bronk 2012b; Bronk et al. 2013). Real-life moral exemplars, such as Mother Theresa, and fictional moral exemplars, such as *To Kill a Mockingbird's* Atticus Finch, provide clear behavioral examples for others to follow. Exemplars are also used in psychological research.

When used in empirical research, exemplars serve a slightly different purpose. Although exemplars in empirical research may also provide behavioral inspiration and guidance, their primary function is to provide an understanding of high-functioning development (Damon & Colby 2013). To understand the full picture of human development, we need to study incomplete, typical, and complete—or at least more complete—examples of development. Exemplars demonstrate a higher level of development than is typical in some particular area (e.g., morality, spirituality, etc.). To understand what a construct, such as spirituality, entails, we need to understand how individuals who are not particularly spiritual, who are spiritual to a typical or common degree, and who are highly spiritual function. "An exemplar approach is necessary for providing an accurate, nondistorted account of any psychological phenomenon under investigation" (2013, 15). All too often, however, researchers fail to capture the higher ends of development; exemplar research is essential for this purpose. In addition to more fully illuminating a particular construct, an understanding of more complete development also sheds important light on potentially useful interventions designed to stimulate growth among individuals at deficient and more typical developmental levels.

It is important to note that exemplars are not exemplary in all areas. They are human, after all. When selecting exemplars for empirical study, it is important to bear in mind that individuals need only be exemplary in one area of scholarly interest (e.g., in terms of their moral commitments, their spiritual lives, etc.). It is quite possible they will be typical or even underdeveloped in other areas (e.g., as parents, as bosses, etc.).

Exemplar research is a strategy for including expert participants in empirical research (Bronk et al. 2013). The exemplar methodology has been applied to explore lesser-understood and multifaceted domains of development. For instance, studies have profiled care exemplars, bravery exemplars, moral exemplars, spiritual exemplars, and purpose exemplars, among others (Bronk 2012a; Colby & Damon 1992; King et al. 2014; Walker & Frimer 2007). Exemplar samples engage the exemplar participant as a collaborator in the investigation.

The exemplar methodology is not new. Just as people have used exemplars as models for thousands of years, so too have scholars used (versions of) exemplar methods to conduct investigations for some time. Although Aristotle did not conduct much empirical research, he was interested in, among other topics, the study of ethics, and as a means of understanding ethical constructs such as wisdom, he embraced an exemplar methodology approach of sorts. In *Nicomachean Ethics*, he wrote, "We approach the subject of practical wisdom by studying the persons to whom we attribute it" (1962, 1140a25). In other words, to understand how a complex construct functioned and developed, Aristotle examined that construct in the lives of individuals who exhibited it in an intense and highly developed manner. This assumption lies at the heart of more contemporary exemplar studies.

In short, *the exemplar methodology is a sample selection technique that involves the intentional selection of individuals, groups, or entities that exemplify the construct of interest in a particularly intense and highly developed manner* (Bronk 2012b; Bronk et al. 2013). In applying the exemplar methodology, researchers intentionally identify and study a sample of individuals who exhibit a particular characteristic—in the case of the present program of research, family purpose—in an exceptional or highly developed manner. In this way, the exemplar methodology features participants who are rare, not from the perspective of the characteristics they exhibit, but in the highly developed manner in which they demonstrate those particular attributes (Damon & Colby 2013).

In our study of family purpose, our unit of analysis was the family, and consistent with the tenets of the exemplar methodology, we developed nomination criteria to identify families that constituted exemplars of family purpose. We shared those criteria with expert nominators (Bronk 2012b; Bronk et al. 2013). Nomination criteria stemmed from our definition of family purpose. In addition to sharing our full definition of family purpose with our nominators, we asked them to identify families that (1) had been engaged in a shared enterprise for at least two—preferably three—generations, (2) found meaning in working in the shared enterprise, and (3) were inspired to engage in the shared enterprise because of how doing so allowed them to contribute to the broader world. Although these criteria did not require that all family members engage in the shared enterprise, (4) they did suggest that shared purpose was likely to be evident among families where most of the members would recognize and value the family's collective aim. We shared these criteria with practitioners who worked with families with shared enterprises and asked them to nominate families. We conducted brief screening interviews with the nominated families to ensure they met our criteria.

This process yielded a sample of (N=87) members of 25 families (12 North American and 13 European families). Across the sample, family enterprises varied in function and size. For instance, one family had owned and operated a small organic farm for three generations, and another had owned and operated a multinational distribution company for more than one hundred years.

Our sample was bimodal in nature; slightly less than half the participants represented middle-income families with small to medium-sized family enterprises, and slightly more than half represented ultra-high net worth (UHNW) families with large, usually international, family enterprises. A few fell somewhere in between. Including UHNW families in our sample was intentional; given the global nature of their organizations, these families have the potential to do great good or cause significant harm. Some scholars have referred to UHNW families as having "the capacity to exercise ... hyperagency" (Schervish & Herman 1988, 32).

Family Purpose Study Findings

The study yielded interesting insights with important implications. One key finding is that family purposes are rare (Bronk et al. under review). We sought to identify which of the 25 nominated families in our sample met our five criteria for shared purpose, as specified by our family purpose definition. Even though we intentionally included families with shared enterprises, who we expected would be more likely than other families to demonstrate shared purpose, and even though we had nominators identify families within this population particularly likely to demonstrate highly-developed forms of shared purpose, only about half of the 25 nominated families in our sample met all five criteria for family purpose: (1) The pursuit of collective, family purpose represents an intention that spans at least two generations. (2) A family purpose is meaningful enough to inspire family members to actively engage in making progress toward it. (3) A family's purpose is consistent with the family's actions in the past, in the present, and in its forward-looking aims. (4) Most members recognize the aim as significant and meaningful to the family. (5) A family purpose is oriented toward a cause beyond the family. The families that clearly and completely met all five of our criteria were designated as exemplar families of shared purpose. They demonstrated a rare and comparatively highly developed form of family purpose.

Other families in our sample met some, but not all the five criteria for shared family purpose. Some families demonstrated budding family purpose, meaning shared purpose was evident among younger but not older family members, and other families demonstrated fading family purpose, meaning shared purpose was evident among older but not younger family members. Still, other families in our sample demonstrated no signs of family purpose. Although some members of these families were committed to contributing to the broader world in their own ways, members of these families lacked a shared approach to doing so.

Based on our finding that purpose was rare, even among our nominated sample, we expect that rates of family purpose are exceedingly rare in the general public (Bronk et al. under review). This finding also points to different trajectories for families that meet some, but not all, of the criteria for purpose. Whereas families with budding family purpose may be expected to develop a fuller sense of family purpose with time, fading family purposes would be expected to wane with time. Of course, additional, longitudinal research is needed to substantiate this expectation.

Subsequent analyses focused only on the exemplar families with shared purpose (12 of the 25 families in the study). Thematic analyses suggested that family purposes can be differentiated by the target of family members' sense of responsibility (Bronk et al. under review). Families found purpose in taking responsibility for different groups of people or causes. For instance, across the sample, three sources of responsibility emerged. Some families found purpose in taking responsibility for the ethical way their organizations were run. These families were committed to providing good jobs to people who needed them, they made intentional efforts to share profits with employees, and they avoided laying off employees, even during COVID-19. Other families found purpose in taking responsibility for customers or end-users. These families demonstrated an extraordinary commitment to serving their customers' needs. Members of one family, which oversaw a nonprofit organization that provided arts education to underserved youth, prayed for the young people they served on a regular basis. In addition to taking responsibility for employees and customers, nearly all the families in our exemplar sample also expressed a strong sense of responsibility for some aspect of the broader world (e.g., working to preserve the environment, supporting their local community, etc.). Most families found purpose in pursuing more than one of these aims. In other words, some families found purpose in taking extraordinary responsibility for both their customers and for some aspect of the world beyond the family, or in taking extraordinary responsibility for both the way their companies were run and for some aspect of the world beyond the family. By definition, a family purpose involves a commitment to some aspect of the broader world, but that commitment can be to employees, customers, and/or the broader society.

Having identified a sample of families with highly developed forms of shared purpose, we also sought to understand the features that supported the development and pursuit of family purpose over time (Bronk et al. under review). In many regards, our sample was more notable for its heterogeneity than for its homogeneity. Some families were in business together, others ran nonprofit organizations together, and still others had shared commitments that were neither business nor nonprofit-oriented (e.g., shared commitment to serving as religious leaders). Families varied in other ways as well (size, geographic homeland, etc.). However, despite their many differences, it was remarkable that they found support for their family's shared aims in such similar ways.

Our analyses revealed that most of the exemplars of family purpose found support for their collective purposes in a shared commitment to moral and/or civic virtues. Multiple family members, and in many cases, all the family members we interviewed, said they shared a commitment to virtues that focused on caring for and contributing to others. These virtues often formed the foundation of their shared family purpose. For instance, interviewees from a fifth-generation U.S. family with a large holding company said their shared family purpose derived from a strong sense of "social responsibility."

The exemplar families with purpose were also notable for their high degree of cohesion. Members of these extended families came together on a regular basis to spend time together, and they tended to get along quite well. Cohesion among the families with purpose was evident both within and across generations. Of course, families without purpose are often cohesive as well, but in the case of the families with shared purpose, this cohesion was essential to bringing the members together around a collective commitment. It is difficult to imagine a family enacting a shared purpose if the members of that family do not get along well.

In addition to being highly cohesive, most of the purposeful families in our sample also identified a purpose champion, or someone in the family who actively supported and promoted the family's shared aim. This person encouraged buy-in among family members. Purpose champions consistently used the beyond-the-family commitment to inspire and motivate other family members to support the family's shared purpose.

Humble leaders were another typical feature of families with shared purpose. Family leaders and other members of the older generations were eager to listen to the concerns and perspectives of the younger family members. Being willing to listen ensured that members of the older generation, who often had more power and say in the direction of the family's purpose, listened to members of the younger generation. Humility and an eagerness to learn from one another were key to ensuring family members from different generations were on the same page regarding the causes they worked to advance. Among several families with purpose, younger members shared the older generations' concerns, but they expressed new concerns too, and families with purpose were eager to hear the younger generations' concerns. This openness increased the likelihood that family purposes would grow to reflect the evolving family concerns.

Yet another consistent feature of families with purpose was a strong sense of family identity. Families with purpose tended to have a strong sense of who they were and what they stood for as a family. Members told us they valued their shared family identity.

Finally, most of the families with purpose had a strong religious foundation. Religious and spiritual beliefs provided family members with a shared touchpoint for their collective purpose. Members of a second-generation family that founded and ran a nonprofit noted that shared religious beliefs helped to keep the family close and work toward its common aim.

Given that families with shared religious beliefs may be particularly likely to pursue collective purposes, another analysis focused on understanding the way religious beliefs supported shared family purposes (Bronk in preparation). Theory suggests several ways religious beliefs may be relevant to the formation and pursuit of a shared family purpose. Religious beliefs may provide an important moral framework for decision-making, and they can serve as a source of family identity that inspires purpose (Abdelgawad & Zahra 2020; Parboteeah et al. 2008). Religious beliefs shared among family members may provide an important source of motivation to serve a higher good, and service to the world beyond the family is a core component of a family purpose (Parboteeah et al. 2008). Two of the families in our sample found purpose in running family foundations, and in this context, religious beliefs informed the mission and grant-making priorities. Other families ran for-profit businesses, and in this context, religious beliefs shaped the values that guided the family's business decisions.

Given that shared religious beliefs seemed theoretically likely to inspire shared purposes, members of our research team analyzed the role they played in our exemplar families of purpose. Findings from this analysis suggest that religious beliefs played at least three different roles in sustaining family purpose (Bronk in preparation). In some families, religious beliefs inspired the development of shared family purposes. Many religions encourage adherents to serve the broader world, and in this way, religious beliefs motivated some families to develop a shared purpose. Among these families, religious beliefs provided the "why" for their family's shared aim. In other families, religious beliefs shaped the way families pursued their collective purposes. Drawing on religious beliefs that encourage adherents to treat others well, these families made decisions regarding how to interact with their employees based on how their faith dictated they should interact with others. In these families, religious beliefs guided the "how" of shared family purpose. Finally, in still other families, religious beliefs inspired the content or "what" of family purposes. One family, for instance, found purpose in serving marginalized youth, and the decision to serve this particular population was inspired, at least in part, by their religious faith, which encouraged them to care for people who were struggling.

Two additional analyses of the family purpose dataset focused on the relationship between family values and family purposes and on the role that values played in the transmission of family purposes across generations. Using Schwartz and Bardi's (2001) basic human values framework, the first of these analyses examined both the values related to family purposes (el Sehity in preparation) and the way those values were passed across generations (Asamer in preparation). Findings suggest values and family purposes influence one another in a bidirectional way. Values shaped the focus of the family's shared purpose, and the family's shared purpose shaped the values prioritized by family members. Particularly purposeful families provided rich accounts of joint, intergenerational spaces where reciprocal influences, both within and across generations, took place. Intergenerational spaces included family holidays, family activities, and values-oriented projects, often coordinated and executed within the shared family enterprise. In short, family values were often discussed and shared in both formal and informal ways. In line with 'Kuczynski and De Mol's (2015) account of values transmission, findings suggest that for values to be shared, all family members must have a role in shaping and being shaped by one another's personally held beliefs. It cannot be assumed that members of the older generation transmit values while members of the younger generation receive them. Instead, members of both generations influence one another in a bidirectional process of formulating, negotiating, and clarifying a shared understanding of the family's values and priorities. These findings suggest the intergenerational values and purpose transmission process may be a dialectical, relational phenomenon.

The final analysis explored the degree to which members of families with purpose shared and identified with family goals and priorities (el Sehity in preparation). Salice and Henriksen (2021) have proposed two forms of shared intentionality: joint intentionality and we-intentionality. Joint intentionality relies on people's ability to be moved by another's intentions, whereas we intentionality relies on people's capacity to see themselves as members of a group and to adopt the group's perspectives. Findings from the present analysis suggest that families with purpose demonstrate signs of we-intentionality, as evidenced by their tendency to identify with their family, including its history and its shared intentions. This finding is underscored by family business research, which suggests that family social interactions can support the collective commitment to family-centered goals (Kotlar & Massis 2013).

What's Next in This Line of Research?

These insights shed important light on the emerging family purpose construct, but much remains to be learned. Given that this study relied on a relatively small sample of exemplars of family purpose, it will be important to investigate the prevalence of family purpose among non-nominated samples. Our analyses suggest family purposes are rare even among nominated samples; how common (or uncommon) are they in the general public? What might less highly developed or approaching-family-purpose forms of the construct entail? These kinds of investigations would require a much larger, more diverse sample of families and likely a survey of family purpose, using measures that have yet to be developed.

In addition to investigating the prevalence of family purpose, it makes sense to further investigate its role in supporting family functioning and societal good. A small body of research suggests that other forms of collective purpose may be highly beneficial to local communities and the broader society (e.g., Holland 2022; Hudson 2022; Quinn & Thakor 2018), but empirical research has yet to directly investigate the benefits of shared family purpose. How do families benefit from committing to a shared aim? Our research suggests shared commitments may help unite exemplar families and offer them a reason for staying together; is this the case for more typical families who only demonstrate some of the construct's criteria? What impact do family purposes have on broader society?

How, if at all, do individual purposes intersect with shared family purposes? In other words, how do individuals with strong purposes in their lives connect with their family's shared purposes? Do they find ways of making the family's purpose their own? Are they likely to find their individual purposes within the family's purpose? Do individual and family purposes often contradict one another? Understanding how family purposes and individual purposes intersect would shed important light on our growing understanding of both family and individual purposes and enhance efforts to bolster both forms of purpose.

Investigations of family purpose should also examine potential downsides of shared family purposes. Do members of families with strong shared purposes ever feel constrained by their shared vision? Do they feel pressure to conform to the family's shared aim? What avenues exist for dissent? How do dissent-supporting avenues function?

Family purposes represent a balance between continuity and change. Family purposes are, by their nature, enduring and stable across time. They inspire generation after generation. However, to remain relevant, family purposes also need to evolve. As society changes, family members' views and priorities are likely to shift. What do family purposes look like over time? What remains constant, and what changes? What are the avenues for change, and what practices help ensure a level of continuity? A long-term longitudinal study of family purposes would be required to investigate these kinds of questions.

These represent only a few of the likely next steps in this line of research. To investigate most of them, larger samples of purposeful families would need to be recruited. This could prove challenging, given the rarity of the phenomenon. However, if family purposes are found to be as beneficial as other forms of collective purpose, then finding ways of recruiting sufficiently large samples to further investigate this promising construct may be worthwhile.

Conclusion

This study represents one of the first empirical investigations of the family purpose construct, a construct that has gained attention for its potential benefits to both the families that pursue them and the communities those families find purpose in serving (EY 2020; Jaffe 2020). Emerging findings suggest that families can demonstrate exemplary forms of shared purpose, budding or fading forms of shared purpose, or no shared purpose at all. Findings also point to the important role religious beliefs can play in uniting family members around a collective, contributory commitment. In addition, findings shed light on the supports for family purpose and on the bidirectional nature of values and purpose development and transmission. Since family purpose is so rare, it seems unlikely we could have learned all that we did about family purpose using any approach other than an exemplar methodology. This methodology allowed us a rare glimpse into the communication styles, values, and priorities of families with shared purpose. We hope this study inspires both future research, using exemplar methodologies, and future research on the family purpose construct.

References

Abdelgawad, S. G., & Zahra, S. A. 2020. "Family firms' religious identity and strategic renewal." *Journal of Business Ethics*, 163, 775–786. DOI: 10.1007/s10551-019-04385-4

Aristotle. 1962. *Nicomachean ethics*. Translated with introduction and notes by Martin Ostwald. Library of Liberal Arts.

Asamer, V. (in preparation). *The transmission of family purpose across generations*.

Bronk, K. C. 2012a. "A grounded theory of youth purpose." *Journal of Adolescent Research*, 27, 78–109. DOI: 10.1177/0743558411412958

Bronk, K. C. 2012b. "The exemplar methodology: An approach to studying the leading edge of development." *Psychology of Well-Being: Theory, Research and Practice*, 2(5). DOI: 10.1186/2211-1522-2-5.

Bronk, K. C. 2013. *Purpose in life: A component of optimal youth development*. New York, NY: Springer.

Bronk, K. C. 2022. "Family purpose in family firms: What it looks like and why it's important." *FFI Practitioner*. Accessed online 24 April 2023. https://digital.ffi.org/editions/family-purpose-in-family-firms-what-it-looks-and-why-its-important/

Bronk, K. C. (in preparation). *The role of religious beliefs in the formation and pursuit of family purpose*.

Bronk, K. C., Hill, P. L., Lapsley, D. K., Talib, T. L., & Finch, H. 2009. "Purpose, hope, and life satisfaction in three groups." *Journal of Positive Psychology*, 4(6), 500–510. https://doi.org/10.1080/17439760903271439

Bronk, K. C., King, P. E., & Matsuba, K. 2013. "An introduction to exemplar research: a definition, rationale, and conceptual issues." *New Directions for Child and Adolescent Development*, 142(4), 1–12.

Bronk, K. C., Mitchell C., Postlewaite, E., Colby, A., Damon, W., & Swanson, Z. (under review). "Family purpose: An empirical investigation of collective purpose."

Bronk, K. C., Reichard, R. J., & Qi, J. 2023. "A co-citation analysis of purpose: Trends and (potential) troubles in the foundation of purpose scholarship." *Journal of Positive Psychology*. https://doi.org/10.1080/17439760.2023.2168563.

Colby, A., & Damon, W. 1992. *Some do care: Lives of extraordinary moral commitment*. New York, NY: Free Press.

Creswell, J., & Poth, C. N. 2018. *Qualitative inquiry and research design: Choosing among five approaches* (4th ed.). Thousand Oaks, CA: Sage.

Damon, W. 2008. *The path to purpose: How young people find their calling in life*. New York, NY: Free Press.

Damon, W., & Colby, A. 2013. "Why a true account of human development requires exemplar research." *New Directions for Child and Adolescent Development*, 142(4), 13–25.

Damon, W., Menon, J. L., & Bronk, K. C. 2003. "The development of purpose during adolescence." *Applied Developmental Science*, 7(3), 119–128. https://doi.org/10.1207/S1532480XADS0703_2.

el Sehity, T. (in preparation). *The bidirectional nature of family values, goals, and purposes*.

EY (December 15, 2020). *What is purpose and why do we need it?* Accessed online 3 March 2022. https://www.ey.com/en_nl/purpose/why-business-must-harness-the-power-of-purpose

Hill, P. L., & Turiano, N. A. 2014. "Purpose as a predictor of mortality across adulthood." *Psychological Science*, 25(7), 1482–1486. DOI: 10.1177/09567976 14531799.

Hill, P. L., Turiano, N. A., Mroczek, D. K., & Burrow, A. L. 2016. "The value of a purposeful life: Sense of purpose predicts greater income and net worth." *Journal of Research in Personality*, 38–42, epub. DOI: 10.1016/j.jrp.2016.07.003.

Holland, C. 2022. "Why a collective vision is essential for your church." *Playlister*. Accessed online 21 February 2023. https://www.playlister.app/blog/why-a-collective-vision-is-essential-for-your-church

Hudson, E. 2022. *The power of collective purpose in schools.* Global Online Academy. Accessed online 21 February 2023. https://globalonlineacademy.org/insights/articles/the-power-of-collective-purpose-in-schools

Jaffe, D. 2020. *Borrowed from your grandchildren: The evolution of the 100-year family enterprises.* Hoboken, NJ: Wiley.

Jaffe, D. T., & Lane, S. H. 2004. "Sustaining a family dynasty: Key issues facing complex multigenerational business- and investment-owning families." *Family Business Review*, 17(1), 81–98.

King, P. E., Clardy, C. E., & Ramos, J. S. 2014. "Adolescent spiritual exemplars: Exploring spirituality in the lives of diverse youth." *Journal of Adolescent Research*, 29(2), 186–212. https://doi.org/10.1177/0743558413502534

Kotlar, J., & Massis, A. D. 2013. "Goal setting in family firms: Goal diversity, social interactions, and collective commitment to family–centered goals." *Entrepreneurship Theory and Practice*, 37(6), epub. https://doi.org/10.1111/etap.12065

Kuczynski, L., & De Mol, J. 2015. "Dialectical models of socialization." In W. F. Overton, & P. C. M. Molenaar (Eds.), *Theory and method (vol. 1) of the handbook of child psychology and developmental science* (7th ed.) (pp. 323–368). Hoboken, NJ: John Wiley & Sons, Inc.

Lavee, Y., McCubbin, H. I., & Olson, D. H. 1987. "The effects of stressful life events and transitions on family functioning and well-being." *Journal of Marriage and Family*, 49(4), 857–873. DOI: 10.2307/351979.

Michael-Tsabari, N., & Lavee, Y. 2012. "Too close and too rigid: Applying the circumplex model of family systems to first-generation family firms." *Journal of Marital and Family Therapy*, 38, 105–116. DOI: 10.1111/j.1752-0606.2012. 00302.x.

Olson, D. 2011. "FACES IV and the circumplex model: Validation study." *Journal of Marital and Family Therapy*, 37(1), 64–80.

Parboteeah, K. P., Hoegl, M., & Cullen, J. B. 2008. "Ethics and religion: An empirical test of a multidimensional model." *Journal of Business Ethics*, 81(2), 387–398.

Pederson, S., & Revenson, T. A. 2005. "Parental illness, family functioning, and adolescent well-being: A family ecology framework to guide research." *Journal of Family Psychology*, 19(3), 404–419. DOI: 10.1037/0893-3200.19.3.404.

Quinn, R. E., & Thakor, A. V. 2018. "Creating a purpose-driven organization: How to get employees to bring their smarts and energy to work." *Harvard Business Review*, 78–85. Accessed online 21 February 2023. https://hbr.org/2018/07/creating-a-purpose-driven-organization

Salice, A., & Henriksen, M. G. 2021. "Disturbances of shared intentionality in schizophrenia and autism." *Frontiers in Psychiatry*. https://doi.org/10.3389/fpsyt. 2020.570597

Schervish, P. G. (2006). The moral biography of wealth: Philosophical reflections on the foundation of philanthropy. Nonprofit and Voluntary Sector Quarterly, 35(3), 345–557. DOI: 10.1177/0899764006288287

Schervish, P. C., & Herman, A. 1988. *Empowerment and beneficence: Strategies of living and giving among the wealthy: Findings from the study of wealth and philanthropy.* Chestnut Hill, MA: Boston College Center on Wealth and Philanthropy.

Schwartz, S. H., & Bardi, A. 2001. "Value hierarchies across cultures: Taking a similarities perspective." *Journal of Cross-Cultural Psychology*, *32*(3), 268–290. DOI: 10.1177/0022022101032003002.

Steptoe, A., & Fancourt, D. 2019. "Leading a meaningful life at older ages and its relationship with social engagement and its relationship with social engagement, prosperity, health, biology, and time use." *PNAS*, *16*(4), 1207–1212. DOI: 10.1073/pnas.1814723116.

Walker, L. J., & Frimer, J. A. 2007. "Moral personality of brave and caring exemplars." *Journal of Personality and Social Psychology*, *93*(5), 845–860. https://doi.org/10.1037/0022-3514.93.5.845

Ward, J. L. 1997. "Growing the family business: Special challenges and best practices." *Family Business Review*, *10*(4), 323–337.

8 Traditions and Exemplars in Spiritual Formation

Toward an Integration of Catholic Theology and Developmental Science

Timothy Reilly

Humans are born into ongoing narrative and spiritual communities. Resulting from this, many children are formed in the spirituality of their communities, often centered on religion. Despite this, there is widespread evidence that many Americans choose to leave their religious communities, eschewing religion altogether or entering new spiritual communities (e.g., Smith & Snell 2009). This is likely in part because of the lack of effective exposure to exemplars and models in their spiritual communities, especially their families (Smith & Adamczyk 2021), alongside the broader decline in participation in such communities in much of the developed world (Smith & Snell 2009). Clear thinking about the processes supporting spiritual formation, especially imitation of spiritual exemplars, may help to understand these trends and to develop strategies for addressing the spiritual and religious changes occurring in our society.

To begin, spiritual formation is about the intentional cultivation of a way of being aligned with particular values within a tradition, and here the focus is on the Catholic faith tradition. Another way of saying this is that all spiritual formation is formation in virtue, as virtue is understood within a tradition (MacIntyre 2007; Reilly & Narvaez 2022). The Catholic tradition is one of many spiritual and religious traditions and one which has received little attention from the perspective of developmental science. As such, Catholicism is emphasized, though the empirical studies drawn on use samples from diverse religious backgrounds.

The 4 Es approach to virtue (Reilly & Narvaez 2022) informs the later sections of the chapter, which focus on the role of exemplars and others in spiritual formation in the Catholic tradition. Thus, the chapter first addresses the 4 Es approach, especially relating it to Catholicism. Then it presents some central ideas from Catholic thought bearing on exemplarity and spiritual formation. Following this, relevant developmental science is considered, with a focus on those aspects that are most relevant to the considerations arising from Catholic theology of formation. The chapter closes with considerations for further exploration and integration between Catholic thought and developmental science.

DOI: 10.4324/9781032648392-11

The 4 Es of Virtue in Catholic Formation

Virtuous development and spiritual formation can be understood in light of the 4 Es: (1) *ends*, (2) *ethic*, (3) *excellence*, and (4) *emergence* (T. Reilly et al. 2022). This approach is roughly aligned with both Aristotelian (Aristotle 2002) and Thomistic (Aquinas 1991) accounts of virtue. Each of these facets of virtue is intertwined with the others, mutually informing how the others should be understood. *Ends* organize the values, both ultimate and instrumental, to be realized by virtue formation. *Ethic* emphasizes virtuous formation as not just acting rightly in a single situation but instead as a characteristic way of being across situations, ideally manifesting in the virtuous functioning of an entire personality. *Excellence* highlights exemplary functioning and expert activity. Finally, *emergence* is about coming to be, and so is most central to addressing formation. I will begin with an example of the 4 Es in a narrower practice, archery, which I do not take to be directed toward the highest *ends*. I will then describe the 4 Es in light of the tradition of the Catholic faith.

In archery, *ends*, *ethic*, *excellence*, and *emergence* all have important and related parts to play. The *ends* of archery are being able to hit one's target, and ideally, to hit that target where you desire to hit the target. So, if an archer is shooting at a standard target, the *end* is typically hitting the bullseye. *Ethic* expresses the actual perceptions, thoughts, motives, and behaviors that make up a personality in part or in whole. Thus, a virtuous archer is able to perceive a target and the context in ways that facilitate accuracy, to think through new conditions and adjust to them, to desire to hit the target for its own sake, and to use a bow of some kind in order to do so. Further, some archers are more *excellent* than others, and so more reliably fire arrows that strike at or near the target, have better motives for doing so and perceive and think more appropriately regarding what is needed to hit a target. Finally, regarding *emergence*, one is not born a virtuous archer; instead, one learns through engagement with others how to fire a bow and aim at a target. Thus, each of the 4 Es is interrelated, and none stand on their own. After all, one can hit a bullseye in many ways, and so achieve the *ends* of archery, while failing to live out the *ethic* of archery. For example, one could walk up to a target without a bow and put an arrow into it or using a firearm on a target, neither of which would be archery.

In considering spiritual formation in the Catholic faith, ultimate *ends* can best be understood as twofold: loving God and loving others (Benedict XVI 2005), with each virtue supporting the pursuit of these ultimate *ends* in light of the particular *end* of the virtue. Thus, the virtue of integrity, which has pursuing harmoniously good commitments as an *end* (Herdt 2020; T. Reilly et al. 2022), is virtuous inasmuch as an individual's commitments are harmoniously ordered to the highest goods of loving God and others. Excellence then manifests as *excellence* directed toward the *end* of loving well, through the development of an appropriate *ethic* or personality. This virtuous *ethic emerges*, in part, from engagement with exemplary individuals and communities, through imitation or otherwise. Thus, the Catholic faith tradition provides clear articulations and expressions of *ends*, *ethic,* and *excellence*, while developmental science especially contributes to a richer understanding of *emergence* as it supports these facets of virtue, which have been less systematically addressed.

A Catholic Understanding of Exemplarity and Formation

Here, I want to acknowledge that I am writing as a developmental psychologist with limited theological training. Nonetheless, there are numerous Catholic theological concepts that bear further consideration in light of, and for, developmental science. These include ideas, discussed in more detail below, about who should be considered exemplary and in what sense (e.g., the imitation of Christ and the communion of saints), the Catholic Christian tradition and narrative (Kerygma, scripture, and revelation), and sanctification. Further, recent accounts emphasize particular approaches to formation (e.g., accompaniment; see Francis 2013) and pillars of formation (John Paul II 1992). This chapter's engagement of these ideas will be a sketch relating to the present topic rather than a full explication.

Catholic thought relating to exemplarity focuses on Jesus Christ and Christian saints. The imitation of Christ (e.g., Paul VI 1964) highlights Jesus of Nazareth as the central figure for imitation and emulation in Christianity, as the exemplar par excellence, while noting Jesus' otherness, given that Jesus is understood as both human and divine. Catholics also acknowledge the Catholic Church as a communion of saints and as the Body of Christ (e.g., DeLorenzo 2017). The communion of saints includes two divisions that are particularly relevant to this chapter, the Church Triumphant (those saints believed to be living in union with God in heaven) and the Church Militant (Catholic Christians on earth who have not yet died). Indeed, the Catholic Church presents itself as seeking to be, roughly speaking, a community of the practice of love (Benedict XVI 2005). This means that, even as Jesus of Nazareth is acknowledged as the height of exemplarity and *excellence*, all Christians are at once expected to strive for exemplarity in love (through the imitation of Jesus) and to follow the example of other excellent Christians regarding love, both those living and beyond the grave. Further, the communion of saints emphasizes universal community of Christians rather than expecting a single Christian to provide a comprehensive model, which can, in this way of seeing only be provided by Jesus of Nazareth.

Turning to narrative, Catholics assert that the biblical Old and New Testaments are divinely inspired texts. These scriptures, especially the four Gospels, are understood as central to understanding Christ and therefore how each Christian is to live, imitating Jesus Christ as a model (Barron 2007). Indeed, these two things, imitation of Jesus and the narrative of scripture, are intertwined in the Catholic tradition, as in the scriptures Jesus directly exhorts his followers to imitate him in particular ways, especially in proclaiming the Good News of redemption and new life (Barron 2007). Further, in light of the communion of saints (DeLorenzo 2017), Catholics understand themselves not to be mere observers in this story but participants through Jesus in God's ongoing redemption of the world.

Sanctification conveys the ideal outcome of Catholic Christian formation, transformation into greater holiness and likeness to Jesus Christ, both individually and communally (Paul VI 1964). However, this is understood to take place not merely, or even primarily, as a result of the initiative and action of individual Christians. Instead, sanctification occurs in response to grace offered by God, generally and in particular ways, through the Sacraments and liturgy (Paul VI 1963). Grace in this sense means participation in the life of God through God's free gift of that life (Aquinas 1991). Sacraments are understood as providing specific graces, allowing Catholics to more fully participate in the life of God (Paul VI 1963), which is manifest through the sacraments, rather than simply imitating it.

Nonetheless, the personal formation of the individual matters for their ability to respond to this grace effectively so as to become like Jesus Christ. Thus, the Catholic Church seeks to assist its members' spiritual formation through accompaniment, walking with those in need of spiritual guidance and formation (Francis 2013), with four pillars of formation (John Paul II 1992; Paul VI 1965). These include (though here I adapt the phrasing slightly): (1) human formation, emphasizing the ability to relate to others and oneself as persons, (2) intellectual formation, forming the mind to seek wisdom and to see and understand the world rightly, (3) contemplative formation, emphasizing the capacity to relate to God through prayer or other activity that leads one to experience oneself as in communion with the divine, and (4) practical formation, relating to living out the Catholic faith well and efficaciously.

These pillars of formation provide a structure for thinking about where and how developmental science relates to Catholic views of spiritual formation. While elucidating all of these ties is beyond the scope of this chapter, a brief overview is provided here for the interested reader. Human formation has many ties to developmental science, especially the psychology of moral and civic character development (e.g., Lapsley et al. 2020). Intellectual formation has clear ties to theories of intellectual character and epistemic virtue, though this scholarship often emphasizes scientific intellection (e.g., Chinn et al. 2014) rather than the broader formation of thought and imagination. Contemplative formation has received less direct attention in social scientific scholarship on virtue development, though it is implicit in theories like Triune Ethics Metatheory (Narvaez 2016), which suggests the centrality of imagination to human views of their relationship to others and the world. Contemplative formation also bears a clear relationship to mindfulness practices like gratitude journaling (Emmons & McCullough 2003) and the Ignatian Examen (Curlee & Ahrens 2022). Practical formation can be thought of as the personalized, contextualized, and agentic living out of the other facets of formation, relating to calling (Hall & Chandler 2004) and purpose (T. S. Reilly & Mariano 2021) development.

Developmental Science, Exemplarity, and Spiritual Formation

In light of the above, Catholic theology is consonant with an important perspective in developmental science (Overton 2013): relational developmental systems theory (RDST). RDST emphasizes individuals as existing within developmental structures and relationships that, at once, influence their development and which they influence. As such, RDST highlights individual-context relationships as dynamic and bidirectional rather than with influence only moving in one direction. For instance, one must consider not only the influence of parents on children but also the influence of children on parents and not only the influence of exemplars on others but also the influence of others on exemplars.

I will use RDST to frame the understanding of exemplarity and spiritual formation in this chapter. RDST is helpful for conceptualizing development as it provides an overarching framework for an understanding of spiritual formation as the development of a virtuous spiritual personality. RDST also has the benefit of having been explored more generally as relating to religion and spirituality (see Balswick et al. 2016; King et al. 2020, 2023). However, little research in developmental psychology speaks directly to Catholic Spiritual formation, so spiritual formation will be considered broadly, seeking to generalize prior work to Catholic applications.

In the sections below, varied facets of developmental science related to spiritual formation are addressed. This begins with personality, considering the *ethic* of the person being formed. Next exemplarity is addressed as it relates to spiritual formation, highlighting *excellence* in pursuit of the highest *ends*. Finally, *emergence* supports the formation of a more *excellent ethic*, both as influenced by contexts and relationships and through an individual's own agency.

Personality: Understanding a Person's *Ethic*

A systematic understanding of personality as a comprehensive *ethic* is necessary for a rich consideration of formation as a personal process, rather than as something that is one-size-fits-all. Two helpful theories in this regard are Knowledge and Appraisal Personality Architectures (KAPA; Cervone & Little 2019) and the three-level actor-agent-author model (McAdams 2013). Both approaches provide insight into both personality functioning and personality development, rather than the largely descriptive approach common in considering personality traits.

Personality arises through varied structures and processes/dynamics (Cervone & Little 2019). KAPA (Orom & Cervone 2009) highlights individual cognitive, behavioral, and affective *structures* and psychological and social appraisal *processes* as driving personality functioning and change. Cognitive, behavioral, and affective structures are understood as psychological schemas within an individual, which may be quite situation-specific (e.g., a schema to remember to thank a friend) or quite general (e.g., a schema for social situations). These schemas and their influence on psychological functioning can be seen as forming the architectural foundation for psychological functioning on which experiences dynamically build (Cervone & Little 2019). The more specific a schema, the smaller an array of situations it would be expected to predict behavior in. Further, these schemas can relate to (1) goals (e.g., planning to wake up for an alarm, Gollwitzer et al. 2006), (2) values like being nice or being able to manipulate others (Cloutier & Ahrens 2020), (3) experiences like seeing how others react to one's request for help (Bosmans et al. 2020), and (4) capabilities like one's ability to preach effectively (Schunk & Zimmerman 1997).

Processes/dynamics in KAPA highlight the moment-to-moment influence of experiences and current circumstances on personality functioning (Cervone & Little 2019; Cloutier & Ahrens 2020). Thus, in novel situations, an individual may be at a loss for how to behave because they cannot recall a relevant schema. A different individual may have substantial prior experience that they perceive as relevant in this new situation and so draw on that experience for responding in this new situation. To use a religious example, imagine two adults attending a Catholic Mass for the first time. One has never attended any kind of religious service, and so is confused and observes from the back. The other has been to an array of Protestant services, and so compares and contrasts these experiences with the Catholic Mass, participating where their existing schema seems to provide enough guidance. In both cases, the individual would then be able to evaluate their experience and respond differently in related situations in the future. The reactions of others to one's presence and participation (e.g., smiles or scowls) could inform this evaluation. These reactions and experiences may also inform their attitudes and beliefs about Catholics, Catholic Mass, and Catholicism on the whole.

McAdams (2013) proposes that personality expresses dimensions of individuals as actors, agents, and authors in varied ways. Individuals are actors inasmuch as they take on consistent social roles and enact traits consistently across situations. They express agency through pursuing plans, exploring and expressing values, and imagining desired futures. Finally, individuals author their lives, telling stories about their past experiences, and through these stories, seek to generate a consistent identity and tell coherent stories about who they have been and hope to become. There is evidence that even young children express authorship and agency through play (Corsaro 1993; Creekpaum 2019), meaning that each of these facets of personality is present throughout life. McAdams' (McAdams 2013) theory can be considered as emphasizing various interrelated schemes in personality, and so is closely related to KAPA (Orom & Cervone 2009).

In summary, individuals have complex integrations of levels of personality differentiated across schemas that are organized by varied goals, values, experiences, and capabilities. These dimensions of personality will be considered in at least two ways below. First, they will be considered as manifest in exemplars, highlighting personality *excellence*. Next, they will be considered as relating to formation, addressing how they relate to personality change and the *emergence* of virtue.

Exemplarity: Living Out an *Excellent Ethic*

The above sets the stage for the consideration of exemplars of various kinds, understood as those who manifest *excellence* in a domain. Psychologists, philosophers, and theologians have written extensively on exemplary individuals, including spiritual exemplars (Barron 2007; King et al. 2014), moral exemplars (Damon & Colby 2015; Giebel 2021; Walker et al. 2010), and creative exemplars (Csikszentmihalyi 1996; Simonton 1999). Especially in preparing to consider formation, exemplary communities deserve attention, including religious families (Dollahite & Marks 2009), other religious communities (Spezio 2017), or communities focused on intellectual formation (Nakamura et al. 2009).

Exemplary individuals manifest *excellent ethics*. Excellent ethics include schemas and appraisals conducive to high-level functioning in the exemplar's domain, but also differentiation, as each exemplar engages in different behaviors and relationships in order to manifest their *excellence*. Walker et al. (2010) found two broad types of moral exemplars communal (more relationally focused) and deliberative (more rationally focused). This study of moral exemplars demonstrates differences between exemplars and non-exemplars at each level of personality: as actor, agent, and author. This indicates that there are many factors in exemplarity, aligning with the claim that exemplarity *should* look different for different individuals (see also Dumler-Winckler 2017). Additionally, studies of exemplary individuals highlight particular qualities that relate to *excellence* generally, including qualities like honesty and integrity, humility, courage, curiosity, and flexible thinking (Reilly 2018). Each of these qualities can be thought of as a potential virtue that results from effective appraisals using well-tuned schemas and so adaptively integrates the structure and appraisal functions of personality (Cloutier & Ahrens 2020).

Exemplary communities offer additional insight. These communities have the potential to support the formation of their members with *excellent ethics*. For instance, some scientific research groups are recognized by peers as developing both excellent and ethical scholars, in part because of a heightened emphasis on fostering integrity and honesty in their members (Nakamura & Condren 2018; Nakamura et al. 2009). Within exemplary religious families, excellent formation of children has been associated with child-centered religious conversation, engagement with religious traditions, rituals, and texts, religious exploration, and exemplary parenting, among other factors (Dollahite & Marks 2019). Finally, though systematic research in this area is sparse, one can consider exemplary spiritual communities like Homeboy Industries (Boyle 2011, 2017). Indeed, Homeboy Industries is inspired by Catholic thought, though not all members have been formally initiated into the Catholic Church. All are welcome in this community, so long as they commit to the radical model of kinship, compassion, and inclusion around which Homeboy Industries is centered (Spezio 2017). This includes a move toward self-forgetfulness as homeboys strive for greater love and communion with others. Further, the members of Homeboy Industries model self-forgetfulness with each other and seek to live out a very different *ethic* than the way of living that led them to join gangs and think of others as enemies.

As such, exemplar individuals, communities, and contexts, through highlighting *excellent ethics*, have much to contribute to spiritual formation. They provide guidance regarding the ideal outcomes of processes of formation, especially with regard to the domain of their exemplarity. This also includes an understanding of what it looks like for individuals to live out various virtues, like humility and integrity. Further, exemplary communities support thinking about formation in virtue, as they must socialize members to be virtuous. Thus, thinking at least theoretically about exemplary Catholic communities informs many of the examples below. As Catholic communities and contexts, these will be considered as directed toward the two highest *ends* mentioned above, loving God and loving others.

Spiritual Formation: The *Emergence* of Virtue

All of the above sets the stage for addressing spiritual formation, which can be considered as fostering *emerging* spiritual virtue. Such formation can occur in a number of ways and likely serves to integrate the functioning of a personality through a global rather than situation-specific spiritual scheme. This is to say that a fully spiritual person should be able to appropriately relate all of their experiences to their spirituality.[1] Further, given individual differences in personality, whether arising from different traits and temperaments or different opportunities and challenges, Catholic formation must be understood as relating to individuals and their unique contexts and qualities. This is true even as the orienting *ends* remain loving God and others (Benedict XVI 2005) for each individual.

Three approaches to understanding emergence are emphasized here, though many others could be considered. First, attachment theory is addressed, considering the developmental consequences of experiences of close relationships. Second, cognitive apprenticeship as an approach considering spiritual practices is broached. Finally, self-regulated learning is explored through social cognitive theory (Bandura 1977), which aligns closely with the KAPA approach to personality (Cervone & Little 2019) above.

Attachment

Attachment emphasizes relationships with supportive others amidst stress for protection and safety (Cherniak et al. 2021). Two central tensions, which contribute to insecure attachments, are (1) a concern about the availability and support of close others and (2) a concern for the responsiveness of close others (Bosmans et al. 2020). Regarding spirituality and religion, this is important as studies demonstrate a close relationship between attachment to parents and religious affiliation (Cherniak et al. 2021). Specifically, those who have a less secure attachment to their parents are also more likely to convert and to be less stable in any religious affiliation. Further, much is known about the relationship between how parents choose to parent and the attachment of a developing child, emphasizing appropriate levels of parental attentiveness, supportiveness, and responsiveness to attachment-related behavior (e.g., Bosmans et al. 2020). Studies have also demonstrated relationships between attachment and benevolent or prosocial behavior (Gross et al. 2017) and gratitude (Scott et al. 2021). Thus, fostering healthy attachment to parents and to God (Beck & McDonald 2004) seems to be one potential key to healthy spiritual formation, both in terms of loving others through benevolent behavior and through gratitude and closeness to God (Nelson et al. 2023).

Apprenticeship in Community

Spiritual formation, as formation in a tradition, happens within particular communities, and in particular practices and activities of those communities. Thus, in social scientific terms, spiritual formation is a sociocultural process. Practices are clusters of activities oriented toward particular ends that are sustained by the community, like navigation, science, midwifery, or writing (Lave & Wenger 1991). Scholars have extensively studied the ways that communities of practice socialize participants to behave in socially valued ways, especially through cognitive apprenticeship (Collins 2006). Relating this to the present chapter, apprenticeship can help us to understand the role of communities in forming others in religious practices and traditions.

Apprenticeship includes a number of components and, at its best, seeks to make not just the overt behavior but the psychological functioning of the master accessible to those being apprenticed (Collins et al. 1991). Thus, the master highlights to the apprentice their goals, motives, perceptions, and evaluations as they engage in an activity. Further, they guide the apprentice's engagement, providing feedback and helping the apprentice to develop more robust strategies and approaches to a task. For instance, a spiritual master might highlight oversights in an apprentice's reading of scripture or suggest new approaches to engaging in prayer. Further, the master will adapt this to the changing abilities of their apprentice, fading support for mastered activities. Eventually, the goal is that the apprentice is able to function at the level of a master in that practice, whether the practice is narrowly construed, as in the practice of reading sacred texts, or broadly construed, as in the practice of being a Catholic Christian. Indeed, "being a Catholic Christian" in this sense is more properly addressed as having been at least cognitively apprenticed in all of the essential practices of Catholic Christianity, like liturgical practices, prayer practices, social practices, and so on. However, even in this, cognitive apprenticeship gives little guidance in thinking about how individuals might appropriately differ in their expression of a practice or tradition.

Social Modeling and Self-Regulation

Self-regulated learning can help prompt understanding of the different ways that individuals might express their personalities within a practice or tradition (Schunk & Zimmerman 1997). Self-regulated learning (Schunk & Zimmerman 1997) provides a widely applicable process for individuals to take up the skills and *ethic* of social models and make them their own. However, positive development based on imitation requires achievable and relatable models, and models that are reinforced rather than punished for the target behavior (Han et al. 2017). The process of self-regulation development has four stages: observation, imitation, self-control, and self-regulation, which will be elaborated upon below (Schunk & Zimmerman 1997).

Self-regulated learning begins with observation and imitation (Schunk & Zimmerman 1997). A learner first sees someone engage in an activity and perhaps hears them describe what they are doing and why, and so develops a schema for engaging in that activity themselves. This can be as simple as learning how to turn on a light switch or as complicated as learning how to write a novel. The learner is then given an opportunity to imitate the observed behavior while being provided social guidance and feedback. Social guidance and feedback are aimed at encouraging more accurate or appropriate imitation. For example, reading a mispronunciation might be encouragingly corrected. The reader could be reinforced for their effort and encouraged for their success in the rest of the reading. Then the teacher models the mispronounced word before asking the student to try it again.

Continuing this example, the self-regulated learning model predicts that imitation, modeling, and feedback contribute to the student learning to read effectively and to reinforce their own accurate reading behavior without external encouragement (Schunk & Zimmerman 1997). This is self-controlled behavior when the learner appropriately reinforces themselves for success on the skill or task because the standards for effective behavior have been internalized. However, at the self-controlled level, the learner may still be reliant on others to present them with a task for them to draw upon the appropriate knowledge. In contrast, those who reach the final stage in this model, the self-regulated stage, are able to adopt their own goals and manage their own learning, recognizing strengths and weaknesses. Thus, a self-regulated learner can take skills they have learned in one domain, such as reading the psalms, and apply them to new goals, such as prayer, without direct guidance in doing so. Such self-regulated processes help to explain manifestations of religious creativity by applying idiosyncratic sets of skills, interests, and resources to generate a novel solution.

In all of this, learning to self-regulate can be considered as a form of socially supported personality formation, in which individuals develop new schemas and so come to be able to think, value, perceive, and act differently. In spiritual formation, this personality change can be considered at low levels, such as learning to distinguish different figures named Joseph in Catholic scripture, and at higher levels, such as learning to properly understand the relationship between Jesus' humanity and divinity (Paul VI 1964). Through spiritual formation, those being formed can be supported in living more virtuously, especially as they learn to coordinate their skills through spiritual self-regulation.

Additional Considerations

The above provides some indication of factors likely to play a role in virtuous spiritual formation. However, there is much more to be said in relating these to the actor, agent, and author (McAdams 2013) model of personality and to considerations of context as differentially supporting spiritual formation. These contextual factors can be considered both in light of religious transmission (Smith & Adamczyk 2021) and more general social-psychological understanding of the effects of messaging and social norms on individual behavior (Walton & Yeager 2020). Here, discussion will be more speculative than accounts of attachment, apprenticeship, and self-regulation above.

The actor, agent, and author approach to personality (McAdams 2013) can be considered as levels of self-regulation, which regulate (1) action, (2) choice, and (3) life narrative, identity, and goals, respectively. Further, individuals can function as exemplars at each of these levels, modeling that to others. Actor-level differences in individuals within a community influence how some youth adapt well to high-stress environments while others struggle (Obradović et al. 2010). More broadly, the actor level helps to understand an individual's "default" behavior, their tendency to perceive the world in particular ways or to act in it without experiencing themselves as thinking or choosing. Thus, if someone has learned to engage in habits or rituals upon entering a church, they may eventually do so automatically and become more aware of other thoughts and choices that they associate with the church, all arising from actor-level factors.

At the agent and author levels, this approach (McAdams 2013) highlights other relationships. For instance, specific agent-level choices can influence later manifestations of self as actor or author. Here, the purpose (Malin et al. 2014) of sharing one's religion with others may contribute to the choice to become a religion teacher. This choice shapes actor-level behavior, through enacting the teacher role and corresponding actions, and supports a teaching-related identity and life narrative, at the author level. Beginning from the author level, transcendent spiritual narratives (King et al. 2022) help to shape future choices and channel development and choice-making, thus influencing the agent level. Thus, thinking of oneself as part of the story of God's work in the world shapes the kinds of choices one makes and the purposes one adopts, through the way it shapes one's perception of one's place in the world.

Turning to consideration of context, research on religious transmission and formation has especially emphasized the role of families (Dollahite & Marks 2019; Smith & Adamczyk 2021). The American Families of Faith Study (Dollahite & Marks 2019; Dollahite et al. 2019) was addressed above and presents extensive research on processes of formation and pathways to spiritual formation in exemplary religious families. This study (Dollahite & Marks 2019) reinforces other research that family factors such as discussing religion, frequent attendance at religious events, authoritative parenting, and the importance of religion to parents all influence religious importance to children when they enter adulthood (Smith & Adamczyk 2021).

The influence of well-targeted messages on individual behavior and psychology, called wise interventions, has come to be understood through the metaphor of seed and soil (Walton & Yeager 2020). In many ways, this can be considered a large-scale approach to facilitating self-regulation. In research on wise interventions, social psychologists examine the effects of brief messages and activities on development (e.g., Walton & Yeager 2020). This arises from recognizing and engaging with psychological *vulnerabilities*, *constraints*, *affordances*, and *opportunities*. *Vulnerabilities* emphasize individual-level risks, such as the risk of feeling excluded, incompetent, or as if one has no choice. *Constraints* emphasize the way that situations limit behavior and support for certain beliefs or *ethics*, for instance, by emphasizing competition and thus foregrounding comparative competence. *Affordances* are the ways that situations provide opportunities or permit certain psychological beliefs, behaviors, and identities to take root as *ethics* through allowing and reinforcing relevant perceptions as opposed to punishing them or constraining them. Finally, *opportunities* are key points in the process of engaging with contexts that might change the psychological direction of someone's *ethic*, such as the transition to college or the beginning of a new relationship. These *opportunities* provide possible psychological turning points in which new seeds for excellence can be planted.

Drawing on this approach, consider the transition from attending and participating in religious activities with parents to attending and participating in these activities without them. This is a potential *opportunity* for formators to plant good seeds, supporting children who had little choice in their spiritual formation at younger or less mature ages in taking ownership of their religious and spiritual commitments. However, as the National Study of Youth and Religion attests, much of the United States seems to be "bad soil," with young people eschewing religion en masse (Smith & Snell 2009), highlighting widespread cultural *constraints* to fostering formation resulting from *vulnerability*. Thus, finding contexts where other young people are enthusiastic about Catholicism is more likely to *afford* most children with better soil, supporting them in choosing to participate in the Catholic Church. In such good soil, youth are more likely to feel supported in this choice, to continue to make the choice, and to experience belonging in doing so, reducing *vulnerability*. However, parents might also plant bad seeds, encouraging *vulnerability* by threatening to punish children for noncompliance even by offering "choice" with regard to spiritual formation, emphasizing a stick rather than a carrot. These bad seeds might result in the child attributing their religious participation more to fear of punishment than to free and meaningful engagement in Catholicism. Alternatively, parents could also undermine a sense of choice through excessive incentives for religious involvement, such as offering the child large rewards for religious attendance. Instead, this theory suggests that this *opportunity* in transition may be best met through genuine encouragement of children to make their own choice with regard to religious involvement alongside candid discussion of the potential consequences of the choice. Doing so would support the seed of spiritual formation in taking root in a new way amidst the transition to adulthood.

Summary

The above provides some insight into the ways that spiritual formation might support the *emergence* of virtue. This includes fostering healthy attachment, cognitive apprenticeship in spiritual practices, and supporting religious self-regulation. Further, considering levels of personality, contexts, and wise interventions adds additional nuance to these processes. Nonetheless, there is much more to learn and study in this regard, especially in engaging with these approaches as they relate to a more fully articulated vision of spiritual formation, taking into account development, in terms of factors like age differences, and the particularities of the Catholic tradition.

Integrating and Exploring Connections between Developmental Science and the Catholic Tradition

What are potential areas for integration and exploration at the intersection of Catholic theology and developmental science? One of these, based on what is addressed above, is around considerations of imitation at the author, agent, and actor levels. Another is new forms of exemplarity, with some foundation in existing developmental science, but which are highlighted by the Catholic tradition as worthy of examination, specifically relational/contemplative and redemptive exemplars. Richer consideration of Catholic spiritual contexts as they relate to formation is also encouraged, with special attention to narratives and the communion of saints. These avenues are potentially fruitful for both developmental science and Catholic Theology. Additional consideration of developmental differences is also addressed. Following this, tentative conclusions and suggestions for future work are presented.

One theme to bring out in additional depth is imitation, as it is only alluded to above. This requires additional consideration of what imitation does and does not mean as related to spiritual formation. Imitation can function, psychologically, in a number of ways. One can imitate the perceived motives of an exemplar (imitation of ends) through different means, as in children's pretend play. One can imitate the behavior of an exemplar (see Schunk & Zimmerman 1997) or even the thinking, valuing, and perceiving of an exemplar, coming to appreciate the actor's agency (Collins et al. 1991). Additionally, one can come to admire an exemplar and their way of seeing and being in the world, and so internally come to appreciate their motivations or excellence (Immordino-Yang et al. 2009). These forms of imitation are not mutually exclusive. Instead, the fullest form of imitation likely involves the confluence of each kind of imitation. However, even in imitating motives, behavior, thinking, valuing, and perceiving together, strict mimicry of a model's behaviors or specific goals may lead to replication of an exemplar's behavior, and so not be properly responsive to new conditions and new goals to be pursued. Instead, drawing on varied exemplars is likely to allow for a personalization of the tradition in the formation of an individual.

Catholic theology adds to this in ways that draw out other possibilities for formation. This is first the case because of grace,[2] which allows the divine to take root in persons and so allows for change beyond that which is possible through imitation. As a result of this, a Catholic perspective suggests that we can go beyond imitation in spiritual formation and be transformed by the divine into the divine, superseding the natural processes described by psychology.

For developmentalists, greater attention to possibilities of relational/contemplative exemplarity and redemptive exemplarity would be helpful. Indeed, such exemplars would likely prove salutary to existing scholarship on humility (Wright et al. 2018), growth mindset (Yeager & Dweck 2020), and a de-emphasis on outcomes and performance orientation, which arise in focusing on outcomes attributed to exemplars (e.g., Mother Theresa's global impact) over exemplary processes (e.g., Mother Teresa and the Missionaries of Charity's practices of prayer, obedience to spiritual authority, commitment to poverty, and seeing the poor as children of God (Barron 2007; Teresa & Heilige 2007)). Relational or contemplative exemplars might include children and mystics, emphasizing those who experience awe, gratitude, wonder, and a sense of connection to the divine and others in virtuous ways that are present but not essential in many social scientific studies of moral exemplarity (e.g., Colby & Damon 1992). Redemptive exemplars, instead, are those who undergo dramatic positive transformations. A Catholic theological account of grace and the sacraments, for instance, suggests the possibility of transformational change, which is present in historical accounts of numerous Catholic saints (e.g., Augustine 1993).

In addition, greater attention to formation in spiritual contexts would be valuable, especially attending to Catholicism. Catholicism provides a general human purpose, namely to love God and our neighbor (Benedict XVI 2005), within a narrative tradition that can serve as a transcendental life narrative. Further, both those Catholics we encounter and those historical Catholics who are part of the Church Triumphant provide narrative models of what it can look like to live out the Catholic tradition in light of the communion of saints (DeLorenzo 2017). These models provide opportunities for cognitive apprenticeship (Collins 2006) in the story-telling and culture of Catholicism. However, this does not preclude the making of various life choices; instead, it may inform these choices and perhaps shape their contours. This is demonstrated, for instance, by the Program for Theological Exploration of Vocation, which drew largely on the Christian tradition to support college students in thinking about their lives in self-transcendent ways (see Clydesdale 2015). Ongoing accompaniment by others in the midst of formation and varied models may provide hope to those who struggle with various challenges in pursuing their purposes.

Little attention, so far, has been given to different periods of development or to differences across individuals in the midst of development. It is clear that while children are born into narrative communities, in infancy and early childhood, children can scarcely be expected to tell narratively rich stories about their own lives, even as they actively seek to imagine and engage with the kinds of stories told by their parents and communities (Corsaro 1993). Further, children differ in important ways, with different interests and potentials. As such, children are invited into the ongoing narratives of their family and community and are differentially prepared to participate in these narratives on the basis of both their age and their developing capacities. This reality deserves additional psychological attention in considering the role of narrative exposure and community practices in later spiritual formation. Such exposure likely serves to model and establish spiritual expectations and set the stage for later spiritual formation, but this must be considered against the backdrop of the existing thinking, feelings, and capacities of children themselves, that is to say, in light of children's prior *ethic*. Thus, approaches to emphasizing optimal environments for children's flourishing, like the Evolved Developmental Nest (Narvaez 2014), bear consideration as possible components of exemplary spiritual communities, especially for youth. Such approaches highlight the potential importance of implicit and biological processes in spiritual development. Furthermore, understanding the implications of different underlying abilities, such as varied abilities in mathematics, language, and reasoning, for variations in spiritual development is needed.

Theologically, developmental psychology provides a number of empirically supported theories to understand processes and potential obstacles in spiritual formation. Amidst widespread concern about religious disaffiliation, developmental science provides insights into the role of social and relational processes in spiritual formation. This provides some low-hanging fruit for translation into practice in the Catholic tradition. While theology provides responses to questions of the ultimate ends of spiritual formation and guidance in considering what excellence consists of, developmental science is especially suited to understanding at least some facets of emergence and the formation of various ethics. This is to say that developmental science has important things to contribute to understanding how one comes to be spiritually formed and comes to live in light of that formation. As such, Catholic theologians interested in formation may seek to engage developmental science in creating contexts and accompanying fellow Catholics in their spiritual formation. Further, they are likely to be assisted in this by considering existing developmental science-engaged accounts of the development of religion and spirituality (King et al. 2023), especially Protestant accounts (e.g., Balswick et al. 2016; Schnitker et al. 2019), while remaining attentive to convergences and differences in theology, anthropology, and tradition. This consideration may support not only improving formation with the Catholic tradition but also richer dialog and engagement with those of other traditions.

Notes

1 For a similar claim relating morality to adaptive moral functioning, see Lapsley et al. (2020).
2 This has recently been addressed as an understudied area in psychology of religion and spirituality (Emmons et al. 2017).

References

Aquinas, T. 1991. *The summa theologica of St. Thomas Aquinas: Vol. II.* Translated by T. McDermott. Notre Dame: Christian Classics.
Aristotle. 2002. *Nichomachean ethics.* Translated by C. Rowe, New York, NY: Oxford University Press.
Augustine. 1993. *Augustine: The confessions.* Translated by G. Clark. New York, NY: Cambridge University Press.
Balswick, J. O., King, P. E., & Reimer, K. S. 2016. *The reciprocating self: Human development in theological perspective.* Downers Grove, IL: InterVarsity Press.
Bandura, A. 1977. *Social learning theory.* Upper Saddle River, NL: Prentice Hall.
Barron, R. 2007. *The priority of Christ: Toward a postliberal catholicism.* Grand Rapids, MI: Brazos Press.
Beck, R., & McDonald, A. 2004. "Attachment to God: The attachment to God inventory, tests of working model correspondence, and an exploration of faith group differences." *Journal of Psychology and Theology,* 32(2), 92–103. https://doi.org/10.1177/009164710403200202
Benedict XVI. 2005. *Deus Caritas Est.* https://www.vatican.va/content/benedict-xvi/en/encyclicals/documents/hf_ben-xvi_enc_20051225_deus-caritas-est.html

Bosmans, G., Bakermans-Kranenburg, M. J., Vervliet, B., Verhees, M. W. F. T., & IJzendoorn, M. H. van. 2020. "A learning theory of attachment: Unraveling the black box of attachment development." *Neuroscience & Biobehavioral Reviews, 113*, 287–298. https://doi.org/10.1016/j.neubiorev.2020.03.014

Boyle, G. 2011. *Tattoos on the heart: The power of boundless compassion.* New York, NY: Simon and Schuster.

Boyle, G. 2017. *Barking to the choir: The power of radical kinship.* New York, NY: Simon and Schuster.

Cervone, D., & Little, B. R. 2019. "Personality architecture and dynamics: The new agenda and what's new about it." *Personality and Individual Differences, 136*, 12–23. https://doi.org/10.1016/j.paid.2017.07.001

Cherniak, A. D., Mikulincer, M., Shaver, P. R., & Granqvist, P. 2021. "Attachment theory and religion." *Current Opinion in Psychology, 40*, 126–130. https://doi.org/10.1016/j.copsyc.2020.08.020

Chinn, C. A., Rinehart, R. W., & Buckland, L. A. 2014. "Epistemic cognition and evaluating information: Applying the AIR model of epistemic cognition." *Processing Inaccurate Information: Theoretical and Applied Perspectives from Cognitive Science and the Educational Sciences*, 425–453.

Cloutier, D., & Ahrens, A. H. 2020. "Catholic moral theology and the virtues: Integrating psychology in models of moral agency." *Theological Studies, 81*(2), 326–347. https://doi.org/10.1177/0040563920928563

Clydesdale, T. 2015. *The purposeful graduate: Why colleges must talk to students about vocation.* Chicago, IL: University of Chicago Press.

Colby, A., & Damon, W. 1992. *Some do care: Contemporary lives of moral commitment.* New York, NY: Free Press.

Collins, A. 2006. "Cognitive apprenticeship." In R. K. Sawyer (Ed.), *The Cambridge handbook of the learning sciences* (pp. 47–60). New York, NY: Cambridge University Press. DOI: https://doi.org/10.1017/CBO9781139519526.008

Collins, A., Brown, J. S., & Holum, A. 1991. "Cognitive apprenticeship: Making thinking visible." *American Educator, 15*(3), 1–18.

Corsaro, W. A. 1993. "Interpretive reproduction in children's role play." *Childhood, 1*(2), 64–74. https://doi.org/10.1177/090756829300100202

Creekpaum, S. 2019. "Child development through play." In M. Charles & J. Bellinson (Eds.), *The importance of play in early childhood education: Psychoanalytic, attachment, and developmental perspectives* (1st ed.). New York: Routledge.

Csikszentmihalyi, M. 1996. *Creativity: Flow and the psychology of discovery and invention.* New York, NY: HarperCollins.

Curlee, M., & Ahrens, A.H. 2023. "An exploratory analysis of the Ignatian examen: Impact on self-transcendent positive emotions and eudaimonic motivation." *Journal of Positive Psychology, 18*(5), 733–742. https://doi.org/10.1080/17439760.2022.2109197

Damon, W., & Colby, A. 2015. *The power of ideals: The real story of moral choice.* New York, NY: Oxford University Press.

DeLorenzo, L. J. 2017. *Work of love: A theological reconstruction of the communion of saints.* Notre Dame: Notre Dame Press.

Dollahite, D. C., & Marks, L. D. 2009. "A conceptual model of family and religious processes in highly religious families." *Review of Religious Research, 50*(4), 373–391. JSTOR.

Dollahite, D. C., & Marks, L. D. 2019. "Positive youth religious and spiritual development: What we have learned from religious families." *Religions, 10*(10), 548. https://doi.org/10.3390/rel10100548

Dollahite, D. C., Marks, L. D., & Wurm, G. J. 2019. "Generative devotion: A theory of sacred relational care in families of faith." *Journal of Family Theory & Review, 11*(3), 429–448. https://doi.org/10.1111/jftr.12339

Dumler-Winckler, E. J. 2017. "The virtue of Emerson's imitation of Christ: From William Ellery Channing to John Brown." *Journal of Religious Ethics*, 45(3), 510–538. https://doi.org/10.1111/jore.12188

Emmons, R. A., & McCullough, M. E. 2003. "Counting blessings versus burdens: An experimental investigation of gratitude and subjective well-being in daily life." *Journal of Personality and Social Psychology*, 84(2), 377–389.

Emmons, R. A., Hill, P. C., Barrett, J. L., & Kapic, K. M. 2017. "Psychological and theological reflections on grace and its relevance for science and practice." *Psychology of Religion and Spirituality*, 9, 276–284. https://doi.org/10.1037/rel0000136

Francis. 2013. *Evangelii Gaudium.* https://www.vatican.va/content/francesco/en/apost_exhortations/documents/papa-francesco_esortazione-ap_20131124_evangelii-gaudium.html

Giebel, H. M. 2021. *Ethical excellence: Philosophers, psychologists, and real-life exemplars show us how to achieve it.* Washington D.C.: Catholic University of America Press.

Gollwitzer, P. M., Bayer, U., Scherer, M., & Seifert, A. E. 2006. "A motivational-volitional perspective on identity development." In R. Lerner & J. Brandtstadter (Eds.), *Action and self-development: Theory and research through the life span* (pp. 283–314). Thousand Oaks, CA: Sage.

Gross, J. T., Stern, J. A., Brett, B. E., & Cassidy, J. 2017. "The multifaceted nature of prosocial behavior in children: Links with attachment theory and research." *Social Development*, 26(4), 661–678. https://doi.org/10.1111/sode.12242

Hall, D. T., & Chandler, D. E. 2004. "Psychological success: When the career is a calling." *Journal of Organizational Behavior*, 25, 1–22.

Han, H., Kim, J., Jeong, C., & Cohen, G. L. 2017. "Attainable and relevant moral exemplars are more effective than extraordinary exemplars in promoting voluntary service engagement." *Frontiers in Psychology*, 8. https://doi.org/10.3389/fpsyg.2017.00283

Herdt, J. A. 2020. "Enacting integrity." In C. B. Miller & R. West (Eds.), *Integrity, honesty, and truth seeking* (pp. 63–94). New York, NY: Oxford University Press.

Immordino-Yang, M. H., McColl, A., Damasio, H., & Damasio, A. 2009. "Neural correlates of admiration and compassion." *Proceedings of the National Academy of Sciences*, 106(19), 8021–8026. https://doi.org/10.1073/pnas.0810363106

King, P. E., Baer, R. A., Noe, S. A., Trudeau, S., Mangan, S. A., & Constable, S. R. 2022. "Shades of gratitude: Exploring varieties of transcendent beliefs and experience." *Religions*, 13(11), 1091. https://doi.org/10.3390/rel13111091

King, P. E., Clardy, C. E., & Ramos, J. S. 2014. "Adolescent spiritual exemplars: Exploring spirituality in the lives of diverse youth." *Journal of Adolescent Research*, 29(2), 186–212. https://doi.org/10.1177/0743558413502534

King, P. E., Mangan, S., & Riveros, R. 2023. "Religion, spirituality, and youth thriving: Investigating the roles of the developing mind and meaning-making." In E. B. Davis, E. L. Worthington Jr., & S. A. Schnitker (Eds.), *Handbook of positive psychology, religion, and spirituality* (pp. 263–277). Cham: Springer International Publishing. https://doi.org/10.1007/978-3-031-10274-5_17

King, P. E., Schnitker, S. A., & Houltberg, B. J. 2020. "Religious groups and institutions as a context for moral development: Religion as fertile ground." In L. A. Jensen (Ed.), *The Oxford handbook of moral development: An interdisciplinary perspective* (pp. 592–612). New York, NY: Oxford University Press. https://doi.org/10.1093/oxfordhb/9780190676049.013.34

Lapsley, D., Reilly, T. S., & Narvaez, D. F. 2020. "Moral self-identity and character development." In L. A. Jensen (Ed.), *The Oxford handbook of moral development: An interdisciplinary perspective* (pp. 685–707). New York, NY; Oxford University Press. https://doi.org/10.1093/oxfordhb/9780190676049.013.40

Lave, J., & Wenger, E. 1991. *Situated learning: Legitimate peripheral participation.* New York, NY: Cambridge University Press.

MacIntyre, A. 2007. *After virtue* (3rd ed.). Notre Dame: Notre Dame Press.

Malin, H., Reilly, T. S., Quinn, B., & Moran, S. 2014. "Adolescent purpose development: Exploring empathy, discovering roles, shifting priorities, and creating pathways." *Journal of Research on Adolescence*, 24(1), 186–199. https://doi.org/10.1111/jora.12051

McAdams, D. P. 2013. "The psychological self as actor, agent, and author." *Perspectives on Psychological Science*, 8(3), 272–295. https://doi.org/10.1177/1745691612464657

Nakamura, J., & Condren, M. 2018. "A systems perspective on the role mentors play in the cultivation of virtue." *Journal of Moral Education*, 47(3), 316–332. https://doi.org/10.1080/03057240.2018.1444981

Nakamura, J., Shernoff, D. J., & Hooker, C. H. 2009. *Good mentoring: Fostering excellent practice in higher education.* San Francisco, CA: John Wiley & Sons.

Narvaez, D. 2014. *Neurobiology and the development of human morality: Evolution, culture, and wisdom (Norton Series on Interpersonal Neurobiology).* New York, NY: WW Norton & Company.

Narvaez, D. 2016. *Embodied morality: Protectionism, engagement and imagination.* New York, NY: Palgrave-MacMillan.

Nelson, J. M., Hardy, S. A., & Watkins, P. 2023. "Transcendent indebtedness to God: A new construct in the psychology of religion and spirituality." *Psychology of Religion and Spirituality*, 15, 105–117. https://doi.org/10.1037/rel0000458

Obradović, J., Bush, N. R., Stamperdahl, J., Adler, N. E., & Boyce, W. T. 2010. "Biological sensitivity to context: The interactive effects of stress reactivity and family adversity on socioemotional behavior and school readiness." *Child Development*, 81(1), 270–289. https://doi.org/10.1111/j.1467-8624.2009.01394.x

Orom, H., & Cervone, D. 2009. "Personality dynamics, meaning, and idiosyncrasy: Identifying cross-situational coherence by assessing personality architecture." *Personality and Assessment at Age 40: Reflections on the Past Person–Situation Debate and Emerging Directions of Future Person-Situation Integration*, 43(2), 228–240. https://doi.org/10.1016/j.jrp.2009.01.015

Overton, W. F. 2013. "A new paradigm for developmental science: Relationism and relational-developmental systems." *Applied Developmental Science*, 17(2), 94–107. https://doi.org/10.1080/10888691.2013.778717

Paul VI. 1963. *Sacrosanctum Concilium.* https://www.vatican.va/archive/hist_councils/ii_vatican_council/documents/vat-ii_const_19631204_sacrosanctum-concilium_en.html

Paul VI. 1964. *Lumen gentium.* https://www.vatican.va/archive/hist_councils/ii_vatican_council/documents/vat-ii_const_19641121_lumen-gentium_en.html

Paul VI. 1965. *Apostolicam Actuositatem.* https://www.vatican.va/archive/hist_councils/ii_vatican_council/documents/vat-ii_decree_19651118_apostolicam-actuositatem_en.html

Paul, John II. 1992. *Pastores Dabo Vobis.* https://www.vatican.va/content/john-paul-ii/en/apost_exhortations/documents/hf_jp-ii_exh_25031992_pastores-dabo-vobis.html

Reilly, T. S. 2018. "Exemplarity and virtue: Understanding virtuous exemplarity in science." *Philosophy, Theology and the Sciences*, 5(2), 149–171. https://doi.org/10.1628/ptsc-2018-0014

Reilly, T. S., & Mariano, J. M. 2021. "Fostering mature purpose beyond the classroom: Considering family and other institutions in agentic purpose commitment." *Estudos de Psicologia (Campinas)*, 38, e210115. https://doi.org/10.1590/1982-0275202138e210115

Reilly, T., & Narvaez, D. 2022. "Virtue in practice: Toward a richer account." In *Moral and intellectual virtues in practices: Through the eyes of scientists and musicians*. Cham, Switzerland: Palgrave MacMillan.

Reilly, T., Narvaez, D., Graves, M., Kaikhosroshvili, K., & de Souza, S. I. 2022. *Moral and intellectual virtues in practices: Through the eyes of scientists and musicians*. Cham, Switzerland: Palgrave MacMillan. https://link.springer.com/book/10.1007/978-3-031-18969-2

Schnitker, S. A., King, P. E., & Houltberg, B. 2019. "Religion, spirituality, and thriving: Transcendent narrative, virtue, and telos." *Journal of Research on Adolescence*, 29(2), 276–290. https://doi.org/10.1111/jora.12443

Schunk, D. H., & Zimmerman, B. J. 1997. "Social origins of self-regulatory competence." *Educational Psychologist*, 32(4), 195–208. https://doi.org/10.1207/s15326985ep3204_1

Scott, V., Verhees, M., De Raedt, R., Bijttebier, P., Vasey, M. W., Van de Walle, M., Waters, T. E. A., & Bosmans, G. 2021. "Gratitude: A resilience factor for more securely attached children." *Journal of Child and Family Studies*, 30(2), 416–430. https://doi.org/10.1007/s10826-020-01853-8

Simonton, D. K. 1999. *Origins of genius*. New York, NY: Oxford University Press.

Smith, C., & Adamczyk, A. 2021. *Handing down the faith: How parents pass their religion on to the next generation*. New York, NY: Oxford University Press.

Smith, C., & Snell, P. 2009. *Souls in transition: The religious and spiritual lives of emerging adults*. New York, NY: Oxford University Press.

Spezio, M. L. 2017. "Faith and imitatio for the understanding of habitus." In G. R. Peterson, J. A. Van Slyke, M. L. Spezio, & K. S. Reimer (Eds.), *Habits in mind: Integrating theology, philosophy, and the cognitive science of virtue, emotion, and character formation*. Leiden, Netherlands: Brill. https://doi.org/10.1163/9789004342958_008

Teresa, M., Heilige. 2007. *Come be my light: The private writings of the "Saint of Calcutta"* (1st ed). New York, NY: Doubleday. http://www.loc.gov/catdir/toc/ecip0715/2007015123.html

Walker, L. J., Frimer, J. A., & Dunlop, W. L. 2010. "Varieties of moral personality: Beyond the banality of heroism." *Journal of Personality*, 78(3), 907–942.

Walton, G. M., & Yeager, D. S. 2020. "Seed and soil: Psychological affordances in contexts help to explain where wise interventions succeed or fail." *Current Directions in Psychological Science*, 29(3), 219–226.

Wright, J. C., Nadelhoffer, T., Thomson Ross, L., & Sinnott-Armstrong, W. 2018. "Be it ever so humble: Proposing a dual-dimension account and measurement of humility." *Self and Identity*, 17(1), 92–125. https://doi.org/10.1080/15298868.2017.1327454

Yeager, D. S., & Dweck, C. S. 2020. "What can be learned from growth mindset controversies?" *American Psychologist*, 75, 1269–1284. https://doi.org/10.1037/amp0000794

9 Modeling Exemplary Practical Wisdom and Discernment in Sociotechnical Communities

Mark Graves

Introduction

The cognitive foundations for morality and spirituality are affected by technological advances in areas such as artificial intelligence (AI), brain-computer interfaces, neuropharmacology, and genetic engineering. These technological advances affect human society, which in turn further propels new technological development. Discernment and moral decision-making and practices must account for these interleaved social and technological changes, especially for exemplars who may need to lead social responses to these changes as well as those involved in the design and development of the new technologies. AI, in particular, requires attention to how this technology affects human morality and spirituality (Jackelén 2021; Vallor 2016), due to the ready ways human moral, religious, and spiritual values can become embedded within them (Anderson & Anderson 2011; Wallach & Vallor 2020), e.g., in caregiving (Coeckelbergh 2012; London et al. 2023). As a foundation for this exploration, ethicists have examined how technology affects the virtues, how virtues can be incorporated into technology, and how developing that technology requires virtuous practices (Vallor, 2016; Gamez et al., 2020; Wallach & Vallor, 2020; Neubert & Montañez, 2020). This chapter explores how one's interpretation of exemplary behavior is affected by technology, how technology might affect exemplary discernment and practical wisdom, and how researchers can use technology to study exemplarity.

A focal point is sociotechnical systems, which characterize the mutual causality of people defining technology that in turn significantly affects people's lives (Edwards 2003; Makarius et al. 2020; Selbst et al. 2019). The human-technology interaction may be constrained or regulated by institutions, as socially constructed structures of rules, norms, or standards of behavior that are sometimes formalized into persistent organizations that continue their structure, function, and process despite changes in personnel (Moore 2002; Singh 2014). As a working definition, a sociotechnical system is a system comprised of interacting human agents, technological artifacts, and institutional norms with a particular function or purpose. The present chapter

DOI: 10.4324/9781032648392-12

predominantly considers AI as the technology, though sociotechnical systems may also include AI acting as an agent (van de Poel 2020).

To examine the spiritual and moral dimensions of sociotechnical systems, I examine how sociotechnical systems structure moral, religious, and spiritual communities. As examined later, a community is a socially cohesive group of people with a shared commitment, and thus a sociotechnical community is a socially cohesive group of people with a shared commitment that uses technology in interpreting and enacting that commitment. To connect the communal and sociotechnical theories, I suggest aligning the shared commitment of a community with the institutional norms of a sociotechnical system. From an organizational perspective, institutions structure religious, moral, and spiritual communities, e.g., an institutional church or faith-based not-for-profit, and the spiritual commitments and moral practices of that community inform and enliven the institutional frame. The institution could range from a short-term commitment to meet as a mutually supportive group to long-lasting institutions like the Roman Catholic church. Of particular relevance to sociotechnical communities is discernment and practical wisdom, because those require a thorough awareness of the moral and spiritual dimensions of a situation, and technology can affect both that awareness and the complexities and opacity of a situation.

In this chapter, I examine the technological influences on exemplarity and moral imitation, especially perception and cognition of moral awareness, and how researchers can use technology to study these topics. Discernment and practical wisdom within sociotechnical communities depend upon moral attention, and in the first part of the chapter, I characterize those spiritual and moral practices and their putative underlying cognitive foundation. To connect the examination of exemplarity in a sociotechnical context, the socio-cognitive processes occurring in exemplary behavior and imitation, and the study of those processes, I depend upon mental and scientific modeling. In the second part of the chapter, I treat exemplars as living, concrete models of those practices and virtues, consider aspirants as creating mental models of the exemplars, and examine scientific modeling as an extension. Scientific modeling supports researchers modeling exemplary practices to better understand human morality and spirituality through technology, and I describe foundational work that suggests ways to examine exemplar and aspirant moral cognition.

Practical Wisdom and Discernment in Sociotechnical Communities

Practical wisdom and discernment each incorporate aspects of what is often separated into morality and spirituality. However, they have a common core of a person making decisions among complex unknowns oriented in a direction that transcends the individual or social norms. To characterize the orientation that transcends the individual, Josiah Royce's (1913/2001) community of interpretation provides a broad framework for committed values that dynamically guide the individual with moral and spiritual implications, and I extend the framework to include sociotechnical systems. Key to the intersection of practical wisdom and discernment are the processes of perception as they feed into and are focused on by decision-making. Moral and spiritual attention is essential for practical wisdom among complex unknowns, including technical opacity, and rapidly changing social implications.

Philosophical, Theological, and Psychological Perspectives

Practical wisdom and discernment depend upon one's morality and spirituality. As these terms have a range of meanings, I characterize spirituality, practical wisdom, and discernment and briefly describe moral attention before examining sociotechnical community and moral attention in more depth. In general, morality is considered within an Aristotelian/Thomistic virtue framework.

As a working definition, spirituality is the experience of striving to integrate one's life toward the ultimate value one perceives, and that ultimate value is mediated through a tradition and its associated communities. The scholar of spirituality, Sandra Schneiders (2005), argues that spirituality refers to the experience of moving toward some ultimate value (or horizon, beyond which one cannot perceive) and integrating that movement into one's lived experience. A focus on ultimacy loosely synthesizes many theological aspects of the world's religions in a framework amenable to psychological study of spiritual development (Emmons 1999), and ultimate value incorporates axiological and teleological aspects of the "Good" and the good life (*eudaimonia*). Royce (1913/2001) identifies community as significant for continually interpreting a tradition and its collective spirituality through the lives of its members, and that shared interpretative process plays an essential role in characterizing emergent spirituality, especially in terms of commitments to shared values and ultimate concerns (Graves 2009, 2017, 2023).

Practical wisdom characterizes the "common sense" that savvy adults bring to complex situations and the skilled methods in bringing about morally good changes that moral exemplars identify. Practical wisdom requires making decisions about proximate goods as a way to obtain the more distal moral goods. For Aristotle, practical wisdom includes an ability to deliberate well and both general and situation-specific understandings of the good. Deliberating well requires several psychological processes to function properly, including moral sensitivity, motivation, and judgment (Darnell et al. 2019; Narvaez & Rest 1995). As expanded later using social cognitive theory (Orom & Cervone 2009), one's general and situation-specific understandings of the good involve both knowledge structures, such as morally relevant schemas, and dynamic appraisals, or evaluations, of one's encounters.

Discernment is a spiritual practice that judges well between two "goods." In Ignatian spirituality, discernment attempts to find God in all things and discover where God is active out of a desire to know and do God's will (Barry 2011). One could judge well spiritually between two directions that appear oriented toward one's ultimate value or morally between two actions that each appear virtuous, e.g., accentuating different virtues. In a moral context, the *phronimos* (exemplar of practical wisdom) weighs the exceptions to the general case and identifies the right action (Hursthouse 2006, 292). Synthesizing the spiritual and moral perspectives requires identifying the ultimate value as the *telos*. Thus, discernment occurs in difficult decision-making when existing moral or spiritual cognitive structures suggest conflicting actions and results in a judgment of which action would better integrate one's life with the ultimate value one perceives, e.g., identifying God's will or evaluating what would better lead to flourishing (*eudaimonia*).

Moral attention is a key aspect of practical wisdom that is closely related to discernment. Moral attention identifies the moral dimension of an experience and the ethical needs of those involved. It is a mental discipline seeking to perceive something outside of oneself and involves both an outward perception of how one sees the particulars of one's situation and an internal self-reflection and discernment to set aside dispositions that would distort perception (Holland 1998, 301, 306, 309). Simone Weil (1951) examined moral attention in the spiritual exercise of prayer and characterized moral attention as the ability to truly see someone who is suffering. For Weil, attention is consciously receptive, and she explicitly draws upon resources in apophatic spirituality to develop moral attention as foundational for ethics, e.g., "the soul empties itself of its own content in order to receive into itself the being it is looking at" (Robert 2012; Weil 1951, 36).

Moral attention, practical wisdom, and discernment are interrelated and are like virtues in the sense that they are motivated and that one could do them well or poorly. One could also consider others to do them exemplarily well and imitate those exemplar behaviors. In particular, one can construct knowledge structures and ways of perceiving the ethical dimension of one's world that align with the knowledge structures of exemplars. The next two sections of the chapter consider these moral and spiritual practices in situations where technology has a significant role.

Sociotechnical Community

Although one can identify historically and internationally regarded exemplars, and moral psychologists have determined methods for studies of more accessible exemplars (Bronk 2012), the focus of this chapter is on communities with a shared moral, spiritual, or religious commitment. Historically, these often arose around religious exemplars and persisted after their lives, and during the past century or so, they also formed around strong and specific commitments to social justice or other value-oriented social change, even if no one individual would be considered a founding exemplar. Communities such as these may also involve technology and technological change. The focus on communities where people align on shared values, yet differ in how they discern and navigate tradeoffs in pursuing those values, provides a philosophically grounded framework for examining exemplarity and imitation in a social context. Considering the communal context of exemplarity also enables study of shorter-lived communities and situations where a collection of people may exhibit sufficient moral exemplarity to evoke imitation, even if the individuals remain flawed or underdeveloped (Reimer 2009).

To clarify complexities of interdisciplinary work, a concrete scenario involving AI elder care is used throughout the chapter as an illustrative example. The technology is slightly speculative, but plausible given current research and has notable ethical implications (Coeckelbergh 2012; Lima et al. 2022; London et al. 2023). The scenario is as follows:

> Bob is the primary caregiver for his elderly mother Ann, who has Alzheimer's disease. From a support group in his Methodist church, he learned about and purchased a recently developed AI personal assistant designed for people with Alzheimer's, which several participants utilize for family members. The highly customizable and adaptive device can answer conversational questions, has exercises designed to stimulate memory, can monitor and control many household devices, can send Bob and trusted others various texts and notifications, and can track people in the house and Ann when she leaves, through a pendant, watch, or locking ankle bracelet. The device also has several privacy settings to limit or share information with the device manufacturer with sharing used to improve its further development and enhance Bob's device and others. The support group is organized by the very empathetic minister, who did a year-long chaplaincy at a well-respected memory care facility, and other members who have parents suffering from dementia include a nationally known Alzheimer's researcher, a best-selling author of spiritual care books, two experienced nurses, a robotics researcher, and a bioethicist teaching at the local college. Bob admires many members of the close-knit group and is grateful for such a supportive and knowledgeable community during this difficult time. He also respects his mother's primary care physician, who has known her since she babysat him as a small child, though Bob wishes his mother's neurologist was more supportive and forthcoming with advice on issues besides the very competent medical treatment.

Royce's (1913/2001) philosophy of community provides a foundation for considering the mutual, shared interpretation of committed values and exemplary behavior in communities such as this. Royce describes community in terms of C.S. Peirce's semiotics as cohering socially through shared lives, interpretations, and commitments. Foundational to the continuous semiotic and interpretive process is that each person in the community interprets a second person to a third, and then this triadic interpretation gets interpreted in turn. Royce characterized the Christian church in terms of a true community interpreting the life of Christ and building upon each other's interpretations, with the Holy Spirit as the shared interpretive process (semiotically, the interpretant). Weakening some of Royce's assumptions, I characterize spirituality more generally as strongly emerging from the interpretive process of long-lasting interpretive communities (Graves 2009; 2013, Chapter 6).

Although the example scenario lacks many aspects of the Pauline church and Royce's full characterization of community, it suffices to examine exemplary behavior around care and compassion and how those values are interpreted through the electronic assistant. The members interpret elder care and technical expertise to each other, which then gets augmented from additional perspectives. Bob must discern how to care for his mother using technologically enhanced awareness and behaviors using a tool that has sufficient decision-making capacity such that it could augment or reduce his or Ann's freedom. By interpreting how others make similar determinations, Bob borrows from their collective practical wisdom and embodies new dispositions in himself (and in the device), drawing upon his ultimate concerns and values as distilled in these specific situations.

Although interpretation is a broad philosophical construct, it has plausible psychological foundation for this context in social-cognitive theory. Drawing upon social-cognitive theories of virtue (Ahrens & Cloutier 2019; Lapsley 2016; Orom & Cervone 2009), behavior is best predicted by a person, situation, and the interaction between them. Behavior depends upon a person's dynamic evaluation of encounters in light of their motivations (i.e., appraisal) as well as their enduring knowledge structures (e.g., schemas). A person's knowledge structures and dispositions depend upon prior experience, are structured to respond to expected future situations, and are selected based on the person's motivations and goals. The schemas represent knowledge, and they structure the person's affordances for perceived objects and encounters—both what an object offers, or affords, as its possible use physically and what situations afford morally (Cooper & Glasspool 2001; Hampson et al. 2021; Rietveld et al. 2018). If a person's commitments and identity motivate a virtuous response to a given situation, then that person interprets the situation or social encounter in light of that virtue and commitment and acts accordingly. In addition, if this motivated appraisal becomes habituated, it affects the knowledge structure, the moral affordances of the person, and possible interpretations of future encounters.

Exemplars illuminate additional dimensions of shared commitments, which some members may perceive and imitate. Within a Roycean community, exemplars interpret well with their lives the shared commitment. Others interpret the exemplar's interpretation of the shared commitment and may imitate that interpretation from their own perspectives. Although most clear in religious exemplars in a religious community, the pattern also occurs where the exemplar interprets well with their life any commitment or excellence to which others aspire. In a sociotechnical context, an exemplar attuned to a situation's social and technical affordances and constraints might attend more perspicuously to inequities or other moral consequences not apparent to others and might courageously call attention to those consequences. Within the example scenario, one might identify ethical implications of the technology that others do not perceive, e.g., to privacy, autonomy, or consequences of offloading care to a device. Repeated attention to issues affecting compassion and care that others miss and wise reconciliation of apparent dilemmas could be considered exemplary.

Because of the shared communal commitments, improvements to an individual's spiritual and moral perceptual knowledge and afforded possible behaviors affect the entire community. There is a reciprocation among members as they interpret the committed value through each other's lives and commitments (King et al. 2023). In a Roycean community, every new interpretation might change the community, as it continues to be interpreted and included in subsequent interpretations, e.g., scholarly and pastoral interpretations of Paul's interpretation of Christ's life continue to affect the Christian community. In general, if someone better interprets a shared commitment within a community's novel situation, then that improves the community by adding a clearer perspective upon which others can build. In the example community, if one of the nurses identifies the repeated kind answers by the AI assistant to repeated identical questions by the person with dementia as exemplary patience, then that interpretation can affect how Bob, the pastor, the robotics researcher, the bioethicist, and others view the assistant and that virtue.

As communities persist, their shared commitments and interpretive practices may result in more formal institutions forming around them. Conversely, one can examine whether certain sociotechnical institutions have aspects of community. Within sociotechnical systems, institutions can depend upon productive crafts that may become virtuous practices, with further development of individual and corporate internal goods, especially if the core practice is supported by institutional practices and commitments (MacIntyre 1984; Moore 2002; Moore & Beadle 2006). Moral identity can foster and resist hindrances to virtuous action and moral agency from institutional and environmental influences, and shared interpretation and meaning can influence people to align their own cognitive schemas with those articulated in the collective for better or worse (Aquino & Reed 2002; Weaver 2006, 251; Wang & Hackett 2020). If an AI or robotics developer has a goal to implement ethical behaviors, such as patience, into the device, then that affects how they perceive and act upon technical tasks within their craft. If they make a strong commitment, then that may affect their moral identity, the actions and practices of others, and even the surrounding institutions. Central to how one perceives or appraises the moral or spiritual implications of a situation is moral attention.

Moral Attention

Although Weil (1951) is primarily concerned with moral attention in a religious context, other philosophers, such as Iris Murdoch (1971), identify moral attention as an ethical construct requiring effort and being of intrinsic value. For Murdoch, attention is a reflective activity of an active moral agent directed upon another individual with a "just and loving gaze" (Murdoch 1971, 33). Moral attention requires awareness that a situation has moral content; skilled recognition or construal of moral issues and sensitivity to their importance and affective response; and an innate tendency to attentively perceive the moral elements of experience (Jordan 2007, 326; Miller et al. 2014, 28–30; Reynolds & Miller 2015, 114). Moral attention depends upon a spiritual self-emptying (or moral formation) in order to perceive the other and the other's needs. Clearly relevant for practical wisdom, moral attention also situates spiritual discernment in a social context, which setting aside Neoplatonic conceptualizations, discernment generally involves.

Moral attention in a sociotechnical context requires identifying the moral dimension within the situations, agents, institutional norms, and behaviors of a sociotechnical system and interpreting it in light of the shared values. In human society, one appraises the ethical needs of others and responds as oriented by the moral schemas with which one identifies. In a sociotechnical context, technology may enhance and/or distort one's perceptions and add affordances upon which one might act. Schemas and other knowledge structures and skills may include highly technical information with far-ranging and opaque ethical implications, and many aspects of one's cognitive processing may be extended to AI and other advanced computational technologies (Heersmink 2017; Skorburg 2019).

Moral attention in imitating exemplars means attending to the moral dimension of their behavior and identifying aspects relevant to one's own moral development and identity formation. Beyond a cognitive recognition, imitating requires learning moral affordances that the exemplar perceives but the aspirant does not yet imagine, habituating new interpretation and behavior, and identifying with one's updated knowledge schemas. In the example scenario, balancing between ethical principles requires moral attention to identify moral dimensions of technical decisions, including those made more difficult by technical complexity and opacity. The schemas and other cognitive structures borrowed from exemplars enable perceiving additional moral affordances, upon which the imitator may choose to act (thus strengthening and identifying with those interpretive habits and virtuous behaviors).

Modeling

Models create a skewed and incomplete representation of something by emphasizing certain aspects, as only some relevant features are ascertained. One can consider exemplars as a model for a virtue or practice, and researchers can create models of those exemplars for further investigation. As a working definition, a model abstracts or idealizes a thing or phenomenon by highlighting significant aspects while deemphasizing less relevant features, where usually the description and analysis of the model inform one's understanding of a targeted, real-world thing or phenomenon. As a model, one attends to exemplar moral character and behavior and deemphasizes bodily and other mental characteristics, unless specifically relevant to the virtue or practice of interest. In the example scenario, exemplary characteristics of care and compassion would be most relevant, as would insights into complex ethical issues, while a community committed to justice for an oppressed group might attend to exemplary characteristics of courage and fortitude.

Three approaches to modeling moral attention are: (i) mental models of those who imitate the concrete human models of exemplary moral behavior; (ii) mathematical and statistical models of exemplar mental schemas as identified in narrative identity interviews; and (iii) computational models of exemplary mental processing and behavior via both cognitive and AI modeling.[1] Viewing exemplars as concrete models of a virtue clarifies what it means to have a virtue and provides a foundation for examining the mental models of the aspirant and scientific models of the researcher. Mental models are an internal representation of how something works (Johnson-Laird 2004). Rather than modeling all aspects of an exemplar, one creates a model that aligns with how the exemplar models virtue, or, for the present chapter, practical wisdom, discernment, and moral attention. Statistical and computational models extend the use of models scientifically as empirical methods to examine the ways exemplar and aspirant schemas might operate.

Exemplarity and Imitation

Exemplars are concrete models of integrated virtue and spiritual formation for a range of virtues (Scarlett 2012; Walker 1999; Zagzebski 2013). They serve as role models, demonstrating how one could behave in a situation, representing the goal as possible to attain, and inspiring others to desire the goal (Morgenroth et al. 2015). Moral aspirants must be initially motivated sufficiently to view virtue as a goal at some level, and the exemplar strengthens that motivation, demonstrates the possibility of acquiring and manifesting the virtue, and shows how it operates skillfully. Some exemplars serve as behavioral models for practical wisdom (Aristotle's *phronimos*) or discernment.

Exemplars have schemas and other cognitive structures used in moral attention. Schemas, along with a person's appraisal of a situation, help determine behavior (Ahrens & Cloutier 2019), and moral schemas capture rationales and judgments used in determining and articulating normative behavior (Narvaez 2005; Narvaez & Bock 2002; Rest et al. 2000). One understands virtue in relation to one's self and construes the virtue in relation to the appraisal (Orom & Cervone 2009). Although schemas capture a mental model of what it is like to have the virtue, individuals only respond virtuously if their identity motivates a virtuous response in the current situation (as an ideal for the aspirant and habitually for the exemplar). These schemas capture the possible moral affordances one can identify within a situation, and thus guide the appraisal and one's expectations for the situation (Hampson et al. 2021; Morgenroth et al. 2015). My claim is that in exemplary moral attention, the schemas are particularly well attuned to appraising the moral dimension of a situation.

In imitating exemplars, the aspirant begins to acquire similar cognitive structures, which are built through repetition and strengthened by practices. Cognitive structures appear to be shared between perceived and generated action (Meltzoff & Decety 2003). Over time, schemas are developed through observation and imitation, strengthened through practice, and incorporated into one's identity. The repetition involves not only the habit formation long associated with virtue and character development but also the transition from episodic memories of exemplar and personal behavior to more generalized schema associated with semantic memory (Renoult et al. 2019). What one knows about a particular virtue is closely intertwined with how one remembers it being expressed, perceives it in situations, and considers it for actions.

The aspirant's mental models of virtuous behavior shift the affordances perceived and facilitate moral attention, which itself is habitually formed. One's possible considerations of action, including moral action, orient the affordances one can perceive. As the aspirant's perceptions and actions align with perceived virtue, their mental schemas gain the ability to identify moral affordances. Attending to exemplary characteristics of others (i.e., using them as a model) increases recognition of moral affordances. With repetition, moral attention is developed, especially in the context of practical wisdom and discernment.

Moral and spiritual development requires identifying with one's commitment to moral and spiritual interpretation and behavior. In aspirants' formation of moral attention and practiced schemas, they may identify with possible behaviors as more like them (in forming narrative identity). Understanding this process of moral identity in relation to the moral schemas affecting appraisal would help explain the process of developing from aspirant to exemplar. Shifting from theoretical to operational investigations of exemplarity, the remainder of the chapter explores ways to investigate the exemplar's and aspirant's cognitive schemas with which they identify and their mental processing.

Text Analysis

One can identify and examine the moral and spiritual schemas with which exemplars and others identify through narrative identity interviews and auto-biographical writing (McAdams 2001). A person's schemas incorporate that person's values. If an interviewer asks questions about a person's identity that elicit responses dependent upon those schemas, then one can expect those values to be implicit in articulating aspects of one's identity (Adler et al. 2017). Similarly, in autobiographical writing, if one activates certain schemas in remembering and reconstructing stories about one's self, then the writing would incorporate values and patterns of thought for those schemas.

The cognitive schemas with which one identifies affect not only perception but also the linguistic statements generated about how one perceives oneself. Interview questions and autobiographical writing prompt the person to elucidate knowledge structures that reflect the person's committed values and identity. These investigations of a person's identity schemas complement both explicit survey questions about a person's values (which may also elicit how a person wishes to be perceived or values that person desires to have) and observations of behavior (which also depend upon the person's appraisal of the current situation). One way to identify these values is through qualitative coding, and another is through computational methods, and computational methods are briefly examined here.

Latent semantic analysis (LSA; Landauer et al. 2007) and other mathematical and statistical methods of associative semantics (Brunila & LaViolette 2022; Firth 1957) can measure similarities between autobiographical statements and formal descriptions of moral and spiritual values. LSA uses similar distributive representations of language as current AI models do, but without additional predictive or generative mechanisms. LSA quantifies the extent to which a value occurs implicitly within the autobiographical statement by using a computational proxy for meaning in order to measure the semantic similarity between the theory-derived value descriptors and the autobiographical text (Reimer et al. 2012). When cognitive schemas incorporate moral or spiritual values, statements generated under the influence of those schemas should be semantically similar to the descriptors of those values (Graves et al. 2022).

Similarities between schemas and formal descriptors suggest the presence of those moral and spiritual values within those schemas and may illuminate relationships between those values within and across exemplars. Schemas capture a snapshot of what it is like to have a particular virtue or committed value. Querying identity narratives activates the schemas associated with identity and elicits a response with latent meaning about that identity. Probing those responses with moral or other value descriptors measures the presence of that value, which creates a quantitative variable. One can compare those variables statistically between responses for an individual or between participants. Computational models probe deeper into the valuation process itself.

Computational Models

One can investigate the mental processing and behavior of imitation and exemplary morality with computational models (Han 2016; Oztop et al. 2006), especially those heavily influenced by cognitive, affective, and social neuroscience. The formation and retrieval of generalized knowledge of schemas (e.g., semantic memory) closely involves the ventromedial prefrontal cortex (vmPFC) and bidirectionally interacts with medial temporal lobes important for episodic memory, with the vmPFC also implicated in associating reward value and emotions with episodic memory (Rolls 2022; Spalding et al. 2015; van Kesteren et al. 2010). Computational models suggest a close connection between goals and values with object properties and their emotional salience stored downstream from sensory cortical regions and upstream from motor cortices (De Martino & Cortese 2023; Martin 2016). The apparent connections between social cognition, valuation, and affect regulation in vmPFC (Delgado et al. 2016; Yoder & Decety 2018) suggest a plausible process for the formation of emotionally salient observations of exemplars to form episodic foundations for more generalized schemas that can guide the aspirant's perception and possible action.

Computational modeling of imitation can draw upon social learning, simulation, and cognitive and social neuroscientific studies of imitation. Social learning theory suggests learning occurs through observation, modeling, and imitation of others (Bandura 1971), and computational and neural models have explored how that learning may take place (Lopes et al. 2009; Olsson et al. 2020). The complexities of social interactions make it difficult to simplify the scenarios enough for modeling without eliminating the essential complexities being studied (FeldmanHall & Nassar 2021). Imitation of action has been linked to mirror neurons, but higher-level and social structures and processes do not map easily to simple neural structures (Heyes & Catmur 2022). Computational models based on findings in neuroimaging have contributed to understanding social cognition (Dolcos et al. 2020; Lockwood & Klein-Flügge 2021), though little research has focused on imitation of higher-level activities by adults.

Computational modeling of mental processing associated with exemplary moral behavior can build upon neuroscientific and other psychological studies of spirituality and moral action in exemplars. A number of substantial investigations have explored the neurological foundations for moral psychology (Murphy & Brown 2007; Sinnott-Armstrong 2008), including those examining moral development and exemplarity (Narvaez 2014; Riveros & Immordino-Yang 2021; Van Slyke et al. 2012). Computational models of moral cognition and the processes involved in moral decision-making draw upon studies in value-based decision-making within social neuroscience and neuroeconomics (Qu et al. 2022). Several studies suggest that the brain incorporates moral considerations into its typical process of valuation, with additional systems involved in moral values and potentially harmful or dishonest responses (Balconi et al. 2023; Greene & Paxton 2009; Hu et al. 2021; Hutcherson et al. 2015; Qu et al. 2022). Multiple models have been developed for altruism (Hu et al. 2021; Tusche & Bas 2021) and the observation of moral character (Bellucci et al. 2019, 2020), though additional work is needed to include modeling of exemplarity.

Computational models can build upon AI techniques to examine the function and learning of moral attention, independent of human neural and psychological structures, with implications for machine and technology ethics. In addition to the computational modeling of exemplarity, additional work is needed to connect the foundational work in valuation with investigations into observation and imitation as well as higher-level examinations of moral identity. Complementary investigations into attention in deep learning and deep reinforcement learning may build upon neuroscientific investigations into attention and extend models beyond the current understanding of human's neurobiological platform (Lindsay 2020). Similar to how text analysis models can identify moral dimensions of identity, more complex computational models may be able to attend to moral dimensions of situations that would not otherwise be obvious. This would support developments in making AI more ethical and could augment human moral attention.

Moving beyond computational modeling of individual human aspirants and exemplars, the incorporation of artificial moral attention within communal interpretation can augment practical wisdom and discernment by identifying moral affordances of technical decisions and otherwise opaque technical operations. In the example scenario, the question becomes how to customize the AI assistant so it attends to factors of care and compassion both for its operation and for other people and avoids the harm caused by failing to attend to those factors. Identifying and recognizing suffering is an important aspect of moral attention, compassion, and, when suffering is present, practical wisdom. A goal would be to customize AI to identify suffering and address and/or communicate it to others, as appropriate, while maintaining Ann's privacy and respecting her autonomy and dignity. The AI assistant augments Bob's moral attention by identifying situations of suffering while he is not present. Over time, he may become more skilled at using the technology in this way. Similar configurations could help other AI systems attend more closely to suffering, and a technical challenge is to configure the AI to assist in moral attention rather than reduce opportunities for human care. In particular, Bob may need to learn to use the AI assistant to augment his moral attention and action without offloading the caretaking duties to the AI.

Exemplars can build upon this augmented attention and incorporate it into their schemas. Further skilled customization of the technology would continue to extend an exemplar's awareness, might help synthesize information for decision-making, could simplify tradeoffs involving practical wisdom, and highlight factors relevant for discernment. Although offloading care to AI could harm human ability to build caring relationships, if the technology is developed well, then it could instead identify more opportunities for compassionate response.

Conclusion

Spiritual and moral practices must account for the increased role of technology within society. This affects how aspirants and exemplars incorporate technology into moral attention, practical wisdom, and discernment. Josiah Royce's philosophy of community emphasizes the importance of shared interpretation of values, and sociotechnical systems provide a structure to examine that collective interpretation and evaluation while engaging with technology. Considering exemplars as concrete models of virtues and practices simplifies investigation of exemplar and aspirant mental models, including through analysis of identity narratives and computational models of neurologically grounded mental processes. AI technology can augment awareness of situations and help focus attention on moral needs, extending aspirant and exemplar opportunities for development and action.

Acknowledgments

Thanks to Timothy Reilly, Emanuele Ratti, Kutter Callaway, and Steve Quartz for their comments on an earlier version of the chapter.

Note

1 Weisberg (2013, Chapters 2–3) distinguishes three kinds of models: (i) concrete models that are real, physical objects representing real or imagined systems or phenomena; (ii) mathematical models that typically capture the dynamic relationships of phenomena as functions and equations; and (iii) computational models, where typically an algorithm's conditional, probabilistic, and/or concurrent procedures capture the causal properties and relationships of their target phenomena.

References

Adler, J. M., Dunlop, W. L., Fivush, R., Lilgendahl, J. P., Lodi-Smith, J., McAdams, D. P., McLean, K. C., Pasupathi, M., & Syed, M. 2017. "Research methods for studying narrative identity: A primer." *Social Psychological and Personality Science*, 8(5), 519–527.

Ahrens, A. H., & Cloutier, D. 2019. "Acting for good reasons: Integrating virtue theory and social cognitive theory." *Social and Personality Psychology Compass*, 13(4), e12444. https://doi.org/10.1111/spc3.12444

Anderson, M., & Anderson, S. L. 2011. *Machine ethics*. Cambridge: Cambridge University Press.

Aquino, K., & Reed, A. 2002. "The self-importance of moral identity." *Journal of Personality and Social Psychology*, 83(6), 1423–1440. https://doi.org/10.1037/0022-3514.83.6.1423

Balconi, M., Angioletti, L., & Fronda, G. 2023. "Are the autonomic and central neurophysiological correlates predictive of moral and economic offers?" *Psychology & Neuroscience*, 16, 31–51. https://doi.org/10.1037/pne0000305

Bandura, A. 1971. *Social learning theory*. New York: General Learning Corporation.

Barry, W. A. 2011. *Letting God come close: An approach to the Ignatian spiritual exercises*. Chicago: Loyola Press.

Bellucci, G., Camilleri, J. A., Iyengar, V., Eickhoff, S. B., & Krueger, F. 2020. "The emerging neuroscience of social punishment: Meta-analytic evidence." *Neuroscience & Biobehavioral Reviews*, 113, 426–439. https://doi.org/10.1016/j.neubiorev.2020.04.011

Bellucci, G., Molter, F., & Park, S. Q. 2019. "Neural representations of honesty predict future trust behavior." *Nature Communications*, 10(1), 5184. https://doi.org/10.1038/s41467-019-13261-8

Bronk, K. C. 2012. "The exemplar methodology: An approach to studying the leading edge of development." *Psychology of Well-Being: Theory, Research and Practice*, 2(1), 5. https://doi.org/10.1186/2211-1522-2-5

Brunila, M., & LaViolette, J. 2022. "What company do words keep? Revisiting the distributional semantics of J.R. Firth & Zellig Harris." *Proceedings of the 2022 Conference of the North American Chapter of the Association for Computational Linguistics: Human Language Technologies*, 4403–4417. https://doi.org/10.18653/v1/2022.naacl-main.327

Coeckelbergh, M. 2012. "'How I learned to love the robot': Capabilities, information technologies, and elderly care." In I. Oosterlaken & J. van den Hoven (Eds.), *The capability approach, technology and design* (pp. 77–86). Springer Netherlands. https://doi.org/10.1007/978-94-007-3879-9_5

Cooper, R., & Glasspool, D. 2001. "Learning action affordances and action schemas." In R. M. French & J. P. Sougné (Eds.), *Connectionist models of learning, development and evolution* (pp. 133–142). London: Springer.

Darnell, C., Gulliford, L., Kristjánsson, K., & Paris, P. 2019. "Phronesis and the knowledge-action gap in moral psychology and moral education: A new synthesis?" *Human Development*, 62(3), 101–129. https://doi.org/10.1159/000496136

De Martino, B., & Cortese, A. 2023. "Goals, usefulness and abstraction in value-based choice." *Trends in Cognitive Sciences*, 27(1), 65–80. https://doi.org/10.1016/j.tics.2022.11.001

Delgado, M. R., Beer, J. S., Fellows, L. K., Huettel, S. A., Platt, M. L., Quirk, G. J., & Schiller, D. 2016. "Viewpoints: Dialogues on the functional role of the ventromedial prefrontal cortex." *Nature Neuroscience*, 19(12), 1545–1552.

Dolcos, F., Katsumi, Y., Moore, M., Berggren, N., de Gelder, B., Derakshan, N., Hamm, A. O., Koster, E. H. W., Ladouceur, C. D., Okon-Singer, H., Pegna, A. J., Richter, T., Schweizer, S., Van den Stock, J., Ventura-Bort, C., Weymar, M., & Dolcos, S. 2020. "Neural correlates of emotion-attention interactions: From perception, learning, and memory to social cognition, individual differences, and training interventions." *Neuroscience & Biobehavioral Reviews*, 108, 559–601. https://doi.org/10.1016/j.neubiorev.2019.08.017

Edwards, P. N. 2003. "Infrastructure and modernity: Force, time, and social organization in the history of sociotechnical systems." In T. J. Misa, P. Brey, & A. Feenberg (Eds.), *Modernity and technology* (pp. 185–226). Cambridge, MA: MIT Press.

Emmons, R. A. 1999. *The psychology of ultimate concerns: Motivation and spirituality in personality*. New York: Guilford Press.

FeldmanHall, O., & Nassar, M. R. 2021. "The computational challenge of social learning." *Trends in Cognitive Sciences*, 25(12), 1045–1057. https://doi.org/10.1016/j.tics.2021.09.002

Firth, J. 1957. "A synopsis of linguistic theory 1930–1955." In *Special volume of the philological society*. Oxford: Oxford University Press.

Gamez, P., Shank, D. B., Arnold, C., & North, M. 2020. "Artificial virtue: The machine question and perceptions of moral character in artificial moral agents." *AI & SOCIETY*, 35(4), 795–809. https://doi.org/10.1007/s00146-020-00977-1

Graves, M. 2009. "The emergence of transcendental norms in human systems." *Zygon*, 44(3), 501–532.

Graves, M. 2013. *Insight to heal: Co-creating beauty amidst human suffering.* Eugene, OR: Cascade Books.

Graves, M. 2017. "Grace and virtue: Theological and psychological dispositions and practices." *Psychology of Religion and Spirituality,* 9(3), 303–308. https://doi.org/10.1037/rel0000129

Graves, M. 2023. "Interaction in emergent human systems." *Theology and Science,* 21(2), 331–339. https://doi.org/10.1080/14746700.2023.2188377

Graves, M., Reilly, T., Kaikhosroshvili, K., & Narvaez, D. 2022. "Moral and intellectual virtues: Computational linguistic analysis of scientists and musicians accounts." In T. Reilly, D. Narvaez, M. Graves, K. Kaikhosroshvili, & S. Israel de Souza (Eds.), *Moral and intellectual virtues in practices: Through the eyes of scientists and musicians* (pp. 109–140). Cham, Switzerland: Springer International Publishing. https://doi.org/10.1007/978-3-031-18969-2_5

Greene, J. D., & Paxton, J. M. 2009. "Patterns of neural activity associated with honest and dishonest moral decisions." *Proceedings of the National Academy of Sciences,* 106(30), 12506–12511. https://doi.org/10.1073/pnas.0900152106

Hampson, P. J., Hulsey, T. L., & McGarry, P. P. 2021. "Moral affordance, moral expertise, and virtue." *Theory & Psychology,* 31(4), 513–532. https://doi.org/10.1177/09593543211021662

Han, H. 2016. "How can neuroscience contribute to moral philosophy, psychology and education based on Aristotelian virtue ethics?" *International Journal of Ethics Education,* 1(2), 201–217. https://doi.org/10.1007/s40889-016-0016-9

Heersmink, R. 2017. "Distributed cognition and distributed morality: Agency, artifacts and systems." *Science and Engineering Ethics,* 23(2), 431–448. https://doi.org/10.1007/s11948-016-9802-1

Heyes, C., & Catmur, C. 2022. "What happened to mirror neurons?" *Perspectives on Psychological Science,* 17(1), 153–168. https://doi.org/10.1177/1745691621990638

Holland, M. G. 1998. "Touching the weights: Moral perception and attention." *International Philosophical Quarterly,* 38(3), 299–312. https://doi.org/10.5840/ipq199838324

Hu, J., Hu, Y., Li, Y., & Zhou, X. 2021. "Computational and neurobiological substrates of cost-benefit integration in altruistic helping decision." *Journal of Neuroscience,* 41(15), 3545–3561. https://doi.org/10.1523/JNEUROSCI.1939-20.2021

Hursthouse, R. 2006. "Xi*—Practical wisdom: A mundane account." *Proceedings of the Aristotelian Society,* 106(1), 285–309. https://doi.org/10.1111/j.1467-9264.2006.00149.x

Hutcherson, C. A., Bushong, B., & Rangel, A. 2015. "A neurocomputational model of altruistic choice and its implications." *Neuron,* 87(2), 451–462. https://doi.org/10.1016/j.neuron.2015.06.031

Jackelén, A. 2021. "Technology, theology, and spirituality in the digital age." *Zygon,* 56(1), 6–18. https://doi.org/10.1111/zygo.12682

Johnson-Laird, P. N. 2004. "The history of mental models." In *Psychology of reasoning.* London: Psychology Press.

Jordan, J. 2007. "Taking the first step toward a moral action: A review of moral sensitivity measurement across domains." *The Journal of Genetic Psychology,* 168(3), 323–359. https://doi.org/10.3200/GNTP.168.3.323-360

King, P. E., Mangan, S., & Riveros, R. 2023. "Religion, spirituality, and youth thriving: Investigating the roles of the developing mind and meaning-making." In E. B. Davis, E. L. Worthington Jr., & S. A. Schnitker (Eds.), *Handbook of positive psychology, religion, and spirituality* (pp. 263–277). Cham, Switzerland: Springer International Publishing. https://doi.org/10.1007/978-3-031-10274-5_17

Landauer, T. K., McNamara, D. S., Dennis, S., & Kintsch, W. 2007. *Handbook of latent semantic analysis.* Mahwah, NJ: Lawrence Erlbaum Associates.

Lapsley, D. 2016. "Moral self-identity and the social-cognitive theory of virtue." In J. Annas, D. Narváez, & Snow, Nancy E (Eds.), *Developing the virtues: Integrating perspectives*. New York: Oxford University Press.

Lima, M. R., Wairagkar, M., Gupta, M., Rodriguez y Baena, F., Barnaghi, P., Sharp, D. J., & Vaidyanathan, R. 2022. "Conversational affective social robots for ageing and dementia support." *IEEE Transactions on Cognitive and Developmental Systems*, 14(4), 1378–1397. https://doi.org/10.1109/TCDS.2021.3115228

Lindsay, G. W. 2020. "Attention in psychology, neuroscience, and machine learning." *Frontiers in Computational Neuroscience*, 14. https://www.frontiersin.org/articles/10.3389/fncom.2020.00029

Lockwood, P. L., & Klein-Flügge, M. C. 2021. "Computational modelling of social cognition and behaviour—A reinforcement learning primer." *Social Cognitive and Affective Neuroscience*, 16(8), 761–771. https://doi.org/10.1093/scan/nsaa040

London, A. J., Razin, Y. S., Borenstein, J., Eslami, M., Perkins, R., & Robinette, P. 2023. "Ethical issues in near-future socially supportive smart assistants for older adults." *IEEE Transactions on Technology and Society*, 4(4), 291–301. https://doi.org/10.1109/TTS.2023.3237124

Lopes, M., Melo, F. S., Kenward, B., & Santos-Victor, J. 2009. "A computational model of social-learning mechanisms." *Adaptive Behavior*, 17(6), 467–483. https://doi.org/10.1177/1059712309342757

MacIntyre, A. C. 1984. *After virtue: A study in moral theory*. Notre Dame, IN: University of Notre Dame Press.

Makarius, E. E., Mukherjee, D., Fox, J. D., & Fox, A. K. 2020. "Rising with the machines: A sociotechnical framework for bringing artificial intelligence into the organization." *Journal of Business Research*, 120, 262–273. https://doi.org/10.1016/j.jbusres.2020.07.045

Martin, A. 2016. "GRAPES—Grounding representations in action, perception, and emotion systems: How object properties and categories are represented in the human brain." *Psychonomic Bulletin & Review*, 23(4), 979–990. https://doi.org/10.3758/s13423-015-0842-3

McAdams, D. P. 2001. "The psychology of life stories." *Review of General Psychology*, 5(2), 100–122.

Meltzoff, A. N., & Decety, J. 2003. "What imitation tells us about social cognition: A rapprochement between developmental psychology and cognitive neuroscience." *Philosophical Transactions of the Royal Society of London. Series B, Biological Sciences*, 358(1431), 491. https://doi.org/10.1098/rstb.2002.1261

Miller, J. A., Rodgers, Z. J., & Bingham, J. B. 2014. "Moral awareness." In *Research companion to ethical behavior in organizations* (pp. 1–43). Cheltenham, UK: Edward Elgar Publishing.

Moore, G. 2002. "On the implications of the practice-institution distinction: MacIntyre and the application of modern virtue ethics to business." *Business Ethics Quarterly*, 12(1), 19–32. https://doi.org/10.2307/3857646

Moore, G., & Beadle, R. 2006. "In search of organizational virtue in business: Agents, goods, practices, institutions and environments." *Organization Studies*, 27(3), 369–389. https://doi.org/10.1177/0170840606062427

Morgenroth, T., Ryan, M. K., & Peters, K. 2015. "The motivational theory of role modeling: How role models influence role aspirants' goals." *Review of General Psychology*, 19(4), 465–483.

Murdoch, I. 1971. *The sovereignty of good*. New York: Routledge.

Murphy, N. C., & Brown, W. S. 2007. *Did my neurons make me do it: Philosophical and neurobiological perspectives on moral responsibility*. Oxford: Oxford University.

Narvaez, D. 2005. "The neo-Kohlbergian tradition and beyond: Schemas, expertise, and character." In G. Carlo & C. Pope-Edwards (Eds.), *Moral motivation through the life span* (pp. 119–163). Lincoln, NE: University of Nebraska Press.

Narvaez, D. 2014. *Neurobiology and the development of human morality: Evolution, culture, and wisdom.* New York: Norton. https://doi.org/10.1080/03057240.2015.1069479

Narvaez, D., & Bock, T. 2002. "Moral schemas and tacit judgement or how the defining issues test is supported by cognitive science." *Journal of Moral Education,* *31*(3), 297–314. https://doi.org/10.1080/0305724022000008124

Narvaez, D., & Rest, J. 1995. "The four components of acting morally." *Moral Behavior and Moral Development: An Introduction,* *1*(1), 385–400.

Neubert, M. J., & Montañez, G. D. 2020. "Virtue as a framework for the design and use of artificial intelligence." *Business Horizons,* *63*(2), 195–204. https://doi.org/10.1016/j.bushor.2019.11.001

Olsson, A., Knapska, E., & Lindström, B. 2020. "The neural and computational systems of social learning." *Nature Reviews Neuroscience,* *21*(4), 197–212. https://doi.org/10.1038/s41583-020-0276-4

Orom, H., & Cervone, D. 2009. "Personality dynamics, meaning, and idiosyncrasy: Identifying cross-situational coherence by assessing personality architecture." *Journal of Research in Personality,* *43*(2), 228–240. https://doi.org/10.1016/j.jrp.2009.01.015

Oztop, E., Kawato, M., & Arbib, M. 2006. "Mirror neurons and imitation: A computationally guided review." *Neural Networks,* *19*(3), 254–271. https://doi.org/10.1016/j.neunet.2006.02.002

Qu, C., Bénistant, J., & Dreher, J.-C. 2022. "Neurocomputational mechanisms engaged in moral choices and moral learning." *Neuroscience & Biobehavioral Reviews,* *132*, 50–60. https://doi.org/10.1016/j.neubiorev.2021.11.023

Reimer, K. S. 2009. *Living L'Arche: Stories of compassion, love, and disability.* Collegeville, MN: Liturgical Press.

Reimer, K. S., Young, C., Birath, B., Spezio, M. L., Peterson, G., Van Slyke, J., & Brown, W. S. 2012. "Maturity is explicit: Self-importance of traits in humanitarian moral identity." *The Journal of Positive Psychology,* *7*(1), 36–44.

Renoult, L., Irish, M., Moscovitch, M., & Rugg, M. D. 2019. "From knowing to remembering: The Semantic–Episodic distinction." *Trends in Cognitive Sciences,* *23*(12), 1041–1057. https://doi.org/10.1016/j.tics.2019.09.008

Rest, J. R., Narvaez, D., Thoma, S. J., & Bebeau, M. J. 2000. "A neo-Kohlbergian approach to morality research." *Journal of Moral Education,* *29*(4), 381–395. https://doi.org/10.1080/713679390

Reynolds, S. J., & Miller, J. A. 2015. "The recognition of moral issues: Moral awareness, moral sensitivity and moral attentiveness." *Current Opinion in Psychology,* *6*, 114–117. https://doi.org/10.1016/j.copsyc.2015.07.007

Rietveld, E., Denys, D., & Van Westen, M. 2018. "Ecological-enactive cognition as engaging with a field of relevant affordances: The skilled intentionality framework (SIF)." In A. Newen, L. De Bruin, & S. Gallagher (Eds.), *The Oxford handbook of 4E cognition* (pp. 40–70). Oxford: Oxford University Press. https://doi.org/10.1093/oxfordhb/9780198735410.013.3

Riveros, R., & Immordino-Yang, M. H. 2021. "Toward a neuropsychology of spiritual development in adolescence." *Adolescent Research Review,* *6*, 323–332. https://doi.org/10.1007/s40894-021-00158-1

Robert, W. 2012. "A mystic impulse: From apophatics to decreation in pseudo-dionysius, Meister Eckhart and Simone Weil." *Medieval Mystical Theology,* *21*(1), 113–132. https://doi.org/10.1558/mmt.v21i1.113

Rolls, E. T. 2022. "The hippocampus, ventromedial prefrontal cortex, and episodic and semantic memory." *Progress in Neurobiology, 217,* 102334. https://doi.org/10.1016/j.pneurobio.2022.102334

Royce, J. 1913. *The problem of Christianity. Lectures delivered at the Lowell Institute in Boston, and at Manchester College, Oxford.* New York: Macmillan.

Scarlett, W. G. 2012. "Spiritual exemplars: An introduction." *Religions, 3*(2), 183–90. https://doi.org/10.3390/rel3020183

Schneiders, S. M. 2005. "Approaches to the study of Christian Spirituality." In A. Holder (Ed.), *The Blackwell companion to Christian spirituality* (pp. 15–33). Oxford: John Wiley & Sons.

Selbst, A. D., Boyd, D., Friedler, S. A., Venkatasubramanian, S., & Vertesi, J. 2019. "Fairness and abstraction in sociotechnical systems." *Proceedings of the Conference on Fairness, Accountability, and Transparency,* 59–68. https://doi.org/10.1145/3287560.3287598

Singh, M. P. 2014. "Norms as a basis for governing sociotechnical systems." *ACM Transactions on Intelligent Systems and Technology, 5*(1), 21:1–21:23. https://doi.org/10.1145/2542182.2542203

Sinnott-Armstrong, W. 2008. *Moral psychology, volume 3: The neuroscience of morality: Emotion, disease, and development* (W. Sinnott-Armstrong, Ed.; Vol. 3). Cambridge, MA: MIT Press.

Skorburg, J. A. 2019. "Where are virtues?" *Philosophical Studies: An International Journal for Philosophy in the Analytic Tradition, 176*(9), 2331–2349. https://www.jstor.org/stable/45211655

Spalding, K. N., Jones, S. H., Duff, M. C., Tranel, D., & Warren, D. E. 2015. "Investigating the neural correlates of schemas: Ventromedial prefrontal cortex is necessary for normal schematic influence on memory." *The Journal of Neuroscience, 35*(47), 15746–15751. https://doi.org/10.1523/JNEUROSCI.2767-15.2015

Tusche, A., & Bas, L. M. 2021. "Neurocomputational models of altruistic decision-making and social motives: Advances, pitfalls, and future directions." *WIREs Cognitive Science, 12*(6), e1571. https://doi.org/10.1002/wcs.1571

Vallor, S. 2016. *Technology and the virtues: A philosophical guide to a future worth wanting.* New York: Oxford University Press. https://doi.org/10.1093/acprof:oso/9780190498511.003.0001

van de Poel, I. 2020. "Embedding values in artificial intelligence (AI) systems." *Minds and Machines, 30*(3), 385–409. https://doi.org/10.1007/s11023-020-09537-4

van Kesteren, M. T. R., Rijpkema, M., Ruiter, D. J., & Fernández, G. 2010. "Retrieval of associative information congruent with prior knowledge is related to increased medial prefrontal activity and connectivity." *The Journal of Neuroscience, 30*(47), 15888–15894. https://doi.org/10.1523/JNEUROSCI.2674-10.2010

Van Slyke, J. A., Peterson, G., Brown, W. S., Reimer, K. S., & Spezio, M. L. 2012. *Theology and the science of moral action: Virtue ethics, exemplarity, and cognitive neuroscience.* New York: Routledge.

Walker, L. J. 1999. "The perceived personality of moral exemplars." *Journal of Moral Education, 28*(2), 145–162.

Wallach, W., & Vallor, S. 2020. "Moral machines: From value alignment to embodied virtue." In S. M. Liao (Ed.), *Ethics of artificial intelligence* (p. 383–412). New York: Oxford University Press. https://doi.org/10.1093/oso/9780190905033.003.0014

Wang, G., & Hackett, R. D. 2020. "Virtues-centered moral identity: An identity-based explanation of the functioning of virtuous leadership." *The Leadership Quarterly, 31*(5), 101421. https://doi.org/10.1016/j.leaqua.2020.101421

Weaver, G. R. 2006. "Virtue in organizations: moral identity as a foundation for moral agency." *Organization Studies, 27*(3), 341–368. https://doi.org/10.1177/0170840606062426

Weil, S. 1951. "Reflections on the right use of school studies with a view to the love of God." In E. Craufurd (Trans.), *Waiting for God*. New York: Harper.

Weisberg, M. 2013. *Simulation and similarity: Using models to understand the world*. New York: Oxford University Press.

Yoder, K. J., & Decety, J. 2018. "The neuroscience of morality and social decision-making." *Psychology, Crime & Law*, 24(3), 279–295. DOI: 10.1080/1068316X. 2017.1414817

Zagzebski, L. 2013. "Moral exemplars in theory and practice." *Theory and Research in Education*, 11(2), 193–206. https://doi.org/10.1177/1477878513485177

Part III

Christian Inquiry into Exemplars and Imitation

10 Martin Luther King Jr.'s Nonviolent War for the Soul of America

Radical Love as Revolutionary Imitation of Christ

Emily Dumler-Winckler

Was not Jesus an extremist for love: "Love your enemies, bless them that curse you, do good to them that hate you, and pray for them which despitefully use you, and persecute you." Was not Amos an extremist for justice: "Let justice roll down like waters and righteousness like an ever-flowing stream." Was not Paul an extremist for the Christian gospel: "I bear in my body the marks of the Lord Jesus." Was not Martin Luther an extremist: "Here I stand; I cannot do otherwise, so help me God." And John Bunyan: "I will stay in jail to the end of my days before I make a butchery of my conscience." ...So the question is not whether we will be extremists, but what kind of extremists we will be. Will we be extremists for hate or for love? Will we be extremists for the preservation of injustice or for the extension of justice? ...Perhaps the South, the nation and the world are in dire need of creative extremists.
       ~Dr. Martin Luther King Jr. "Letter from a Birmingham Jail"

Extremists are exemplars. So Dr. Martin Luther King Jr. suggests in his famous "Letter from a Birmingham Jail."[1] Extremists exemplify, represent, or actualize an ideal (or its antithesis) by embodying various virtues or vices. As the ellipses in the epigraph indicate, King's list includes other extremists for justice, truth, and love. His sermons, speeches, and letters are littered with ordinary *and* extraordinary exemplars.[2] Extremism, then, is not the problem, as the "white moderate" claims. The problem, rather, is the moderation of white Christians who think they can share the same ideals and exemplars while remaining moderate.[3] The question "is not whether we will be extremists, but what kind of extremists we will be. Will we be extremists for hate or for love? Will we be extremists for the preservation of injustice or for the extension of justice?"[4] Ironically, King suggests, the white moderate serves as a greater obstacle to justice than extremists of injustice. Initially disappointed to be dubbed an "extremist" by fellow clergymen in Birmingham, King came to embrace the moniker. In doing so, he identified himself with a long tradition of Christian "creative extremists" in love, justice, preaching good news, conscientious objection, and what he would elsewhere call "creative dissent," and "transformed nonconformity."

DOI: 10.4324/9781032648392-14

In *The Radical King*, Cornel West reaffirms that King was indeed an extremist: a radical, revolutionary, Christian.[5] According to West, the domestication of King over the past half century has obscured the radical nature of his thought, life, and work: his example. King and other radicals like Nelson Mandela have been "Santa-Clausified—tamed, domesticated, sanitized, and sterilized—into nonthreatening and smiling old men with toys in their bags and forgiveness in their hearts."[6] The fundamental motif of "the radical King," West notes, is "radical love" which is "Christocentric in content and black in character."[7] This love is radical in a dual sense: *rooted* in revolutionary Christianity, the Black prophetic tradition, and Black freedom struggle, it seeks to *uproot* the spiritual, social, political, and economic evils of white supremacy in America and beyond.[8] Accounts of King's nonviolent "love ethic" that ignore its dually radical nature threaten to further tame his example, that is, what he exemplifies or represents to us today.[9]

One of my central aims in this chapter is to show that King's commitment to nonviolent resistance as a mode of revolutionary social change grew out of his radical commitment to an understanding of the love ethic of Jesus; another is to locate King and his commitment in a long and diverse Christian tradition of the imitation of Christ; and a final aim is to show that his commitments to love and forgiveness as central to revolutionary social change make him more radical, not less.[10] For King, radical love is Christocentric in the sense that it entails imitating Christ's radical love of God and neighbor, integrating conviction and commitment, belief and action, theory and practice, and example and doctrine. As Jesus is the extremist for love *par excellence*, the Christian life has often been understood as an effort to imitate or follow the way of Jesus. The imitation of Christ is at the heart of the personal, communal, and sociopolitical transformation of the beloved community. Following Christ is never as simple as exclusively or directly following Jesus's example. Rather, his example is mediated and refracted through what I have elsewhere called a long "tradition of dissent."[11] Following or imitating Christ inevitably entails emulating or innovating on the example of a diverse array of other "extremists" for love, justice, truth, and beauty—Christian and non-Christian alike. Paul's exhortation to "follow me as I follow Christ" resounds and multiplies with each new generation. King extends traditions and exemplifies practices of spiritual transformation that constitute sociopolitical transformation, demonstrating that radical personal change is integral to radical social change.

The "white moderate" of King's day was doubly deceived.[12] Ignoring Jesus's extremism, they could not recognize King's likeness to Christ. Domesticate Jesus and King appear all the more extreme. A half century later, a white moderate society has ironically managed to Santa-Clausify both extremists. To the extent that American Christians and American culture more broadly domesticate Jesus and King and spurn or ignore their extremism, they misconstrue the exemplarity of each; they neglect the radical nature of the love ethic and vision for social change central to each.

From early on in his studies, ministry, and activism, King was clear-eyed about the radical nature of Jesus' love ethic: the call to love God, neighbors, strangers, and even enemies. His central questions were not whether but *why* and *how* Christians ought to practice this radical love, and *whether* doing so might transform enemies as well as social, political, and economic institutions and structural injustice. Like these questions, King's responses grew from the variegated soil of philosophical examination, theological conviction, spiritual discipline, and communal practice. It is one thing to know that Jesus calls his followers to love their enemies; another thing to know how, why, and to what effect, and still another to practice such radical love.

As for *how* to love one's enemies, the first section of this chapter considers King's treatment of the teachings and example of Jesus. Anger, lament, and radical forgiveness are indispensable. The second section considers King's turn from Jesus' teaching to his example in two sermons, "Love in Action" and "Transformed Nonconformity." For King, to follow Christ's radical love is to participate in a tradition of transformed nonconformity to the world and even to former exemplars. As for *why* one should love even enemies, the second section turns to King's enduring conviction that hate begets hate, love begets friendship.

Still, for the activist and organizer, crucial questions remained: could Jesus' love ethic transform sociopolitical systems, structures, and institutions and demolish systemic evils from Jim Crow to the Vietnam War to global poverty? Karl Marx, Fredrich Nietzsche, and Reinhold Niebuhr posed profound philosophical and theological challenges to Jesus' love ethic. King would face and overcome these challenges with the help of exemplars like Gandhi and W. E. B. Du Bois.[13] But his commitment to Jesus's love ethic also faced a number of practical challenges and tests, which would only be overcome through the highly experimental practices of nonviolent resistance and organizing from Montgomery to Memphis. The final two sections examine his response to these theoretical and practical challenges.

How to Love Even Enemies: On Forgiveness, Justice, and Anger

For King, Jesus' radical teachings and example are clear, an unequivocal call to love God, neighbor, self, stranger, and even enemies. In the thick of Jim Crow America, the immense difficulty of this love ethic was not lost on this son of a Black Baptist minister. The primary question then was not *whether* Christians ought to love, but rather *how* those with their "backs against the wall" might follow this way, love one another and even enemies.[14] King turned to the teachings and example of Jesus for guidance and found forgiveness central to each. And yet, far from fodder for King's domestication, his insistence on love and forgiveness as the means to radical sociopolitical change is one of the most radical and demanding aspects of his legacy.

That forgiveness is central to King's radical love ethic and nonviolent resistance becomes clear in two sermons that he preached during and after the bus protest in Montgomery, Alabama, and revised for inclusion in the sermon book, *Strength to Love* (1963).[15] In "Loving Your Enemies," King reflects on Jesus' teaching, while in "Love in Action," he turns to Jesus' example on the cross.

"Loving Your Enemies" begins with Jesus' teaching in the Gospel of Matthew's Sermon on the Mount:

> You have heard that it hath been said, Thou shalt love thy neighbor, and hate thine enemy. But I say unto you Love your enemies, bless them that curse you, do good to them that hate you, and pray for them which despitefully use you, and persecute you; that ye may be children of your Father which is in heaven.
>
> (Matthew 5:43–45)[16]

Of all of Jesus's teachings, his admonition to "love your enemies," King notes, is probably the most difficult to follow. Some affirm the ideal but insist on its practical impossibility. Others, like Nietzsche, see the ideal itself as confirmation of the weak, anemic, life-denying, and cowardly nature of the Christian love ethic. Both views render Jesus an "impractical idealist" (43). In contrast, King insists that Jesus is a "practical realist:" "Far from being the pious injunction of a utopian dreamer, the command to love one's enemy is an absolute necessity for our survival. Love even of enemies is the key to the solution of the problems of our world" (44).

Taking the practical objections seriously, King begins with the question, "*How do we love our enemies?*" His reply comes in three parts. First and foremost, Christians "must develop and maintain the capacity to forgive" (44). Forgiveness is power. Like physical power, forgiveness must be continually exercised and cultivated, or it will atrophy. Forgiveness becomes habitual through practice, repeatedly forgiving friends and enemies alike. "Not seven times," Jesus and King insist, "but seventy times seven" (33, Matthew 18:21–22). This is just how virtuous habits work: "A man cannot forgive up to four hundred and ninety times," King does the math, "without forgiveness becoming a part of the habit structure of his being. Forgiveness is not an occasional act; it is a permanent attitude" (33). Why then is forgiveness imperative for loving one's enemies?

The power of forgiveness, for King, is integrally related to the power of love. The two powers grow stronger or weaker together. Some may suppose that human beings can love without forgiving or forgive without loving. King argues, rather, that those "devoid of the power to forgive" are "devoid of the power to love" (44). One can only begin "the *act* of loving one's enemies" by accepting "the necessity, over and over again, of forgiving those who inflict evil and injury upon us." No forgiveness—no love.

Not only repetition but also initiation is crucial. "The forgiving act must always be initiated," King affirms, "by the person who had been wronged, the victim of some great hurt, the recipient of some tortuous injustice, the absorber of some terrible act of oppression" (44). The oppressor may or may not repent and may not even request forgiveness. In either case, the injured person is the only one who can forgive, and this act does not ultimately depend on the wrongdoer's repentance.

Those who have endured great evils, as had King, may object that forgiveness should not (or ultimately cannot) be foisted on victims of injustice.[17] Such impositions create a double burden, a double harm. The last thing victims of injustice or harm need is to be *told* to forgive their perpetrators. King's injunction may be read as making such demands. But it may also be read in the indicative rather than imperative mood: it is just the case that the act of forgiveness "must always be initiated by the person who has been wronged." No one else can initiate this act on their behalf. Forgiveness is thoroughly voluntary.[18] As Hannah Arendt writes in *The Human Condition*, "Forgiving … is the only reaction which does not merely re-act but acts anew and unexpectedly, unconditioned by the act which provoked it and therefore freeing from its consequences both the one who forgives and the one who is forgiven."[19]

Far from passive, acquiescent, or condoning injustice, King suggests that radical forgiveness is central to both radical love and the quest for justice. The latter is not as obvious as the former. For King's account of forgiveness resembles recent accounts that see forgiveness as at odds with—or certainly not an aid to—justice for the following reasons: (1) forgiveness is voluntary, gratuitous, and unconditional and so gives wrongdoers better than they justly deserve (whether retribution, vengeance, hostility, or resentment); and (2) forgiveness does not depend on the wrongdoers' repentance or reparation of wrongs and so leaves unjust relations in place.[20] King affirms both points and yet insists that while forgiveness exceeds the demands of justice—giving wrongdoers better than they deserve—it does not contravene or ignore these demands.

Forgiveness does not entail justifying, excusing, accepting, condoning, or "ignoring what has been done or putting a false label on an evil act" (45). On the contrary, the person who forgives an enemy name rather than overlooks the injustice, denouncing rather than ignoring the evil in which they participate. To forgive means, rather, "that the evil act no longer remains as a barrier to the relationship. Forgiveness is a catalyst…. lifting of a burden or the cancelling of a debt" and so creates the possibilities for new relationship. Forgiveness does not mean forgetting in a basic sense, but it does mean that "the evil deed is no longer a mental block impeding a new relationship" (45). The forgiver thereby breaks the cycle of hatred, violence, and oppression, creating the possibility of right relationship. Forgiveness does not establish or guarantee justice or reparations, but it is a necessary condition for the restoration of right relationship. Forgiveness and reparation are both conditions of justice.

In her book *Anger and Forgiveness*, Martha Nussbaum's domesticates King's views in the ways that West rightly laments, depicting King as an exemplar not of forgiveness, but of "non-anger" or "anti-anger,".[21] Gandhi, King, and Mandela, she claims, "all repudiated anger as a matter of both theory and practice."[22] Not only that, "non-anger" is far more central to their nonviolent revolutionary action than love or forgiveness. Indeed, she argues that even "unconditional forgiveness" is morally problematic because it assumes a prior anger and remains backward-looking rather than "transitional" or forward-looking.[23] In keeping with her Stoic propensities, she argues that "anger is always normatively problematic whether in the personal or in the public realm."[24] For her, anger necessarily involves the desire for retribution, vengeance, or what she calls a "pay-back wish."[25]

Others have rightly addressed the weakness in Nussbaum's definitions (for instance, of anger and "non-anger"), distinctions (for instance, between "transitional" and "unconditional" forgiveness), and lack of distinctions (for instance, between anger, retribution, and resentment).[26] My concern here is not only her peculiar account of anger, but also that she misrepresents King's view of anger and its relation to love, forgiveness, and justice. I will focus on the latter.

Following ancient philosophers and theologians, King seems to have understood anger as an emotion or passion that can be harnessed by habits of virtue or vice.[27] For him, anger is not inherently vicious, nor, as Nussbaum assumes, connected to the desire for retribution, vengeance, or payback.[28] As a parent may be angry with their child, or a friend with a friend, without desiring retribution, so anger does not necessarily or even usually entail resentment, hatred, bitterness, or a wish to harm.[29] Rather, we have good reasons to distinguish these affects and their effects. Anger may or may not be a fitting response to any given occasion. Even when fitting, anger comes in various degrees and kinds: we can have too much or too little anger with respect to some slight, offense, or injustice. Activists and organizers have distinguished between hot and cold anger.[30] At its best, as the Hebrew prophets attest, anger is a righteous response to injustice. As West describes King, "radical love produced a seething in his soul, a holy anger and righteous indignation."[31] In stark contrast to Nussbaum, then, for King, anger is *not* "always normatively problematic." The question is whether it is rooted in and expresses love and justice rather than hatred and injustice.

For King, anger is not an ethical problem, but neither alone is it a practical solution. History had taught W. E. B Du Bois, as King put it, that "it is not enough for people to be angry—the supreme task is to organize and unite people so that their anger becomes a transforming force."[32] King was convinced, by Howard Thurman, Mahatma Gandhi, and finally by his own practice of nonviolent resistance, that righteous anger could be organized, disciplined, and mobilized for the cause of justice: "nonviolent resistance… controlled anger and released it under discipline for maximum effect."[33] He held that "even very violent temperaments can be channeled through nonviolent discipline… [to express] their very legitimate anger."[34] This discipline and mobilization are the points of training in nonviolent direct action and "self-purification."[35] King knew anger intimately, describing the anger he felt after his home was bombed.[36] He chose to harness that anger for the struggle of nonviolent resistance.[37]

Forgiveness and anger are not then ultimately at odds, as Nussbaum argues. Forgiveness may diminish or replace anger, but it need not. One can forgive an enemy while remaining angry about the ongoing injustice and harnessing that anger for resistance and justice. Indeed, King does not exemplify the absence of anger, and thereby the absence of "unconditional forgiveness." Rather, he exemplifies the intermingling of righteous anger and forgiveness, justice and love. Far from normatively problematic, anger founded in radical love and justice is a righteous response to injustice. The ethical question is how one uses or channels such anger.

In sum, forgiveness is crucial for love of enemies and for justice. Like love, forgiveness exceeds certain demands of justice, giving wrongdoers better than what they deserve. But acts of forgiveness need not preclude anger, blame, denunciation, accountability, protest, or calls for reparations. Importantly, forgiveness does not entail justifying, excusing, or condoning either the wrongdoing or the wrongdoer.

Secondly, in response to the practical question—*"how do we love our enemies?"*—King suggests that it helps to recognize the ethically mixed, imperfect nature of all human beings: enemies are not purely evil and non-enemies (including ourselves) are not purely good. Rather, like their enemies, Christians are mixed bags of better and worse, virtues and vices, and incontinences, whereby, like the Apostle Paul, we do what we do not want to do. King's stringent belief that all humans are created in the image of God led him to repeatedly affirm that there is some good even in our worst enemies (46). Not only that, but we are each "tragically divided against ourselves" which means that "there is some good in the worst of us and some evil in the best of us" (45–46). Recognizing this admixture enables us to forgive enemies, even as we seek forgiveness from God and one another. As Jesus taught his disciples to pray, "forgive our debts, as we forgive our debtors" (Matthew 6:12).

Thirdly, those who practice radical forgiveness and love recognize that the ultimate goal is not to "defeat or humiliate the enemy but to win his friendship and understanding" (46). Radical love begins not with *philia* (friendship) or *eros* (romantic love) but with *agape,* "the love of God operating in the human heart" (46). But if friendship is not the inception of radical love, it is nonetheless the goal. King repeatedly emphasized that radical love is "much deeper than emotional bosh," not to be "confused with some sentimental outpouring." He was not calling his Black congregation to *like* their enemies: the white supremacists who bombed their churches and homes, those intent on maintaining racial exploitation and domination. But he did insist that the *love* of enemies just might make friends of former enemies.

Jesus: Exemplar of "Love in Action" and "Transformed Nonconformity"

In "Love in Action," King turns from Jesus's teaching to his example. The epigraph for the sermon is Jesus' famous petition from the cross: "Father, forgive them; for they know not what they do" (Luke 23:24). Herein, Jesus embodies or exemplifies his own teaching on love and forgiveness. King argues that Jesus bridges the supposed Humean gulf between "is and ought," between the ideal and real: "never in history was there a more sublime example of the consistency of word and deed" (33). Jesus not only instructs his followers to love their enemies—an "absolute necessity for spiritual maturity"—he provides an example with his own life. Jesus' lament over Jerusalem and anger in the temple in the week leading up to his death culminate in this prayer from the cross.

Here a new question arises, namely, does forgiveness depend on (as the second part of the prayer might suggest) humanity's "intellectual and spiritual blindness": "they know not what they do" (35).[38] Those who cried "Crucify him," King insists, were not "bad men but rather blind men," not evil but rather misguided. In the modern era, a similarly "tragic blindness" led to the pseudo-scientific, pseudo-philosophical, and pseudo-theological doctrines of white supremacy, slavery, and racial segregation: "What a tragedy! Millions of Negroes have been crucified by conscientious blindness" (38).

The same year that King published *Strength to Love* (1963), James Baldwin published *The Fire Next Time*. Here, Baldwin seems to refuse King's distinction between the badness and blindness of those who crucify. The unforgivable sin of white Americans is that "they have destroyed and are destroying hundreds of thousands of lives and do not know it and do not want to know it."[39] Willful rather than conscientious ignorance, then, "is the crime of which I accuse my country and my countrymen," he continues, "and for which neither I nor time nor history will ever forgive them."

In the end, King recognizes both "intellectual and moral [or willful] blindness" (40). Those who draw on "pseudo-scientific" theories of white supremacy "do not know, *or they refuse to know*, that the idea of an inferior or superior race has been refuted by the best evidence of the science of anthropology" (38).[40] Jesus also laments the willful ignorance of his fellow citizens, "Oh! Jerusalem, Jerusalem, the city that kills the prophets...! How often have I desired to gather your children together... but you were not willing" (Luke 13:34).

One can hardly blame Baldwin for joining nature, time, history, and society in refusing to forgive those who wreak horrific destruction. Maria Mayo suggests that during the mid-crucifixion, even Jesus was not able to forgive his enemies.[41] The fatherly petition could just as well have read, "Forgive them Father, for I cannot." In this reading, Jesus does not exemplify forgiveness, but rather the limits of forgiveness for the oppressed. The ethical thrust of this view is that Christians should stop telling victims of oppression to forgive their enemies. Surely, this is right. Nonetheless, King reads the prayer as confirmation that those on the underside of the Roman and American Empires *can* love and forgive enemies, and that the Jewish rabbi who had taught and practiced forgiveness also exemplified it to the end. The cross is the ultimate reminder of "man at his worst" and "Christ at his best" (41).

As the epigraph for this chapter suggests, in life and teaching, King held that "Jesus was an extremist for love."[42] He practiced on the cross what he preached on the mount: "Love your enemies, bless them that curse you, do good to them that hate you, and pray for them which despitefully use you, and persecute you." Accused of being an extremist, King first thought that the white moderate gravely misunderstood the way he moderated between "two opposing forces in the Negro community:" the force of complacency, on the one hand, and the force of bitterness and hatred, on the other. Rather than emulate "the 'do-nothingism' of the complacent or the hatred and despair of the black nationalist," he advocated the "way of love and nonviolent protest." Nevertheless, he grew to appreciate the label. He aspired to emulate Jesus and the wide array of his followers, who were extremists for radical love and forgiveness, nonviolent resistance, and nonconformity.

King is clear that Jesus's exemplification of radical love is of a piece with "transformed nonconformity." Jesus Christ, he proclaims, is "the world's most dedicated nonconformist, whose ethical nonconformity still challenges the conscience of mankind" (13). Ironically, despite the fact that "Christians have a mandate to be nonconformists," King found the "tragic tendency to conform" nowhere more evident than in the church (12, 15). The point here is twofold: (1) King's radical embrace of nonconformity, resistance, and civil disobedience is rooted in the Christian Black radical tradition and any who emulate Jesus's nonconformity; and (2) imitation, emulation, and discipleship always involve a measure of conformity and nonconformity to the exemplars themselves, even more so when the exemplar is a nonconformist! In his sermon by the title, "Transformed Nonconformist," King reflects this dual nonconformity: to the pattern of this world (Romans 12:2) and to the precise example of others.[43]

In the wake of the horrors of the Jewish Holocaust and the Second World War, the Jewish-Polish, social psychologist, Solomon Asch, famously developed conformity studies to understand when and why people tend to conform to social consensus against their better judgment.[44] Asch was concerned with over-imitation or conformity, which he thought his studies confirmed.[45] King shows greater familiarity with sociologists and psychologists who were touting the benefits rather than dangers of conformity, suggesting "that morality is merely group consensus .... [and] that mental and emotional adjustment is the reward of thinking and acting like other people" (11). If conformity is a "byword of the modern world," nonconformity for its own sake (or conformity masquerading as nonconformity) has become the byword of the late-modern world (12). King recognizes that nonconformity for its own sake is no better than conformity.

Nonconformity alone will not do: the Christian mandate is to be transformed, disciplined nonconformists. King must have been reading Ralph Waldo Emerson: not only his essay "Self-Reliance" which he cites in the sermon but also Emerson's so-called "Divinity School Address" to the Harvard graduates (1838). In the address, Emerson declares that it is by the "religious sentiment" that "the universe is made safe and habitable, not by science or power."[46] King echoes, "The hope of a secure and livable world lives with disciplined nonconformists, who are dedicated to justice, peace, and brotherhood. The trailblazers in human, academic, scientific, and religious freedom have always been nonconformists" (16). Nonconformity is not only for trailblazers but also for all who would come into their own. As King cites Emerson, "Whoso would be a man [*sic*] must be a nonconformist" (17). This twentieth-century nonconformist grasps the central anthropological insight of the nineteenth-century nonconformist: the world is made habitable for and by transformed nonconformists who see and resist "evils with a humble and loving spirit" (18).

Why Love Even Enemies: On the Power of Love and Hate

Having addressed the practical question, *how* to love an enemy, King turns to the theoretical question, *why* should Christians love their enemies. "Because Jesus said so or did so" seems insipid and unsatisfying, especially for the oppressed and nonconformists. Here, King examines the immense power of love and hate, attending to their respective salubrious and destructive effects on self, enemy, and community. First, he thinks obviously, "returning hate for hate multiplies hate, adding deeper darkness to a night already devoid of stars."[47] Hate begets hate; violence begets violence. The only way to break the chain of hate and thwart the "descending spiral of destruction" is to refuse hatred, to meet hate with love.

Second, hatred destroys the hated and haters alike: "hate scars the soul and distorts the personality." That hatred destroys the hated is obvious enough:

> We have seen [hatred's] ugly consequences in the ignominious deaths brought to six million Jews by a hate obsessed madman named Hitler, in the unspeakable violence inflicted upon Negroes by bloodthirsty mobs, in the dark horrors of war, and in the terrible indignities and injustices perpetrated against millions of God's children by unconscionable oppressors" (47).

King is hardly naïve about the nature or extent of modern evils; the mass destruction hatred wreaks on the hated. Less obvious is the moral fact that hatred also destroys the hater. Without a hint of hyperbole, he writes, "hate is just as injurious to the person who hates" (48). Here he draws support from modern psychiatrists and psychologists who have come to recognize and affirm "what Jesus taught centuries ago: hate divides the personality and love in an amazing and inexorable way unites it" (48).[48]

Third, love is "the only force capable of transforming an enemy into a friend" (48). This reason may appear as flaccid as "Jesus say so." Those with an enemy's boot on their neck may reasonably reply, no thanks! As the feminist and abolitionist, Sarah Grimké, wrote, "all I ask of our brethren is that they will take their feet from our necks and permit us to stand upright on the ground which God designed us to occupy."[49] To stand upright, to take a stand, is not yet to make an enemy a friend. But it does create the conditions for friendship, namely non-domination. Whereas hate has the power to destroy hater and hated alike, love has the power or potential to transform lover and beloved. Love is at once the potent and "creative force, so beautifully exemplified in the life of our Christ... [and] the only way to create the beloved community" (50).

In a speech he delivered at the annual convention of the Southern Christian Leadership Conference (SCLC) (August 16, 1967), King lamented that philosophers have too often contrasted power and love as "polar opposites, so that love is identified with resignation of power, and power with a denial of love."[50] The cost of these Nietzschean and Christian fallacies is dire, for "power without love is reckless and abusive, and that love without power is sentimental and anemic" (172). So, King reaffirms love as a supremely powerful weapon in the ongoing struggles for justice (175). The famous discourse on love in 1 Corinthians 13 is refurbished: freedom fighters could have the most articulate speech, gifts of prophecy, scientific prediction, academic achievements, and institutions of learning, "but if you have not love, all of these mean absolutely nothing" (176).

Why love? It remains the only way to stop the cycle of hatred and violence, salvage one's own soul, and transform enemies into friends. King was convinced of these tenets early on. The question of whether or not love could instigate sociopolitical as well as personal revolutions would become the experiment of his life. King gradually became convinced of the power of Jesus's love ethic and nonviolent resistance to sociopolitical transformation.[51] To his untimely death, he was committed to testing this theory in practice.

Sociopolitical Revolution: Theo-Philosophical Challenges and Exemplars

Following West, Gary Dorrien acknowledges four key intellectual and spiritual sources for King (in order of importance)—"prophetic Black church Christianity, prophetic liberal Christianity, prophetic Gandhian nonviolence, and prophetic American civil religion."[52] Rooted in this soil and cultivated by mentors like Howard Thurman, Bayard Rustin, Mordecai Johnson, and Benjamin Mays, Jesus' love ethic was central to his faith and theology. This ethic received its severest philosophical and practical challenges in his work as an activist and organizer in the freedom struggle. Karl Marx and Friedrich Nietzsche presented the strongest philosophical challenges. On King's telling, in his essay "Pilgrimage to Nonviolence," he never doubted the power of love for individual and interpersonal transformation. Reading Marx and Nietzsche, however, led him to question and almost despair "of the power of love in solving social problems."[53]

In different ways, Marx, Nietzsche, and Reinhold Niebuhr each argue that love is impotent as a revolutionary sociopolitical force. For Marx, religion, along with its illusory happiness and love, is famously an opiate of the masses.[54] Far from solving social problems, the love ethic of Jesus consecrates and perpetuates them. Thus, "the abolition of religion as the *illusory* happiness of the people is the demand for their *real* happiness."[55] In Nietzsche's *Genealogy of Morals* and *Will to Power*, King found a rejection of Christian virtues of love and humility: the cowardly and impotent response of the powerless toward the powerful and strong.[56] Niebuhr also grew critical of pacifism, understood as "a sort of passive nonresistance to evil expressing naïve trust in the power of love" (46). Faced with such cultured and realist despisers, King too doubted whether the love ethic of Jesus could be applied to sociopolitical and economic transformation among groups, nations, and classes.

King's encounter with the thoughts, writings, and work of Mahatma Gandhi was a turning point. West observes, "the Gandhian method of love-motivated (agapic) nonviolent resistance provided the radial King with a response to Marx and an answer to Nietzsche."[57] And as James Cone recalls, "Martin often said that, 'Christ furnished the spirit and motivation [for nonviolent resistance], while Gandhi furnished the method."[58] Introduced to the ideas of civil disobedience while studying Henry David Thoreau at Morehouse and to pacifism through a lecture by Dr. A. J. Muste at Crozer, King became increasingly curious about Gandhi's life, teachings, and movement of nonviolent resistance after hearing a sermon by Dr. Mordecai Johnson in Philadelphia. In King's words:

> As I delved deeper into the philosophy of Gandhi my skepticism concerning the power of love gradually diminished, and I came to see for the first time its potency in the area of social reform .... Gandhi was probably the first person in history to lift the love ethic of Jesus above mere interaction between individuals to a powerful and effective social force on a large scale. Love for Gandhi was a potent instrument for social and collective transformation. It was in this Gandhian emphasis on love and nonviolence that I discovered the method for social reform that I had been seeking for so many months (45).

In Gandhi, King found something new under the sun: the first person in history to exemplify the efficacy of Jesus's love ethic for large-scale social transformation. Other theorists of civil disobedience, abolition, and nonviolent resistance concur that there is, indeed, something new in the idea that society can be permanently improved through organized collective nonviolent action for social change.[59] Power and efficacy are crucial. King's study of Gandhi convinced him that "true pacifism is not nonresistance to evil, but nonviolent resistance to evil. Between the two positions, there is a world of difference. Gandhi resisted evil with as much vigor and power as the violent resister, but he resisted with love instead of hate" (46). Nonviolent direct action is not passive; it does resist, but it does so in love and hope.

Dorrien thus rightly notes that from his early days in the movement, King said he "came to Gandhi through Jesus, not the other way around."[60] King also went further by portraying Gandhi as an imitator of Christ, grafting him into a long line of nonconforming imitators. Having just returned from a two-month trip to India as a guest of Prime Minister Jawaharlal Nehru and the Gandhi Memorial Trust of India, on March 22, 1959, he preached a Palm Sunday Sermon on Gandhi. A perfectly fitting subject for the holy day, "this man, more than anybody else in the modern world, caught the spirit of Jesus Christ and lived it more completely in his life" (24).

The sermon used two Biblical texts to analyze and understand Gandhi as a modern imitator of Christ: Jesus' teaching that "I have other sheep which are not of this fold" (John 10:16), and "the works that I do, shall he do also. And greater works than these shall he do because I go unto my Father" (John 14:12). As for the first, King admits the strange irony "of the modern world that the greatest Christian of the twentieth century was not a member of the Christian Church" (26). As for the second, put simply, "this man took the message of Jesus Christ and was able to do even greater works than Jesus did in his lifetime."

The former claim, that Gandhi is a sheep not of this fold, sounds akin to Karl Rahner's account of anonymous Christianity.[61] But the statement has less to do with soteriology, revelation, and confession, than with ethical action: what it means to follow Christ. Gandhi was directly influenced by the Sermon on the Mount, Thoreau, Tolstoy, and the Biblical injunctions to "turn the other cheek" and "resist evil with good."[62] Still, he was not a member of the Christian church. King's point seems to be that one can know and follow the way of Jesus and so be a "Christian" (etymologically, "little anointed one"), without joining the Christian Church.

As for greater works, Gandhi exemplified the imitation of Christ, not because he did precisely what Jesus did, but because he did even greater things. Gandhi used nonviolence to break the backbone of the British Empire, embodied "absolute self-discipline," and practiced internal criticism. This revolutionary saw the splinter of colonialism and racism in his opponent's eye, but also the plank in the eyes of those who maintained the racial caste system in India. King concludes with a question and commission, "Who today will follow Christ in his way and follow it so much that we'll be able to do greater things even than he did because we will be able to bring about the peace of the world and mobilize hundreds and thousands of men to follow the way of Christ?" (37). Through nonviolent resistance, Jesus' love ethic could be a mobilizing force for the masses, perhaps even overturning the American empire.

King had other exemplars, not of this fold: exemplars of the power of radical love closer to home. James Cone notes that the Black Power movement had an impact on the exemplars King publicly admired and extolled. Prior to Black Power, "white personalities had dominated King's idea of excellence and the black models were ones whom whites had portrayed as Negroes worthy of emulation (i.e. Booker T. Washington, George Washington Carver, Roland Hayes, Jesse Owens, Joe Louis, Marion Anderson and Jackie Robinson)."[63] After Black Power, "King made fewer references to whites as persons to imitate; he began to name black persons as models of excellence" including names less acceptable to mainstream whites. Speaking about the Poor People's Campaign in Clarksdale, Mississippi (March 19, 1968), King said, "We're going to let our children know about Countee Cullen and Langston Hughes.... [and] that the only philosophers that lived were not Plato and Aristotle, but W. E. B. Du Bois and Alain Locke came through the universe."[64] "The Dilemma of Negro Americans" in, *Where do we go from Here?* (1968), includes a lengthy list of more than thirty-two Black poets, musicians, athletes, and literary lights from W. E. B. Du Bois and Richard Wright, to Ralph Ellison and James Baldwin. Indeed, less than two months before he was killed, King depicted Du Bois as an exemplar of Black power and radical love.

In a speech given at Carnegie Hall, "Honoring Dr. Du Bois" (February 23, 1968), King notes that Du Bois encompassed at least three careers: first, as a pioneer sociologist; second, as a global activist and organizer; and third, as a historian.[65] Above and beyond the long list of amazing accomplishments that King catalogs, he considers "Dr. Du Bois *the man*" as a model and exemplar of radical love and black power (118):

> This lifestyle of Dr. Du Bois is the most important quality this generation of Negroes needs to emulate. The educated Negro who is not really part of us, and the angry militant who fails to organize us, have nothing in common with Dr. Du Bois. He exemplified black power in achievement and he organized black power in action. It was no abstract slogan to him (119).

A comment as thick with praise as blame, Du Bois is the exemplar of black power *par excellence*: a model of achievement and organized black power, a rejection of intellectual elitism and disorganized militancy. Recall, while anger is perfectly legitimate, King remarks, "History had taught [Du Bois] it is not enough for people to be angry—the supreme task is to organize and unite people so that their anger becomes a transforming force" (119). Ultimately, Du Bois's life was rooted in and animated by a radical love and faith in his own people (118). To conclude, King observes, "Dr. Du Bois' greatest virtue was his committed empathy with all the oppressed and his divine dissatisfaction with all forms of injustice" (120). And so, the refrain follows: may we too be divinely dissatisfied, until "justice will roll down like waters from a mighty stream" (121).

As exemplars of radical love, Gandhi and Du Bois provided King with distinct solutions to the challenges posed by Marx, Nietzsche, and Niebuhr. By embodying the virtues and ideals of love, justice, and nonviolent resistance, they instilled hope in the power of Jesus' love ethic to organize movements for mass sociopolitical and economic change. Exemplars provide a model to admire and emulate; they can also prove the viability of an ideal or theory in practice. As Du Bois described John Brown: "he did not use argument but was himself an argument."[66]

Still, King understood that the power of exemplars is not without hazards. One hazard, we have seen, is the temptation to over-imitate or conform too narrowly to a particular example. As Emerson put it, "Genius is always sufficiently the enemy of genius by over influence."[67] Another hazard is the tendency to imagine exemplars as altogether inaccessible, exceptional, and thereby inimitable. A thick description of character development and complexity is one way to guard against each. King carefully avoids these dual temptations, whether depicting Jesus, Gandhi, or Du Bois. Yet another hazard is having inadequate exemplars and models or too narrow a range, as Cone suggests of the early King's excessively Western, white, or white-sanctioned exemplars. As a remedy, King would eventually name a wide range of Black exemplars and democratize exemplarity, recognizing so-called ordinary, everyday exemplars, role models, heroes, and (occasionally) heroines.

Six months before his assassination, King gave an address, "What is Your Life's Blue Print?" to a group of students at Barratt Junior High School in Philadelphia. While emphasizing the uniqueness of each student's blueprint, King suggests that certain foundational elements should be common to all: first, a belief in one's own dignity, worth, or "somebodiness;" second, a commitment to excellence in various fields of endeavor; and third, a commitment to "the eternal principles of beauty, love, and justice."[68]

King dwells on the second point. One way to offset the hazards of exemplarity is to multiply exemplars. There is not one blueprint, type, model, or mold, but many. So, he points to "noble examples of black men and black women," "new and blazing stars of inspiration" who have "risen up and plunged against cloud-filled nights of affliction." The list of stars includes: "Booker T. Washington rose up ... Marian Anderson rose up ... Roland Hayes... George Washington Carver... Jackie Robinson ... Willie Mays ... Jesse Owens ... and Joe Louis and Muhammad Ali, with their educated fists."[69] Each, in their own way, was involved in the struggle for freedom and justice, not by doing what another could do best but by doing what they could do best.

Yet, the other danger of exemplarity, namely exceptionalism, remains. To those youth who may have despaired of being the best at anything—whether literary arts, opera, science, running, or boxing—King has another remedy. "If it falls to your lot to be a street sweeper," King suggests, "sweep streets like Michelangelo painted pictures ... like Beethoven ... like Leontyne Price... like Shakespeare ..." (67). The idea is not merely to praise the exceptional, or do precisely what they do, but to pursue excellence as they did in your own domain. Leaving structural injustices to the side in this instance, King's affirms, "if you can't be the sun, be a star .... Be the best of whatever you are" (67). He makes a similar point in *Where Do We Go From Here*, recognizing that not all will achieve the heights of various professional careers. Many will be laborers in the factories, fields, and streets. His refrain remains: "No work is insignificant. All labor that uplifts humanity has dignity."[70]

King understood that the development of radically loving street sweepers and minor stars is also crucial to the larger struggle for freedom and justice. Not everyone can or *should* be Gandhi, Du Bois, Ida B. Wells, or Fannie Lou Hammer. The supposed impotency of Jesus's love ethic is overcome not only in exemplars of radical love but also in those they helped to inspire and organize: the masses of exemplary street sweepers, laborers, and minor stars struggling for justice with love in their own way, place, and time. This multiplication of exemplars means that the imitation of Christ is not only Christological but at once pneumatological, reflecting the many-membered body of Christ.

Sociopolitical Revolution: Practical Challenges and Practices

Having confronted philosophical and theological challenges to the impotency of Jesus' love ethic and nonviolent resistance, King would encounter a number of practical challenges in his time as an activist and organizer. Early on, he encountered the first three tests of nonviolent resistance in the face of white supremacist terror and courts in Montgomery, Alabama. From a Birmingham jail, he defended the methods of nonviolent resistance against the attacks of the so-called "white moderate." Finally, Black Power directly challenged both King's conception of Jesus and his use of nonviolent resistance in the Black freedom struggle.

The Montgomery bus boycott would provide the first practical tests of King's commitment to Jesus's love ethic and nonviolent resistance. The movement for nonviolent resistance in America was born in the Black church. Before Gandhi became a household name in Montgomery, it was the principle of "Christian love" and Jesus of Nazareth's Sermon on the Mount that "stirred the Negros to protest with the weapon of love."[71] In his memoir, *Stride Toward Freedom* (1958), King recalled the "50,000 Negroes who took to heart the principles of nonviolence, who learned to fight for their rights with the weapons of love, and who, in the process, acquired a new estimate of their own human worth."[72] Such gains were hard won.

The first two tests arrived in the form of white-supremacist acts of terror: King's house bombing and dynamite thrown on the lawn of E. D. Nixon. Both events threatened to ignite violent resistance. On the evening of January 30, 1956, King's home was bombed, and an armed crowd quickly gathered on his lawn. When some threatened violence, King insisted that they must continue to "meet violence with nonviolence," appealing to Jesus' teaching in the Sermon on the Mount, "Love your enemies...."[73] A similar scene followed the bombing at Nixon's house. These events led to King's decisive break with arms. He got rid of the one weapon he owned and took other pragmatic nonviolent measures for self-defense.

The third test came when white opponents changed their tactics from physical to legal terror and intimidation. A jury "composed of seventeen whites and one Negro" found the bus boycott illegal.[74] Fearing that the protesters would be battle-weary or filled with despair, King found instead that, "those who had previously trembled before the law, were now proud to be arrested for the cause of freedom" (17). In keeping with traditions of abolition, civil disobedience, and nonconformity, he reflects, "I was a convicted criminal, but I was proud of my crime. It was the crime of joining my people in a nonviolent protest against injustice" (20). His people, specifically the Black church, helped King to face and overcome the first three practical tests—physical and legal terror—to Jesus's love ethic and nonviolent resistance.

Seven years later, from a Birmingham jail, King would face a new challenge to the methods of "self-purification" and nonviolent direct action in the verbal attacks by white clergymen and the broader "white moderate" culture.[75] His response is the famous, "Letter from a Birmingham Jail."

> I have been gravely disappointed with the white moderate. I have almost reached the regrettable conclusion that the Negro's great stumbling block in his stride toward freedom is not the White Citizen's Counciler or the Ku Klux Klanner, but the white moderate, who is more devoted to "order" than to justice; who prefers a negative peace which is the absence of tension to a positive peace which is the presence of justice; .... Shallow understanding from people of good will is more frustrating than absolute misunderstanding from people of ill will (135).

The letter is a brilliant attempt to convert the white moderate clergy, and white moderate culture more broadly, to the extremism of Jesus and his followers. The white moderate's claim to champion the same ideals and follow the same exemplars while remaining moderate is inconsistent. If they would follow Jesus, they must become extremists like King; the values and ideals displayed in their own exemplars demand it. The white moderate is gravely mistaken; he thinks he can follow Jesus while remaining more devoted to the racist social "order" than to justice, to the absence of tension than the presence of justice.

Throughout the letter, King places himself and the larger Civil Rights movement in a long tradition of prophetic justice, one with which the clergy themselves claim to identify. To the objection that King is an outsider, he notes that he was invited through organizational connections, but more basically, he is in Birmingham "because injustice is here" (128). Like the Hebrew prophets and the Apostle Paul, who spread the gospel to the far corners of the Greco-Roman world, "I must constantly respond to the Macedonian call for aid" (128).

To the objection and anxiety about civil disobedience as a method, King appeals to the age-old distinction between just and unjust laws. "One has not only a legal but a moral responsibility to obey just laws. Conversely, one has a moral responsibility to disobey unjust laws. I would agree with St. Augustine that 'an unjust law is no law at all'" (133). Like the antebellum abolitionists before him, King appeals to civil disobedience "evidenced sublimely in the refusal of Shadrach, Meshach, and Abednego to obey the laws of Nebuchadnezzar .... [and] practiced superbly by the early Christians" (134). Nonviolent resistance and direct action are simply radical extensions of prophetic *imitatio Christi* traditions.

Finally, King denounces their mythic and "tragic misconception of time" (136). Time itself does not remedy social evils. Any gains in social justice come "through the tireless efforts of men [*sic*]willing to be coworkers with God" (131–132). In the realm of justice, patience is not a virtue. Rather, King urges participation, action, impatience, divine dissatisfaction, or the "fierce urgency of now." As he concludes the "Beyond Vietnam" speech (1967), "In this unfolding conundrum of life and history there is such a thing as being too late" (217).

King ends the address, with a tone of disappointment and lament; disappointment with the white church and its leadership, its failure to denounce segregation and racism in moral and theological terms, its misplaced praise for law enforcement and "law and order," its failure to serve as a thermostat rather than thermometer of social mores; lament about the false dichotomy between the gospel and social justice (139–145). He concludes with an unhappy yet hopeful prediction that "one day the South will recognize its real heroes. They will be the James Merediths ... the oppressed, battered Negro women ... the young high school and college students, the ministers ... and elders... these disinherited children of God" who took a stand for the most sacred values in our "Judeo-Christian heritage" (144). The allusion matters. King reportedly carried a copy of Thurman's *Jesus and the Disinherited* with him at all times. The charge could not be more severe. The South (the white South) has not recognized Jesus among those with their "backs against the wall"; they have not fed the hungry, clothed the naked, satiated the thirsty, visited the prisoners, welcomed the stranger, or broken down the dividing wall of segregation.[76] Instead, they mock, imprison, and crucify the least of these.

As the nightmare of the Vietnam War compounded the racial nightmare in America in the years that followed, the hope that the white South or America broadly would one day recognize their real heroes must have appeared as a distant dream. Though many failed to see the connection at the time, King's denunciation of the Vietnam War in "Beyond Vietnam: A Time to Break Silence" was of a piece with his commitment to nonviolent directed action and the love ethic of Jesus. As Vincent Harding puts it, "nothing in the life of … Jesus … provided any indication that it was possible to love neighbors while also burning them, bombing them, targeting them for missiles, or undermining their search for revolutionary, life-affirming change—even Marxist led change."[77] King was never a principled or absolute pacifist. Especially early on, he argued that although all war is horrible, it might be necessary or preferable to surrender "to a totalitarian system—Nazi, fascist, or communist."[78] The advent of the nuclear age threatened to obliterate just war calculus, but by all counts, the Vietnam War failed to meet those criteria. King's outspoken criticisms of the War earned him new enemies and Harding's fitting moniker: America's "inconvenient hero."[79]

The final practical and theological challenge King encountered in his commitment to nonviolent resistance and the radical love ethic of Jesus came from the rise of the Black Power movement.[80] Black Power had deep roots in traditions of racial pride and black nationalism and in the work of Richard Wright and Malcolm X. Following the shooting of James Meredith in 1966, Stokely Carmichael and other organizers of the Committee on Racial Equality (CORE) and the Student Nonviolent Coordinating Committee (SNCC) gave rise to a new phase of the movement by making "Black Power" a slogan during the Memphis-to-Jackson Freedom March. The challenges from the Black Power movement were at least threefold: first, the movement challenged King to think and speak in new ways about the racial images and imaginary of Jesus himself; second, it challenged his commitment to nonviolent resistance as an effective means of social revolution; and third, it challenged him to translate organizing tactics used in the south into western and northern cities like Watts and Chicago alongside Black Power organizers.

First, King diminished the importance of Jesus's skin color for his exemplarity before and after the rise of Black Power. Nonetheless, according to Cone, his racialized descriptions of Jesus changed after Black Power. Before Black Power, King allegedly responded to a question, "Why did God make Jesus white, when the majority of people in the world are non-white?" by affirming that "the color of Jesus' skin is of little or no consequence …. The significance of Jesus lay, not in color, but in his unique God-consciousness." Nonetheless, King concluded that "He would have been no more significant if his skin had been black. He is no less significant because his skin is white."[81] After Black Power, he insisted with a group of Black ministers that Jesus "was not a white man." Unlike Malcolm X and later Cone, King did not go so far as to say that "Jesus was black." But he did seem to see the importance in denying Jesus' whiteness, particularly given the preponderance of white images of Jesus and their effects on the racist imagination of white Christianity.

Second, King sympathized deeply with the disappointments, anger, and aims that animated the Black Power movement; their central disagreement regarded the use of violence as a means. In his chapter "Black Power" in *Where Do We Go From Here: Chaos or Community?* (1968), King notes that Black Power is a reaction to the failures of white power, "born from the wounds of despair and disappointment."[82] Black power advocates are rightly disappointed, King insists, with the gulf that remains between legal reform and enforcement, with the injustices that plague urban cities in the north, with the militaristic U.S. government that praises Black nonviolence against whites at home and exploits Black violence in Vietnam, with "a federal administration… more concerned about winning an ill-considered war in Vietnam than about winning the war against poverty here at home;" they're rightly disappointed with "timid white moderates," with white legislators, and with a "Christian church that appears to be more white than Christian" (35–37). Moreover, Black Power has legitimate goals and aims: social, political, and economic strength for Black communities; freedom, dignity, and political power for Blacks; the pooling of Black financial resources to achieve economic security; and the affirmation of Black personhood (37–39).

Nevertheless, King thought that "negative values… prevent [Black Power] from having the substance and program to become the basic strategy for the civil right movement" (45). He disliked the slogan "Black Power" because it seemed to suggest "black domination rather than black equality" (34). At a deeper level, he worried that "Black Power is a nihilistic philosophy," which ultimately rejects hope, "the one thing that keeps the fire of revolutions burning" (45, 47). The "ultimate contradiction of the Black Power movement," he claimed, is that "revolution, though born of despair, cannot long be sustained by despair" (46). He also initially rejected Black Power's "implicit and often explicit belief in black separatism," an idea he found as unrealistic and impractical as "politically unsound and morally unjustifiable" (49, 50).

But the most "destructive feature of Black Power," King claims, "is its unconscious and often conscious call for retaliatory violence" (56). Through repeated conversations with the leaders of Black Power, he knew that many were rejecting nonviolence and arguing for the use of violent tactics and riots. Lamentably, he thought, "They don't quote Gandhi or Tolstoy. Their Bible is Franz Fanon's *The Wretched of the Earth*" (56). As with separatism, King is convinced that violent rebellion will not effectively achieve Black Power's aims. Courageous insurrectionists, like Denmark Vesey and Nat Turner, demonstrate, he maintains, that under a powerful white militaristic state, Black "violent rebellion is doomed from the start" (58). From his porch in Montgomery, King understood that hatred and violence are ineffective both because they intensify the fears of the white majority, and because they "leave them less ashamed of their prejudices toward Negroes"

(63). Only a mass movement of nonviolence could demonstrate, as it grew stronger, that "its power would be used creatively and not for revenge .... Violence is the antithesis of creativity and wholeness" (62). And here we find a hermeneutical key to the text's subtitle, *Chaos or Community*: "violence only adds to the *chaos*... It destroys *community* and makes brotherhood impossible" (63).

To reiterate, King's concern about Black Power is not about power itself but rather its abuse. "Nonviolence is power, but it is the right and good use of power" (61). Here, James Baldwin's letter to his nephew is exemplary. In the face of white ignorance, willful ignorance, and knowing inaction, "if the word *integration* means anything this is what it means: we, with love, shall force our brothers to see themselves as they are, to cease fleeing from reality and begin to change it" (63). The subtle suggestion is that only the power of love has such force; only love has the power to appeal to conscience, create self-awareness, and transform agents (61).

King's conclusion in, "Black Power," provides a fitting conclusion for this essay. King had criticized the white moderates for their moderation, and for failing to follow exemplars, whether extremists for injustice or justice. He now criticized Black Power for unwittingly imitating white power and white extremists for injustice:

Occasionally in life one develops a conviction so precious and meaningful that he will stand on it till the end. This is what I have found in nonviolence. One of the greatest paradoxes of the Black Power movement is that it talks unceasingly about not imitating the values of white society, but in advocating violence it is imitating the worst, the most brutal and the most uncivilized value of American life (66).

Paradoxically, he argues, Black Power imitates white violence: the very forms of white power, of terror, of extremism for injustice, that King repeatedly faced in the freedom struggle. In stark contrast to the imitation of Christ, for all of its talk of rejecting the values of white society, Black Power paradoxically imitates "the worst, the most brutal, and the most uncivilized value of American life," namely violence.

On imitation, King quotes at length from the end of Fanon's *The Wretched of the Earth*: "Humanity is waiting for something other from us than... an imitation" of European states, institutions, and societies (67). King admits that the words are brave, challenging, and inspiring. The problem is, again paradoxically, that Fanon and those who quote him continue "to imitate old concepts of violence .... This is the one thing about modern civilization that I do not care to imitate" (69). King ardently agrees, "Humanity is waiting for something other than the blind imitation of the past," of colonialism, slavery, and what Saidiya Hartman calls, "the afterlife of slavery" (68).[83] They are waiting not for more violence but for dissenters, transformed nonconformists, nonviolent resisters, and radically loving revolutionaries. In short, they are waiting for "creative extremists."

As his life, teaching, preaching, and example made clear, King's commitment to nonviolent resistance as a revolutionary force stemmed from his commitment to imitate Jesus and a long, diverse, prophetic tradition of dissent. But prophets are more demanding than their monuments, more threatening alive than dead. Following King's assassination on April 4, 1968, as if predicting the ways that his famous "I have a Dream" speech would be used to affect his "Santa Clausification," Carl Wendell Hime Jr. wrote the poem "A dead man's dream":

A dead man's dream

<blockquote>

      Now that he is safely dead
Let us praise him
          build monuments to his glory
    sing hosannas to his name.
      Dead men make
such convenient heroes: They
         cannot rise
   to challenge the images
           we would fashion from their lives
      And besides,
it is easier to build monuments
   than to make a better world.
      So, now that he is safely dead
we, with eased consciences
        will teach our children
   that he was a great man... knowing
   that the cause for which he lived
is still a cause.
   and the dream for which he died
      is still a dream,
    a dead man's dream.[84]

</blockquote>

For those with eyes to see, ears to hear, as Hime, Harding, West, Cone, and many (but perhaps always too few) others have, Jesus was an inconvenient hero. To the extent that the white moderate today makes convenient heroes of Jesus and King, they fail to grasp the extremism of both exemplars and the demands of following their way. King was and remains an "inconvenient hero."[85]

Notes

1 King (Jr.) (2015), 127–46.
2 For an explicit treatment of how my own account of exemplarity (and that of others like King) differs from Linda Zagzebski's prominent account, see her recent

text, Zagzebski (2017), *Exemplarist Moral Theory*, and my article (forthcoming), "The Trouble with Zagzebski's Semantic Theory of Exemplarity."

3 King (Jr.) (2015), 138. I am grateful to Andrew Peterson for his feedback on a first draft of this essay, especially on this point.

4 A note about the use of the term "we" is in order. Too often, the term "we" denotes a lack of awareness about positionality, privilege, in-group, or the insiders that the royal "we" assumes. Given my position as a white cis-gender woman engaging in Dr. King's work, the use of the term may be particularly fraught in this chapter. It is crucial to notice the distinct and multiple ways that King's use of "we" and address in his letters, sermons, and other writings may imply Black Christians, Blacks more broadly, Christians more broadly, and/or human beings broadly. For instance, while some sermons were given to the Black church, King revised them for publication with a wider audience, and his claims about Jesus's teachings appear to be directed at all Christians. When I use the term in this chapter, "we" refers to the audience I address, whomever you, dear reader, may be. As Bernard Williams puts it: "The best I can say is that 'we' operates not through a previously fixed designation, but through invitation…It is not a matter of 'I' telling 'you' what I and others think, but of my asking you to consider to what extent you and I think some things and perhaps need to think others" (see Bernard Williams *Shame and Necessity*, 171n.7). Even if this invitational and dialogical "we" is not without problems, I seek to avoid what Robert Brandom calls an "I-we" account of discursive social practices that "mistakenly postulate the existence of a privileged perspective—that of the 'we,' or community" and fail to distinguish between what a given community "*takes* to be true and what *is* true" (99, 600). See Brandom (1994), 599–600; and Stout (2004), 277.

5 King (Jr.) (2015), xiii, xv.

6 King (Jr.) (2015), 74. On the one hand, I am aware that writing about King's love and forgiveness as a white woman could risk either a similar taming effect or appropriation. Assuredly, neither is my aim. On the other hand, it seems to me that it would be negligent at best to write about the imitation of Christ in modern radical religious traditions, particularly in America, and not deal squarely with "the most significant and effective organic intellectual in the latter half of the twentieth century whose fundamental motif was [Christocentric, black] radical love" (xv). Myisha Cherry rightly cautions against those in positions of power or privilege telling victims of abuse or oppression to love and forgive. That is also not my aim. Rather, my aim here is to examine King's commitment to nonviolence as part of modern radical religious traditions of imitating Christ, as well as the theological, philosophical, and practical challenges and responses he developed through his work in the freedom and justice struggle. See Cherry (2017, 2021).

7 King (Jr.) (2015), xv.

8 King (Jr.) (2015), xi.

9 See, for example, King (Jr.) (2015), 45. King may have borrowed the term "love ethic" from Howard Thurman's, *Jesus and the Disinherited*, (1996), 89–91.

10 While scholars like West, Vincent Harding, and Gary Dorrien have noted the radical nature of King's commitment to Jesus's love ethic and nonviolent resistance, they have not theorized the role of imitation and exemplarity in his own work or located his work explicitly in a longer tradition of the "imitation of Christ." At the same time, recent scholars such as Karuna Mantena have expounded King's theory and practice of non-violent resistance without addressing its theological roots in his commitment to Jesus's love ethic, which served as the basis for his interest in Gandhian nonviolence. Mantena rightly rejects the dichotomy often drawn between principled versus strategic nonviolence, but proceeds to suggest that King's commitment was primarily animated by his belief in violence's "*futility*" and the "viability"

of nonviolence. See Karuna Mantena (2020), "Showdown for Nonviolence" in Shelby and Terry, *To Shape a New World*, 84–85.
11 Dumler-Winckler (2022).
12 King (Jr.) (2015), 135.
13 King (Jr.) (2015), 97.
14 Thurman (1996), 3.
15 King Jr. *Strength to Love* (2010), xiv. Despite having revised several of the sermons "for the eye," King remained convinced that "a sermon is not an essay to be read but a discourse to be heard," and expressed misgivings about publishing this book of sermons in 1962.
16 King Jr. (2015), 43. All references to these two sermons are drawn from this text, *Strength to Love*, unless otherwise noted.
17 See Mayo (2015); Cherry (2017, 2021).
18 On negative velleity, see Bowlin, (2016), 145. One may wish the world or circumstances were different than they are. One may wish that one did not have enemies to forgive. But, given these realities, the act of forgiveness is still voluntary.
19 Arendt, Canovan, and Allen (2018), 241.
20 Again, I am grateful to Andrew Petersen for drawing out this point. For one such account of forgiveness, see Stump (2020), 438n.47.
21 Nussbaum (2018), 212–13. Interestingly, most recent accounts of forgiveness have not considered King's account. See Potts (2022), Couenhoven (2019), and the series on forgiveness in the *Journal of Religious Ethics* (2013). Nussbaum's (2018) is an exception.
22 Nussbaum (2018), 212, 225. Nussbaum also claims, falsely in my view, that "Both men [Gandhi and King] hold… that anger is inherently wedded to a payback mentality: Gandhi says that resenting means wishing some harm to the opponent…" (221). Even if this were true of resentment, there are good reasons to distinguish between resentment and anger. She admits that King "allows some scope for real anger" but that this expression makes him "less saintly than Gandhi" (221).
23 Nussbaum (2018), 75.
24 Nussbaum (2018), 5.
25 Nussbaum (2018), 28, 38, 212.
26 See Srinivasan (2018); Srinivasan (2016); Jackson (2018); Jaycox (2020).
27 Aristotle (1999), *Nicomachean Ethics*, Book IV; West (2016).
28 Nussbaum (2018), 28, 31. Nussbaum claims that anger is almost always about a "pay-back wish." While the angry person has three options or "roads": "the road of status," "the road of payback," or "Transition-anger" the latter, in which anger quickly transitions into compassion or hope, is the exception to the norm. In her view, anger itself could not be the effect or source of radical love.
29 Nussbaum (2018), 36. Again, Nussbaum admits that "transition anger" flourishes in parent-child relations but does not think that it is more widespread.
30 Rogers and Moyers (1990).
31 King (Jr.) (2015), 222.
32 King (Jr.) (2015), 116. See also, Rogers and Moyers (1990).
33 King (Jr.) (2010), 18, 34.
34 King (Jr.) (2015), 151.
35 King (Jr.) (2015), 129. For a contemporary account that makes a similar case see Cherry, *The Case for Rage*; and Cherry (2018).
36 King (Jr.) (2015), 11.
37 Ibid.
38 I am aware of the ableist problems with the metaphor of blindness. I keep it here to because it is the central metaphor King's uses to describe ignorance as the root of sin.
39 See James Baldwin (1998), 292. See also Richard Rorty (1999), 12, and Eddie Glaude Jr. (2020), 41.

40 Here King demonstrates his familiarity with "great anthropologists like Ruth Benedict, Margaret Mead, and Melville J. Herskovits" as well as with those who "pressed for a justification of their belief in the inferiority of the Negro" turn to the "pseudo-scientific" theories of phrenology (38).
41 Mayo (2015), 48, 162.
42 King (Jr.) (2015), 139.
43 King Jr. (2010), 11.
44 For Asch's key publications and experiments, see Asch (1951, 1952, 1956).
45 Hodges and Geyer note that while Asch thought his studies demonstrated the human tendency to conform, they in fact show a remarkable tendency toward pragmatic non-conformity. Hodges and Geyer (2006).
46 Emerson (1971), *Volume I.*, 79
47 King Jr. (2010), 47.
48 King Jr. (2010), 48. Here King cites a study and essay by Dr. E. Franklin Frazier, "The Pathology of Race Prejudice."
49 Grimke, Grimke, and Perry (2015), 35.
50 King (Jr.) (2015), 171.
51 Cone (2012), 127. As James Cone notes, "Justice, love, and hope—these three themes shaped the heart of King's theology", which was central to the "freedom struggle of the poor."
52 Dorrien (2018), 21.
53 King (Jr.) (2015), 45. Dorrien notes that King's rendering of his intellectual development overemphasized the role of white theologians and philosophers he encountered in seminary, as well as his familiarity with Gandhi's work, while taking for granted the role of the black church in his intellectual and spiritual formation. But he also insists, paces David J. Garrow, Keith D. Miller, and David Levering Lewis, that King was powerfully influenced by his time in seminary and he took his theological studies seriously. So too, while King knew very little about Gandhi at the outset of the Montgomery campaign, he did later study and endorse Gandhi's approach to non-violent resistance. See Dorrien (2018), 19, 263–67.
54 Marx (1977), 131.
55 Ibid.
56 King (Jr.) (2015), 44, 56, 171.
57 King (Jr.) (2015), 3.
58 Cone (2012), 77.
59 Chernus (2004), x.
60 Dorrien (2018), 266.
61 Rahner, Imhof, and Biallowons (1986), 207.
62 Again, it is notable that resisting evil, rather than "non-anger," is at the heart of Gandhi's and King's nonviolent resistance.
63 Cone (2012), 230.
64 Citation from Cone (2012), 230.
65 King (Jr.) (2015), 115. At a time when sociology as a field was nascent and the "scientific inquiry of Negro life" was virtually neglected, Du Bois was "pioneering in the field of social study of Negro life" (115). Severely underfunded, Du Bois produced two classics before the twentieth century—*Suppression of the African Slave Trade* (1896) and *The Philadelphia Negro* (1899)—adding other monumental works in the twentieth century such as the *Souls of Black Folks* (1903), *John Brown* (1909), and *Black Reconstruction in America* (1941). The sociologist became a historian and biographer to correct the "conscious and deliberate manipulation" of history by white historians who had "for a century crudely distorted the Negro's role in the Reconstruction years" (116). Amid his scholarly contributions, Du Bois became a national and international organizer, working

with others to found the NAACP, calling a Pan-African Congress in 1919, 1921, and 1923 to address the dangers of imperialism, and serving as chairman of the Peace and Information Bureau. A radical throughout his life.

66 Redpath (2018), 157. W.E.B. Du Bois (2001), 204.
67 Shakespeare is one of Emerson's favorite examples: "That which each can do best, none but his Maker can teach him … Shakspeare will never be made by the study of Shakspeare." Emerson, "Self-Relience," (1971), 47. King's conceptions of exemplarity, imitation, and self-reliance seem to have been strongly influenced by Emerson himself and other Emersonian perfectionists. Emerson, "The American Scholar" (1971). On Emersonian Perfectionism see Cavell (1991, 2003); and Stout (2004), 57.
68 King (Jr.) (2015), 65, 66, 68.
69 Readers may notice the striking resemblance between this list and the one that Cone suggests that King abandoned after Black Power. He does, however, add Muhammad Ali. King (Jr.) (2015), 67–68.
70 Jr, Harding, and King (2010), 136.
71 King (2010), 71.
72 King, xxix.
73 King (Jr.) (2015), 10. As his own anger grew after the event and threatened to become "corroding hatred," he reminded himself that the racism and white supremacy of his enemies are products of the cultures and systems in which they were raised. "So these men are merely the children of their culture" (11). Cone argues that King gradually grew more amenable to the separatism of Malcolm X in his final years due to continued disappointment with white's ability to shift the culture of white supremacy. See Cone (2012), 229, 232.
74 King (Jr.) (2015), 14.
75 Same as Endnote no. 12.
76 Thurman (1996), 1.
77 Harding (2008), 13.
78 King (2010), 83.
79 Harding (2008), 3.
80 I follow King's capitalization of "Black Power" throughout.
81 Cone (2012), 230–31. Cone does not provide a clear citation for this quote, and the only other works that suggest King saying this all point to this passage in Cone.
82 Jr, Harding, and King, *Where Do We Go from Here*, 33. All in text citations from "Black Power" reference this source. With his characteristic charity, King admits, "If Stokely Carmichael now says that nonviolence is irrelevant, it is because he, as a dedicated veteran of many [nonviolent] battles, has seen with his own eyes the most brutal white violence against Negroes and white civil rights workers, and he has seen it go unpunished" (34).
83 Hartman, *Lose Your Mother*, 6.
84 Same as Endnote no. 79.
85 Same as Endnote no. 79.

References

Arendt, Hannah, Margaret Canovan, and Danielle Allen. 2018. *The Human Condition: Second Edition*. 2nd edition, Enlarged edition. Chicago, IL; London: University of Chicago Press.
Aristotle. 1999. *Nicomachean Ethics*. Translated by Terence Irwin. 2nd edition. Indianapolis, IN: Hackett Publishing Company, Inc.
Asch, S. E. 1951. "Effects of Group Pressure upon the Modification and Distortion of Judgments." In *Groups, Leadership and Men; Research in Human Relations*, 177–90. Oxford, England: Carnegie Press.

Asch, Solomon E. 1952. *Social Psychology*. Englewood Cliffs, NJ: Prentice-Hall.

Asch, Solomon E. 1956. "Studies of Independence and Conformity: I. A Minority of One Against a Unanimous Majority." *Psychological Monographs: General and Applied* 70, no. 9, 1–70. https://doi.org/10.1037/h0093718.

Baldwin, James. 1998. *James Baldwin: Collected Essays: Notes of a Native Son/ Nobody Knows My Name/The Fire Next Time/No Name in the Street/The Devil Finds Work/Other Essays*. Edited by Toni Morrison. New York, NY: Library of America.

Bowlin, John R. 2016. *Tolerance among the Virtues*. Princeton, NJ: Princeton University Press.

Brandom, Robert. 1994. *Making It Explicit: Reasoning, Representing, and Discursive Commitment*. Cambridge, MA: Harvard University Press.

Cavell, Stanley. 1991. *Conditions Handsome and Unhandsome: The Constitution of Emersonian Perfectionism: The Carus Lectures, 1988*. Chicago, IL: University of Chicago Press.

———. 2003. *Emerson's Transcendental Etudes*. Stanford, CA: Stanford University Press.

Chernus, Ira. 2004. *American Nonviolence: The History of an Idea*. Maryknoll, NY: Orbis Books.

Cherry, Myisha. 2017. "Forgiveness, Exemplars, and the Oppressed." In *The Moral Psychology of Forgiveness*, edited by Kathryn J. Norlock, 55–72.

———. 2018. "Love, Anger, and Racial Injustice." In *The Routledge Handbook of Love in Philosophy*. New York, NY: Routledge.

———. 2021. "Racialized Forgiveness." *Hypatia* 36, no. 4: 583–97. https://doi. org/10.1017/hyp.2021.49.

———. 2021. *The Case for Rage: Why Anger Is Essential to Anti-Racist Struggle*. Oxford University Press.

Cone, James H. 2012. *Martin & Malcolm & America: A Dream or a Nightmare*. 20th Anniversary edition. Maryknoll, NY: Orbis Books.

Couenhoven, Jesse. 2019. "The Possibilities of Forgiveness." *Journal of Religious Ethics* 41, no. 3 (2013): 377–81. https://doi.org/10.1111/jore.

Dorrien, Gary. 2018. *Breaking White Supremacy: Martin Luther King Jr. and the Black Social Gospel*. New Haven, CT: Yale University Press.

Du Bois, W. E. B. 2001. *John Brown*. Edited by David R. Roediger. New edition. New York, NY: Modern Library.

Dumler-Winckler, Emily. 2022. *Modern Virtue: Mary Wollstonecraft and a Tradition of Dissent*. New York, NY: United States of America: Oxford University Press.

Emerson, Ralph Waldo. 1971. *Collected Works of Ralph Waldo Emerson, Volume I: Nature, Addresses, and Lectures*. 1st edition. Cambridge, MA: Belknap Press: An Imprint of Harvard University Press.

Grimke, Sarah, Angelina Grimke, and Mark Perry. 2015. *On Slavery and Abolitionism: Essays and Letters*. New York, NY: Penguin Classics.

Harding, Vincent. 2008. *Martin Luther King: The Inconvenient Hero*. Revised edition. Maryknoll, NY: Orbis Books.

Hodges, Bert H., and Anne L. Geyer. 2006. "A Nonconformist Account of the Asch Experiments: Values, Pragmatics, and Moral Dilemmas." *Personality and Social Psychology Review: An Official Journal of the Society for Personality and Social Psychology, Inc* 10, no. 1: 2–19. https://doi.org/10.1207/s15327957 pspr1001_1.

Jackson, Timothy P. 2018. "Not Far from the Kingdom: Martha Nussbaum on Anger and Forgiveness." *Journal of Religious Ethics* 46, no. 4 (December 2018): 749–70.

Jaycox, Michael P. 2020. "Nussbaum, Anger, and Racial Justice: On the Epistemological and Eschatological Limitations of White Liberalism." *Political Theology* 21, no. 5 (July 2020): 415–33. https://doi.org/10.1080/1462317X.2020.1747810.

King, Martin Luther Jr, Dr, Vincent Harding, and Coretta Scott King. 2010. *Where Do We Go from Here: Chaos or Community?* Illustrated edition. Boston, MA: Beacon Press.

Glaude, Eddie S. Jr. 2020. *Begin Again: James Baldwin's America and Its Urgent Lessons for Our Own.* 1st edition. New York, NY: Crown.

King, Martin Luther (Ed.). 2010. *Strength to Love: Gift Edition.* Minneapolis, MN: Fortress Press.

King, Martin Luther Jr. 2010. *Strength to Love.* Minneapolis, MN: Fortress Press.

King, Martin Luther Jr. 2015. *The Radical King.* Beacon Press.

King, Martin Luther. 2010. *Stride toward Freedom: The Montgomery Story.* Edited by Clayborne Carson. Edition Unstated. Boston, MA: Beacon Press.

Mantena, Karuna. 2020. "Showdown for Nonviolence." In *To Shape a New World: Essays on the Political Philosophy of Martin Luther King, Jr.* Edited by Tommie Shelby, and Brandon M. Terry. Cambridge, MA: Belknap Press: An Imprint of Harvard University Press.

Marx, Karl. 1977. *Critique of Hegel's "Philosophy of Right."* Edited by Joseph O'Malley. Translated by Annette Jolin. Cambridge: Cambridge University Press.

Mayo, Maria. 2015. *The Limits of Forgiveness: Case Studies in the Distortion of a Biblical Ideal.* Minneapolis, MN: Fortress Press.

Nussbaum, Martha C. 2018. *Anger and Forgiveness: Resentment, Generosity, Justice.* Reprint edition. New York, NY: Oxford University Press.

Potts, Matthew Ichihashi. 2022. *Forgiveness: An Alternative Account.* New Haven, CT: Yale University Press.

Rahner, Karl, Paul Imhof, and Hubert Biallowons. 1986. *Karl Rahner in Dialogue: Conversations and Interviews 1965–1982.* New York, NY: Crossroad Pub Co.

Redpath, James. 1860. *Echoes of Harper's Ferry.* Boston, MA: Thayer and Eldridge.

Rogers, Mary Beth, and Bill Moyers. 1990. *Cold Anger: A Story of Faith and Power Politics.* Denton, TX: University of North Texas Press.

Rorty, Richard. 1999. *Achieving Our Country: Leftist Thought in Twentieth-Century America.* New Ed edition. Cambridge, MA: Harvard University Press.

Srinivasan, A. "2018. The Aptness of Anger." *Journal of Political Philosophy* 26, no. 2 (June 1, 2018): 123–44. https://doi.org/10.1111/jopp.12130.

Srinivasan, Amia. 2016. "A Righteous Fury." *The Nation* (January 1, 2016).

Stout, Jeffrey. 2004. *Democracy and Tradition.* Princeton, NJ: Princeton University Press.

Stump, Eleonore. 2020. *Atonement.* Oxford: Oxford University Press.

Thurman, Howard. 1996. *Jesus and the Disinherited.* Reprint edition. Boston, MA: Beacon Press.

West, Ryan. 2016. "Anger and the Virtues: A Critical Study in Virtue Individuation." *Canadian Journal of Philosophy* 46, no. 6 (December 2016): 877–97. https://doi.org/10.1080/00455091.2016.1199232.

Zagzebski, Linda. 2017. *Exemplarist Moral Theory.* 1st edition. New York, NY: Oxford University Press.

11 Imitating God

Thomas Jay Oord

Exemplarity through imitation of God has an underdeveloped history in Christianity. Imitating Jesus, famously advocated by Thomas à Kempis in his book *The Imitation of Christ (De Imitatione Christi)*, is better known. By "Christ," most who advance this approach have Jesus of Nazareth in mind. Although Christian creeds ascribe both divinity and humanity to this Nazarene, the imitation most advocate pertains to being like the human Jesus.

Those who address the possibility that humans can imitate God often connect the idea to their being made in God's image and likeness (Gen. 1:26–28). Of what the image and likeness consist of is debated; what remains after sin is also contested.[1] But those who believe humans can imitate God often build their argument, in part, from the conviction that God and creatures share something in common.

In this essay, I explore ontological and ethical issues of exemplarity as they pertain to imitating God. I build from a passage in the Apostle Paul's letter to Jesus' followers in Ephesus. Paul instructs them to "be imitators of God, as beloved children, and walk in love, as Christ loved us ..." (Eph. 5:1,2a).

In my exploration of imitating God, I look at Augustine's theology. I'm especially interested in his views of God and of love. I address Thomas à Kempis too, because Augustine's thought influenced him. I then explore an open and relational theological framework and why I believe it to be more helpful overall than an Augustinian one.

My constructive claim is that imitating God means loving like God loves. This means I need a definition of love, and I define it as acting intentionally, in relational response, to promote overall well-being. A robust theistic ethics of exemplarity can portray God as exemplar and divine love as imitable.

The Apostle Paul's Logic of Exemplarity

To understand what Paul means when he asks the Ephesians to imitate God, we should look at his arguments leading to that request. Paul begins this portion of his letter to Jesus' followers by saying, I "beg you to walk in a manner worthy of the calling to which you have been called" (Eph. 4:1). In subsequent paragraphs, he identifies what "walking" includes. It means developing

DOI: 10.4324/9781032648392-15

virtues, including humility, gentleness, patience, desire for unity, and "bearing with one another in love" (Eph. 4:2–3). Paul says his readers should "speak the truth in love" (Eph. 4:15). This means growing up into Christ as a whole body, which grows by "building itself up in love" (Eph. 4:16).

Paul contrasts the virtuous walk he promotes with how the "gentiles" walk. He believes futility, ignorance, hardness of heart, and alienation from God characterize the non-virtuous walk. Those who live this way lose sensitivity, abandon themselves to licentiousness, are greedy, and become impure. Readers should "put away" that life with its lusts and "clothe yourselves with a new self." A renewed self is "created according to the likeness of God in true righteousness and holiness" (Eph. 4:17–24).

Turning from an old life involves developing particular practices. It means "putting away falsehood," being angry without sinning, giving up stealing, and taking on work. This life builds up others and puts away bitterness, wrangling, slander, and malice. It involves, says Paul, being "kind to one another, tenderhearted, forgiving one another, as God in Christ has forgiven you" (Eph. 4:25–32).

What is God Like?

In what seems to be the summary of his argument, Paul writes the words on which I focus: "Therefore be imitators of God, as beloved children, and walk in love, as Christ loved us and gave himself up for us, a fragrant offering and sacrifice to God" (Eph. 5:1–2). In this passage and those preceding it, love is prominent.[2]

If humans are to heed Paul's charge to imitate God, they must have some idea about the one they try to imitate. It's impossible to imitate intentionally something of which we have absolutely no understanding. This raises a *giant* question: How should God be understood?

Although made in God's image, biblical writers portray humans as dissimilar to God in various ways. For instance, many passages say God is a universal Spirit without a body. God is "spirit," says Jesus (Jn. 4:24), and *Yahweh* is described as *ruach* by writers of the Hebrew scriptures. God is said to be invisible: "No one has ever seen God" (Jn. 1:18; 4:12). In fact, we have reasons to doubt that we perceive God with any of our five senses. Spirit is universal too (Ps. 139). This presents obstacles to comparing a ubiquitous God with localized creatures.

These dissimilarities between the Creator and creatures raise questions. How can we imitate an incorporeal, invisible, and universal Spirit? How does a universal God act? And if God cannot be seen, how would we know when we imitate God?

Three options outlined below do not make good sense of what it means to imitate God. One says, "God alone does everything." This is theological determinism, or monergism. If true, we do nothing. All our actions are divinely determined. Paul seems to assume his readers can act when choosing to imitate God, but theological determinism affords no place for free creaturely activity.

A second option says, "God does nothing." God does not act, at least not in our universe. Deists who believe God initiated the universe but no longer act embrace this approach. If God does nothing, however, we have nothing to imitate, and Paul's instruction makes no sense.

The third option, which we cannot take, is popular among leading theologians. It claims divine action is unlike anything we might think or imagine. God is utterly unknowable, and the divine ontology is entirely unlike ours. I call this "absolute apophatic theology."

At least in some of his writings, Augustine advocates this third approach. He uses the category "accidents" to talk about how God differs entirely from creatures. Creatures have accidental properties, which "can be either lost or diminished," Augustine says. They exist "in relation to something." He offers the following list: "friendships, relationships, services, likenesses, equalities, and anything else of the kind." He adds "places and times, acts and passions" to the list. According to Augustine, "in God, *nothing* is said to be according to accident."[3] Only creatures have accidental properties. This means God can't love, act, relate, be a friend, or experience time like we do. God is unlike us in every way, in part because of God's indivisible aseity.

At times in his work, Augustine describes God as loving, creating, saving, revealing, and so on. Those descriptions don't fit his philosophical commitment to the notion that God has no accidents and is indivisible. The best one can say is that the Augustinian God mysteriously *does* things in a nonacting, timeless, unresponsive, and nonexperiential way. That's *nothing* like what we know as "doing."[4] It's impossible to imitate Augustine's God.

Representing the Augustinian tradition, Michael J. Dodds explains what this approach entails. "We should be cautious about trying to say anything about how God acts," says Dodds. "God is totally other." For this reason, "the mode or manner of divine activity will ever escape us." After all, says Dodds, "God's action is fundamentally different from that of creatures."[5]

If Augustine is right, we cannot imitate God. And Paul's charge is inconceivable.

Augustine on God's Love

Augustine's theology not only portrays God as utterly unknowable. His view of love cannot sustain Paul's command that Ephesians imitate God by walking in love. Let's look briefly at Augustine's thoughts.

Augustine's most sustained exposition of love comes in *Teaching Christianity* (*De Doctrina Christiana*).[6] Rather than think love is about doing good or promoting well-being, which is how love is typically understood, Augustine says, "love is a kind of craving,"[7] or what some call "acquisitive desire."[8] Augustine uses words like "cling" and "obtain" as synonyms for love. To love someone or something is to be inclined toward it, yearn for it, or seek satisfaction in it. Love desires.

Augustine divides the objects of desire into those we use and those we enjoy. "Enjoyment consists in clinging to something lovingly for its own sake," he says, "while use consists in referring what has come your way to what your love aims at obtaining."[9] We rightly love what is most valuable, he explains, and we use other objects in service to what is greatest.

In a section headed "God Alone is to be Enjoyed," Augustine explains how this applies to loving God and others. "Among all the things there are," says Augustine, "those alone are to be enjoyed, which we have noted as being eternal and unchanging. The rest are to be used in order that we may come at last to the enjoyment of [that which is eternal and unchanging]."[10] His point: only God is worthy of desire. We should use people and creation "so that we may proceed from temporal and bodily things to grasp those that are eternal and spiritual."[11]

Augustine realizes that saying we should use people seems inappropriate. "We have been commanded, after all, to love one another," he admits. "But the question is whether people are to be loved by others for their own sake, or for the sake of something else." That which is worthy of love for its own sake, says Augustine, "constitutes the life of bliss." Because people cannot bring true bliss, we should use them.[12]

Augustine's understanding of love opposes most of Christian Scripture and much of how love is used in common speech. Biblical writers use Hebrew and Greek words translated as "love" and mean acting to do good or promoting well-being. According to Scripture, to love is to show compassion, be kind, offer salvation, help enemies, be generous, and more. The vast majority of biblical love language differs from Augustine's.[13]

God's Doesn't Love Us

Because Augustine understands love as craving for what is most valuable, he comes to an odd conclusion: God doesn't love us. At least God doesn't love us in the ways Augustine understands love. We discover this in a subsection titled, "God Does Not Enjoy Us, But Makes Use of Us."

To explain himself, Augustine reminds us of what he considers love's true object. "There still seems to be some uncertainty about what we have been saying," he admits, "that we enjoy that thing which we love for its own sake."[14] And we should use what does not make "us perfectly happy or blissful," he says. Then Augustine poses a question to himself: "How does [God] love us?"

According to his own categories, Augustine is asking, "Does God use or enjoy us?" If God "enjoys us," says Augustine, "it means he is in need of some good of ours, which nobody in his right mind could possibly say. Every good of ours, after all, is either God himself, or derived from him."[15] To enjoy us, God must find something in us worth enjoying. According to Augustine, however, we have nothing to offer that God doesn't already have.

The only way God can love (desire) us, according to Augustine's categories, is to use us. "He does not enjoy us, but makes use of us," he states flatly. "Because if he neither enjoys us nor makes use of us, I cannot find any way in which he can love us."[16]

Even saying God "uses us" is not correct if we take Augustine's thoughts seriously. After all, he believes God needs nothing. Augustine can't say God enjoys us for our own sake or uses us for the sake of something else. God "does not make use of us, either" he finally confesses. At least not "in the same way as we use things." He explains: "Our making use of things is directed to the end of enjoying God's goodness." But "God's making use of us is directed to his goodness."[17] According to his own categories and vision of God, however, this explanation makes no sense.

In Augustine's theological framework, God only loves Godself. God is concerned only with the divine life because only that which is eternal and unchanging deserves ultimate concern.[18] God is self-oriented.

Augustine's view differs radically from Jesus' view of love. For instance, Jesus is quoted as saying, "God so loved the world that he gave his only Son" so that humans can experience eternal life (Jn. 3:16). Augustine's views oppose Paul's claim that "God proves his love for us in that while we still were sinners, Christ died for us" (Rm. 5:8). It also stands in opposition to the Psalms, which speak of God's steadfast love (*hesed*) for creation, even when creatures fail to love in response. Augustine's view of love stands at odds with the vast majority of the Bible, which repeatedly says God wants our good.

Thomas à Kempis and *The Imitation of Christ*

Augustine's views shaped Thomas à Kempis's classic work, *The Imitation of Christ*. In their translation, Aloysius Croft and Harold Bolton claim the book is, after the Bible, "the most widely read book in the world."[19] While this may be an exaggeration, there is little doubt that the work, written around 1420, has been widely influential.

The book is mistitled. Few passages in *The Imitation of Christ* speak of imitating Christ;[20] the author gives few references to what biblical writers say Jesus said and did. I also found no explicit references to imitating God. Thomas à Kempis offers advice for personal piety, sacred practices, enhancing one's interior life, communion, and the development of the soul.

The few passages that speak of imitating Jesus, call upon readers to suffer by "bearing the cross, "denying ourselves," and "despising the present life."[21] Readers are commanded to submit and obey; they should fear God. Just as Christ offered himself "a complete sacrifice to appease the divine wrath," so readers ought to offer themselves wholly to Christ.[22]

Contemporary readers like me will find the copious references to divine wrath and punishment unattractive. For instance, Thomas à Kempis says, "I deserve only to be scourged and punished because I have offended You often and grievously."[23] And he says the fear of hell should motivate us to do what is right. For "even if love does not as yet restrain you from evil, at least the fear of hell does. The man who cast aside the fear of God cannot continue long in goodness..."[24]

Many contemporary readers will also find unappealing the persistent references to rejecting the world. One of the earliest passages in the book puts it this way: "This is the greatest wisdom—to seek the kingdom of heaven through contempt of the world. It is vanity, therefore, to seek and trust in riches that perish ... It is vanity to follow the lusts of the body and to desire things for which severe punishment later must come."[25]

Not only is healthy love for the world rarely, if ever, mentioned, but Thomas à Kempis also rejects healthy self-love. "If you wish to learn and appreciate something worthwhile, then love to be unknown and considered as nothing. Truly to know and despise self is the best and most perfect counsel. To think of oneself as nothing," he says.[26] For "what power there is in pure love for Jesus—love that is free from all self-interest and self-love!"[27] After all, "to find the Creator," we must "forsake all creatures."[28]

In quotes like these and many others, we find the Augustinian notion of love as desire. Notice, for instance, that Thomas à Kempis says we should "love to be unknown." This reflects Augustine's view that love is desire, and we should desire God.

The last paragraphs of *The Imitation of Christ* ask readers to put aside their reasoning and rely instead on "sincere and unflinching faith." For "whatever you cannot understand, commit to the security of the all-powerful God." "All reason and natural science ought to come after this faith, not go before it, nor oppose it." After all, says Thomas à Kempis, God is "eternal, incomprehensible, and infinitely powerful." God "does great and inscrutable things in heaven and on earth, and there is no searching into His marvelous works."[29]

In sum, Thomas à Kempis never talks about imitating God. And his references to imitating Christ derive from an Augustinian theology that's world-denying and punishment-oriented. It's difficult to make much sense of St. Paul's command to imitate God and walk in love if we think Augustine and Thomas à Kempis portray God and love rightly.

Summary and Transition

I have drawn from the writings of Augustine and Thomas à Kempis to address what it might mean for humans to imitate a loving God. If Augustine is correct that God only loves Godself, our imitating God *might* mean we should only love ourselves. Thomas à Kempis clearly rejects this, however, because he believes human self-love is misguided. Augustine does too.

Another interpretation says that imitating God means only loving God. This eliminates loving our neighbors and ourselves for their/our own sakes.

This approach opposes the majority biblical witness, which calls followers of Jesus to love neighbor, God, themselves, and all creation in the sense of wanting their well-being. The prominent New Testament phrase "love one another" makes no sense in Augustinian theology.

Another response to Augustine and Thomas à Kempis is to appeal to mystery. God is a mystery because God is entirely unlike us. But doing so means we cannot make sense of Paul's charge to imitate God. Affirming absolute apophatic theology also means there are no similarities between divine and creaturely love. Instead of conceiving with reason what it means to imitate God by walking in love, we follow Thomas à Kempis and play the mystery card.

Below, I summarize my points:

- The Apostle Paul instructs his Ephesian readers to imitate God.
- This imitation seems to involve humans loving like God loves.
- To imitate God's loving requires some understanding of who God is and how God acts.
- Differences between God and us place into question whether we can imitate God.
- Theologies that say God does everything, does nothing, or is entirely unlike us are unhelpful.
- Augustine portrays God as entirely unlike creatures.
- Augustine understands love to mean desire rather than promoting well-being, and he says creatures should only love God. And God only loves Godself.
- Thomas à Kempis builds from Augustine's theology, and, as a result, he does not help us understand how we might imitate God.

An Open and Relational God

Open and relational theology offers a better framework for imagining how humans might imitate God. While the framework is broad, those who adopt it share a common commitment to thinking that God and creatures are relational and the future is open.

By "relational," open and relational theologians believe God is an agent who gives and receives with creatures. God is passible. As an experiencing agent, God influences others, and others influence God. Rather than being entirely dissimilar, therefore, the Creator and creatures share the ability to act and relate.

By "open," open and relational theologians believe God experiences time moment by moment, analogous to how creatures experience time. Rather than timeless, God is "inside" time and everlasting. The past is the past for God and creation; present is present; the future is open and yet to be determined.

Open and relational theologians say God's acting is like creaturely acting, at least in some ways. The basic meanings of "act," "relate," "experience," and "love" apply to the Creator and creatures; God exemplifies the ontological principles of existence.[30] To put it another way, divine action is neither entirely different nor mysterious. God is part of the causal network of existence as one cause among others.

Differences between Creator and creation exist, of course. God experiences everlastingly, for instance, while creaturely experiencing is temporary. God relates with all, but no creature can relate with all others. God loves by nature; creatures can choose whether to love. And so on.

God is transcendent and immanent: different from creatures in some ways, but like them in others. Without similarities, we cannot make constructive claims about how God and creatures love. Without differences, we cannot distinguish the Creator from creatures. Without similarities, we cannot imitate God.

Detecting the God Who Can Be Imitated

God's invisibility and universality raise obstacles that must be overcome when formulating an *imitatio dei* theology. To offer a coherent view of divine exemplarity, we need to overcome those obstacles. I offer conceptual tools below to do so.

Our five senses cannot perceive an invisible and incorporeal spirit. "No one has seen God," to cite scripture again (Jn. 1:18). We can't literally see God walking in the garden, for instance. Our eardrums literally don't vibrate in response to sounds from divine vocal cords. We cannot see, taste, hear, smell, or touch a spiritual being.[31]

Biblical writers sometimes talk about encounters with an embodied God, of course. God walked in the garden with Adam and Eve, Genesis tells us (Gen. 3). Jacob wrestled with the Lord (Gen. 32), and Moses saw God's butt (Exod. 33). John heard a voice from heaven saying, "This is my beloved Son. Listen to him" (Mt. 3:17). And so on.

If God's being or composition is spiritual, however, these descriptions cannot be literally true. God doesn't literally have a body and doesn't literally walk, speak, get red in the face, kiss, and so on. Scriptures that say God does such activities are metaphorical. Metaphors are important but should not be interpreted literally.

Believers are right to assume the Spirit's action behind or beneath something we admire or respect. When we see a beautiful sunset, a doe licking her newborn fawn, a soldier turning the other cheek, an act of kindness for an elderly person, and more, theists might infer that the Spirit inspired each. A loving, good, true, and beautiful Spirit inspires but does not entirely cause everything loving, good, true, and beautiful that occurs in the world.

Theists can do more than infer God's activity behind what they observe, however. Open and relational theologians argue for access to God that involves non-sensory perception.[32] This way of knowing provides knowledge of other aspects of life, like causation, values, emotions, freedom, and more.

It also assumes a robust empiricism, which says we draw from experience to know our world and God's activity.

John B. Cobb, Jr. explains it like this: "If God is present and working in us, ... there is non-sensory perception of God all the time ... Instead of speaking of new spiritual senses, we can think of non-sensuous experience of the divine presence in our lives and awareness of its salvific effects."[33] In short, non-sensory perception detects the actions of the Spirit.

The idea of non-sensory perception fits the language of theists who talk about encounters with God. Believers speak of detecting the divine, for instance, as a "still small voice," "intuition," a "feeling," a "holy nudge," an "inclination," one's "moral compass," a "hunch," an "inkling," "divine insight," an inaudible "call," a "light," our "better angels," one's conscience, and more. Although not fully accurate, this language describes the direct perception of the Spirit.

To sum up, our sense perceptions cannot detect what an invisible Spirit does. This creates obstacles to imitating God. We can *infer* the Spirit's activities, however. We directly detect God's activity through non-sensory perception. This detection of divine action helps as we consider what it means to imitate God.[34]

What Is Love?

Having cleared some conceptual obstacles, I return to the Apostle Paul's advice to imitate God. In the sections leading up to "be imitators of God," Paul points to moral issues, virtues, and, in particular, love. Immediately following the charge to imitate God, Paul writes, "walk in love, as Christ loved us and gave himself up for us, a fragrant offering and sacrifice to God" (Eph. 5:1–2).

Paul thinks his readers can imitate God by "walking" in love. Other translations say, "live a life of love." "Walking" does not literally mean using legs. It refers to acting in love. But if we are to imitate divine love, we must have some clarity about what love is.

I find it helpful to define love in the following way: to love is to act intentionally, in relational response to God and others, to promote overall well-being.[35] To put it another way, love purposefully acts in relationships to foster flourishing.

To clarify this definition, I address its three clauses. The phrase "to act intentionally" points to action and motives. Love is not simply a feeling, although feelings often play a role in acts of love. A lover *does* something. And an act of love involves some deliberation, even if this deliberation is fleeting.

The phrase "to act intentionally" addresses intentions. A lover acts purposely. We should not regard an action as loving if it is accidental. Acts done with the motive to harm should not be labeled "acts of love," for instance, even if they have beneficial consequences. To put it another way, the lover acts prospectively, hoping to promote well-being. Motives matter.

I also use "to act intentionally" to account for the self-determination—freedom—inherent in love. Lovers are choosers and, to some degree, responsible for their actions. Freedom is always limited, however. Concrete circumstances, environmental constraints, bodily factors, genetics, neurology, historical pressures, and other conditions limit what is genuinely possible at any moment.[36] But acts of love require that lovers have genuine, albeit limited, freedom.

The phrase "in relational response to God and others" covers a range of important issues. The relational aspect suggests that love requires more than one person. Agents beyond the lover influence her. Love is relational; lovers respond.

Love includes, but is more than desire. To express love, in fact, we must sometimes act contrary to our desires, yearnings, or wants. We might have a strong desire to get revenge, for instance, but love calls us to forgive. We might want to express ourselves sexually in an illicit way, but love calls us to exert self-control.

My reference to God in this love definition points to the conviction that we cannot understand love well without reference to divine activity. God is the source of love and acts in each moment to empower and inspire creaturely love. God also relationally receives information, feelings, and activities, and then God responds by empowering and calling creatures to seek the common good.[37] To put it in the Apostle John's language, we love because God first loves us (1 Jn 4:19).

While God is the source, power, and inspiration for creaturely love, God is not love's sufficient cause.[38] Lovers relate to creaturely others. The "others" to whom lovers respond need not be human. We can respond to animals, other creatures, our environments, and more. Whether our love can or will be reciprocated by others is another issue.

The last phrase of my love definition, "to promote overall well-being," points to the beneficial consequences at which love aims. Overall well-being includes the good of enemies and strangers, families and friends, societies, animals, other creatures, inanimate creations, and basic elements of existence. Even God's well-being is enhanced by love. Love enhances multifarious dimensions of existence.[39]

The word "overall" suggests that our assessment of how love promotes good includes but reaches beyond our own good. "Self-love" has an appropriate place in the economy of "overall well-being." But sometimes love also requires self-sacrifice. A life well lived includes many aspects of well-being.

The aim for "overall" well-being points to the justice dimension of love. Actions that privilege the few to the detriment of the whole are not loving. Actions that deny basic rights and goods are also not loving. Cornel West is fond of saying, justice is what love looks like in public.[40] I like to say that love seeks overall flourishing, and acting for the common good seeks justice for all.

Conclusion: We Can Imitate God When We Love

I'm ready now to bring together my arguments. Here are bullet point summaries of what I've argued above in the second half of this essay:

- Open and relational theology says both God and creatures are relational.
- God and creatures act moment by moment and move into an open future.
- Because open and relational theology claims similarities exist between God and creatures, it provides a framework to make sense of imitating God by loving like God loves.
- Although God is universal, invisible, and incorporeal, God acts, relates, and loves analogously to how creatures act, relate, and love.
- Love is best defined as acting intentionally, in relational response to God and others, to promote overall well-being.
- Because creatures share similarities with God and because the definition of love applies to creatures and the Creator, we can imitate God.

In an open and relational theological framework, therefore, Paul's admonition to his readers in Ephesus makes sense. It's attainable. We imitate God when we act intentionally, in relational response to God and others, to promote overall well-being. The God who loves persistently is our example of what it means to love well.

Imitating God makes sense in open and relational theology.

Notes

1 See essays in Rosenberg et al. (2018). My own essay in this book argues for "relational love" as the best category for conceiving how creatures are in God's image.
2 Elias E Meyer argues that writers of Hebrew scriptures mean by imitating God does *not* always involve imitating the ways of love. See Meyer (2009), 373–83.
3 Augustine, *Trinity* V:17.
4 For my full criticism of Augustine, see Oord (2023a), Chapters 5–6.
5 Dodds (2017), 161, 169, 171. For my review of Dodds's book, see Oord (2013), 191–94. Thomistic theology, in the tradition of Thomas Aquinas, is susceptible to criticisms like these. Although Aquinas claims God is a primary cause working through secondary causes, if we ask what the primary cause *does*, we get answers that have nothing in common with what we know as "doing." Dodds explains: "these causes do not belong to the same order" (191). This means that "when a primary and secondary cause act together, the effect belongs entirely to both" (192). In other words, this is a version of compatibilism, with all the incoherence that comes from saying God entirely causes something and creatures also cause it. Dodds admits the proposal leads to incomprehensibility: "we must hold firmly to two apparently contradictory truths. God does whatever creatures do, and that creatures themselves do whatever they do" (208). Compatibilism is inconceivable; we should reject versions of primary-secondary causation that assume it.
6 Augustine (1996).
7 Augustine, *Eighty-Three Different Questions*, 35, 2.

8 See, for instance, Ramsey (1950), 122. See also Avis (1989).
9 Ibid., Book 1, paragraph 4.
10 Ibid., Book 1, paragraph 22.
11 Ibid., Book 1, paragraph 4. Many have criticized Augustine for his views on sex. For a sustained theological criticism, see Jeanrond (2010).
12 Ibid., Book 1, paragraph 20.
13 I explore in detail various biblical meanings of love in *Pluriform Love*.
14 Augustine (1996), *Teaching Christianity*, Book 1, paragraph 31.
15 Ibid.
16 Ibid., Book 1, paragraph 32.
17 Ibid.
18 When reflecting on the Trinity, Augustine says God ceaselessly loves Godself. This love is contemplation and enjoyment of the divine life. (Augustine, *On the Trinity*, 9, 2.) His appeal to intra-Trinitarian love, however, does not solve his problems regarding God's love for creatures and creation. God simply doesn't love them. God neither loves creatures by enjoying them nor using them— except insofar as in using them, God loves Godself. And God does not intend to promote their well-being.
19 Kempis (2003), viii. The book was likely written by several members of the Brethren of Common Life in the Netherlands. Thomas Hemerken of Kempen (Thomas a Kempis) later compiled and translated the book into Latin. I'll follow the common practice of referring to Thomas a Kempis as the author.
20 For a scholarly book that focuses on what Jesus says and does as recorded in the Bible, see Burridge (2007). Burridge's book, however, has very little to say on what it might mean to imitate God.
21 Thomas a Kempis (2003), 108.
22 Ibid., 126.
23 Ibid., 102.
24 Ibid., 24–25.
25 Ibid., 2.
26 Ibid., 3.
27 Ibid., 40.
28 Ibid., 78.
29 Ibid., 139.
30 I agree with Alfred North Whitehead on this point. See Whitehead (1978), 521.
31 An important exploration of what it means to perceive God is found in Alston (1991).
32 For details on nonsensory perception of God, see Griffin (1993). See also Cobb (1995).
33 Cobb (1995), 75. I compare Wesley's view of spiritual sensations with non-sensory perception in Oord (2002), 121–35.
34 Many of these ideas and more are elaborated on in Oord (2023b).
35 I provide a more expansive explanations of this love definition in Oord (2010) and Oord (2023a).
36 Daniel Day Williams makes this point nicely in Williams (1969), 116.
37 I explain what it means for God to be an ideal recipient and contributor in Oord (2010), Chapter 6.
38 I address the importance of denying that God can act as a sufficient cause in *The Uncontrolling Love of God*, Chapter 7.
39 Partha Dasgupta uses the phrase "pluralist outlook" for what I call the multifarious dimensions of existence. See his book, Dasgupta (2001), 14.
40 West (1989), 271.

References

Alston, William P. 1991. *Perceiving God: The Epistemology of Religious Experience.* London: Cornell University Press.

Augustine, 1982. *Eighty-Three Different Questions* Washington, D.C. : Catholic University Of America Press..

Augustine, 1996. *Teaching Christianity* (De Doctrina Christiana), edited By John E. Rotelle, O.S.A, translated by Edmund Hill, O.P., Hyde Park, NY: New City.

Augustine, 1982. *Trinity.*

Avis, Paul. 1989. *Eros and the Sacred.* Harrisburg, PA: Morehouse.

Burridge, Richard A. 2007. *Imitating Jesus: An Inclusive Approach to New Testament Ethics.* Grand Rapids, MI: Eerdmans.

Cobb, John Jr. 1995. *Grace and Responsibility: A Wesleyan Theology for Today.* Nashville, TN: Abingdon.

Dasgupta, Partha. 2001. *Human Well-Being and the Natural Environment.* Oxford: Oxford University Press.

Dodds, Michael J. 2017. *Unlocking Divine Action: Contemporary Science and Thomas Aquinas.* Washington, D.C.: Catholic University of America.

Griffin, David R. 1993. *Founders of Constructive Postmodern Philosophy: Pierce, James, Bergson, Whitehead, and Hartshorne.* Albany, NY: State University of New York Press.

Jeanrond, Werner. 2010. *A Theology of Love.* London: T & T Clark.

Kempis, Thomas à. 2003. *The Imitation of Christ,* translated by Aloysius Croft and Harold Bolton, Garden City, NY: Dover.

Meyer, Esias. 2009. "The dark side of the Imitatio Dei. Why imitating the God of the Holiness Code is not always a good thing." 22. 373–83.

Oord, Thomas J. 2002. "Grace and Social Science: Nonsensory Perception of God in a Constructive Postmodern Wesleyan Philosophy," *Jnanadeepa: Pune Journal of Religious Studies,* 5,. no. 2. 121–35.

Oord, Thomas J. 2010. *Defining Love: A Philosophical, Scientific, and Theological Engagement.* Grand Rapids, MI: Brazos.

Oord, Thomas J. 2013. "Unlocking Divine Action," *Christian Scholar's Review* 43, no.2, 191–94.

Oord, Thomas J. 2023a. *Pluriform Love: An Open and Relational Theology of Well-Being.* Grasmere, ID: SacraSage.

Oord, Thomas J. 2023b. *The Death of Omnipotence and Birth of Amipotence.* Grasmere, ID: SacraSage.

Ramsey, Paul. 1950. *Basic Christian Ethics.* Chicago, IL: University of Chicago Press.

Rosenberg, Stanley. et. al., eds. 2018. *Finding Ourselves after Darwin: Conversations on the Image of God, Original Sin, and the Problem of Evil.* Grand Rapids, MI: Baker.

West, Cornel. 1989. *The American Evasion of Philosophy.* Madison, WI: University of Wisconsin Press.

Whitehead, Alfred N. 1978. *Process and Reality: An Essay in Cosmology,* corrected edition, edited by David Ray Griffin and Donald W. Sherburne, New York, NY: Free; orig. ed., 1929.

Williams, Daniel D. 1969. *The Spirit and Forms of Love.* New York, NY: Harper and Row.

12 Challenging Aristotle's Privileged Virtue with Christ

Lily M. Abadal

Introduction

This chapter will directly engage what I call Aristotle's "privileged virtue thesis," which essentially holds that only a very small number of very privileged people have access to the kind of external goods and mentors that will allow them to flourish through the acquisition of the virtues. Another way of putting this is that virtue is so rare because good formation and mentorship are rare. Aristotle's thesis is a difficult one to refute given what we know about social learning and the necessary conditions for true moral inspiration to spontaneously occur. Effective moral exemplars must be more than extraordinarily virtuous people that we fancy to imitate, they must also have a specific type of relationship with the student of virtue. Jennifer Herdt recalls this in *Putting on Virtue*, "What is crucial in order for one's desires to be transformed into those of a virtuous person … is that one *love and be loved* by the moral exemplar set before one."[1] As Herdt explains, this requirement is particularly poignant given that virtue is not a mechanical feat that can be produced through compliance. Instead, it requires cultivating affection for what is good. If we contend, as most virtue ethicists would, that moral exemplars are necessary for the acquisition of virtue and recognize the lack of suitable mentors among us, it is no wonder that Aristotle argues virtue is a privilege. However, this chapter will suggest that Christ provides a unique challenge to Aristotle's privilege of virtue thesis because of the type of moral exemplar Christ is. Moreover, I contend that Peter Abelard's theory of atonement, particularly its moral exemplarist dimensions, will be especially helpful in helping us understand why. Consequently, the chapter will proceed in three sections. First, I will clearly articulate Aristotle's privilege of virtue thesis as expressed in the *Nicomachean Ethics* and spell out the necessary and sufficient conditions for effective moral exemplars. Second, I will briefly detail Abelard's theory of atonement, which will help us reflect upon why Christ is uniquely positioned *qua* moral exemplar to transform human affections so that genuine virtue can be formed. Finally, I will argue that Christ challenges Aristotle's privileged virtue thesis by making virtue theoretically available to more than the privileged few.

DOI: 10.4324/9781032648392-16

Aristotle and the Privilege of Virtue

For Aristotle, formation of the virtues is complex and far from egalitarian. Simply put, not everyone can cultivate it. We might even call it a privilege to be able to do so. This is not due to the fact, as some may intuit, that people are born with personalities that make it more difficult for them to be courageous, etc. In fact, Aristotle would contend that moral virtue is acquired, not natural; it must be molded through painful processes of habituation and learning (1103a19–26).[2] Instead, it is largely because formation of virtue requires a host of environmental conditions and external goods[3] for it to take shape and hold.[4] An individual must be reasonably attractive, have several friends, be of considerable wealth or noble birth, and born into a society with proper laws that help instill a reverence for the good. Though crude to our modern ears, Aristotle is not without reason. Attractiveness makes it more likely that a child will be favored by teachers, peers, and potential mates. This translates into more attention and affirmation of their value. Friends provide opportunities to practice virtues and insight into our vices and limitations.[5] Wealth and noble birth make it possible for considerable leisure to build such friendships, sufficient study, and virtue-forming practices like chess, painting, or baseball. Most importantly, wealth supplies the resources available for magnificent deeds. Finally, lawless societies procure heightened fears and anxieties about survival and safety, making it difficult to focus on much else.

These environmental conditions and external goods are often outside of our control.[6] We can imagine instances in which a child is born with an unfortunately large nose, a number of odd quirks that their peers find annoying, without access to quality schools and programs because their parents lack skilled work and financial resources, or whose lives are amidst a war-torn country without rule of law and no means to migrate elsewhere. This means children born without unfortunately large noses, adequate socialization, and who go to excellent schools in countries with laws and protections to keep them safe are at a considerable advantage in their quest for the good life, that is, to cultivate virtues. They are indeed privileged. But, perhaps the most important privilege of all, more rare than reasonable attractiveness or familial wealth, is the access some have to genuinely exemplary moral exemplars and mentors. Let us explore why by digging into the specifics of what is needed for moral development.

As Kristian Kristjansson reminds us, "Nowhere does Aristotle produce a clear-cut, comprehensive account of moral development, let alone a meticulously worked-out stage theory similar to that of, for instance, Kohlberg."[7] Despite this fact, he does say enough about what is required for virtuous activity and the conditions under which that virtuous activity can be formed for us to discern the necessary conditions for it to develop both intellectually and emotionally. Perhaps the best place to start is outlining what strictly qualifies as virtuous activity. This definition is clear enough; virtue of character is "about feelings and actions, and these admit of excess, deficiency, and an intermediate condition" (1106b18–20). More specifically, though, virtue requires "having these feelings at the right times, about the right things, towards the right people, for the right end, and in the right way" (1106b21–23). Virtue is not simply about right action. It is not simply about right intention. It can't be reduced to a mere habit, although it is procured through habituation. The truly virtuous person must consistently maintain a delicate mean between excess and deficiency—one propelled by affection for the ultimate end.

Susan Meyer outlines three necessary conditions that further specify virtue's demands: (1) the virtuous agent must act with knowledge; (2) the virtuous agent must "act on decision" for the sake of the right end; and (3) the virtuous agent must act from "a firm and unchangeable disposition."[8] The first of these conditions requires that the agent acts voluntarily. In other words, virtue cannot be forced or coerced. The second speaks to the motivation of the agent. We can understand this as the teleological dimension; prudent reasoning must be in service to the right end, and this right end must be desired. Finally, virtuous action results from a settled disposition, which lends to the ease with which it is performed.

The second condition Meyer points out is particularly relevant to our consideration of moral exemplars. It suggests that the process of shaping virtue, especially in the young, requires much more than conditioning; it demands inspiration. Loving the fine and the good will prove more complicated than just telling the student of virtue that they ought to do so or explaining why the fine and good is, in fact, fine and good. Indeed, Aristotle warns that no argument can convince an immoral person to become good.[9] To state it plainly, we cannot reason our way to developing affections. Moreover, habituation into virtuous feelings presupposes a motivation to perform virtuous actions *for* the right ends. In other words, we cannot suppose that prolonged right action will eventually procure virtuous motivations. Here we are forced to question how a person comes to rightly love in such a way that "they find nothing pleasant that conflicts with reason" (1152a3). As it turns out, a great deal of this transformation requires a parallel transformation of motivation.

Alasdair MacIntyre points out this difficulty, claiming that "All education into the virtues, especially the education of the young, has to begin by discovering some way of transforming the motivations of those who are to be so educated."[10] They must "come to value goods just as and insofar as they are goods, and virtues just as and insofar as they are virtues."[11] He goes on to explain that the wrong motivations for imitating virtue procure something that may appear virtuous—that is, it may conform to the requirements of virtue, justice, or the like—but is actually "counterfeit virtue."[12] Moreover, the wrong motivations for acting with apparent virtue can actually procure vices. For instance, a child who is simply motivated to act bravely to please their father will not develop practical reason and courage sufficient for acting bravely in instances where their father is not watching or when they have reason to believe their father would not be pleased. Thus, the desire to act courageously *for the sake of* gaining their father's favor is an insufficient motivation to cultivate the virtue of courage.

This task of cultivating virtuous motivations is a difficult conundrum and seems to greatly depend upon who attempts, or does not attempt, to form the young in virtue. We are, after all, dependent, rational animals.[13] Before considering how this goes right, it might be helpful to imagine the ways it can go wrong. First, if a child simply has no one in his or her life who takes an active interest in forming them well, it is safe to say they will struggle to cultivate good and fine desires. After all, formation is both social and intentional. Second, perhaps a child has parents and teachers deeply invested in her moral formation, but these mentors are seriously mistaken about what constitutes good formation. While well-intentioned, they lack a proper conception of the good and may present a distorted version of it as desirable, leading to the malformation of the child's desires. We might also imagine instances in which these parents and teachers have a proper conception of the good but lack virtue themselves. They can present a vision of the good life that the child should aspire to but fail to live it themselves in some significant way. This, of course, creates a situation in which the child comes to distrust the plausibility of the vision or the sincerity of the person articulating it. Thus, they search for competing visions or easier paths. We can especially imagine situations in which children are victims of trauma or abuse where this might especially be the case.

Putting all of this together, if a child has hope of becoming virtuous, she must have a mentor or teacher invested in her moral development. That mentor or teacher must have a correct conception of the good and model that vision reliably and consistently. In other words, the mentor/s must be virtuous. If the mentor is virtuous, we can presume that their life will evidence the desirability of virtue itself. They will be respected by their peers, giving some indication to their protégé that they have qualities worthy of admiration. They will not agonize over important decisions or struggle to overcome vices that impede the success of their relationships. They will have deep friendships that are a source of joy. They will value the child and communicate that care consistently and reliably. They will be fair with discipline and reasonably merciful. Most importantly, the child will enjoy the company of that mentor and experience the effects of their goodness. All of this, of course, will translate into their desire to mimic that person—to want to be like them. As a result, we might conclude that cultivating virtuous motivation is not simply possible by sheer force of will or through strength of reason. Instead, it is deeply relational, as it involves an intimate encounter with someone worthy of our imitation.

Jennifer Herdt sheds light on this reality in *Putting on Virtue*. It is worth considering her reflections on Aristotle's *Nichomachean Ethics* at length:

> A proper upbringing is not achieved simply through 'compelling power' nor through such power in concert with laws that offer a summary of instructions for virtuous action, nor through these joined with exemplars of virtuous action, offered for imitation. What is crucial in order for one's desires to be transformed into those of a virtuous person (such that one not only performs the actions characteristic of a virtuous person but does so with the accompanying enjoyment in doing the right things for the right reasons in the right ways) is that one love and be loved by the moral exemplar set before one.[14]

Herdt's point is that it is not enough to point at some virtuous person and claim them as our moral exemplar. There is too much distance between exemplar and protégé for that to render any serious moral development. Absent a relationship with that exemplar, the student of virtue couldn't possibly know how they react when the chips are down or see how they make decisions in times of stress. They wouldn't experience the effects of their goodness either—they wouldn't feel what it's like to be in the presence of someone virtuous.

At this point, we have arrived at a very high bar for what sort of mentors are needed for virtuous formation. Given that a very small number of people qualify as genuinely virtuous, it is also the case that very few children have access to genuinely virtuous mentors. We can't deny that many children do, indeed, have people in their lives who love them. However, these people may not have a sound vision of the good life or the ability to live virtuously themselves, making them unfit moral exemplars worthy of imitation. Thus, we are stuck with the harsh reality that the means to virtuous formation are reserved for those fortunate few who happen to love and be loved by the moral exemplars set before them. Or are we?

Abelard's Atonement Theory

In this section, I would like to consider how Christ may solve the scarcity of genuine moral exemplars problem presented by the Aristotelian vision outlined above. To do this well, it will require a careful but brief exploration of Peter Abelard's soteriology, which emphasizes the psychological transformation that occurs within Christians through atonement. I turn to Abelard here not only because his theory of atonement is often characterized as "exemplarist," but also because he shows a keen understanding of how moral transformation takes shape in human beings and what the unique role of Christ is in that process. Though exploration of Abelard's atonement theory takes us a little astray from the discussion of virtue formation, we must establish the context in which we find Abelard's Christian exemplarism that is important to personal transformation and the cultivation of virtue. This is especially significant in order to avoid misappropriating Abelard with Pelagianism.[15] Afterward, I will connect the subjective dimension of Abelard's atonement theory to our earlier discussion, suggesting that Christ can become a universal moral exemplar of the sort needed for genuine virtue formation.

To begin, Abelard's theory of atonement has a long history of misinterpretation. In most standard Christian theology anthologies, Abelard is accused of being an advocate and inventor of the moral exemplar theory of atonement—Christ came to be an example of holiness, and by following his example, we can merit salvation through working out our sanctification.[16] This unorthodox account is normally highlighted as a contrast to orthodox explanations of Christ's saving work, such as Anselm's satisfaction theory or Luther's penal substitution theory.[17] The dissatisfaction with Abelard's moral exemplarism is that it apparently refuses some objective transaction, in which Christ's saving work accomplishes salvation on behalf of sinners. Richard Swinburne, for instance, emphatically dismisses Abelard's account in *Responsibility and Atonement* because "Abelard's exemplary theory of the atonement, that Christ's life and death work to remove our sins by inspiring us to penitence and good acts, contains no objective transaction."[18]

However, in recent years, secondary scholarship has tackled this mistake. Thomas Williams explains in the *Cambridge Companion to Abelard* that Abelard's atonement theory does not refuse acknowledgment of an objective transaction: "The exemplarist reading denies any such objective benefit and therefore misses a key aspect of Abelard's theory of the Atonement."[19] Likewise, Phillip Quinn describes Abelard as a hierarchical pluralist—his atonement theory has a number of moving parts, one of them being penal substitution; however, the dominant motif is exemplarism.[20] In other words, simply because Abelard could be described as exemplarist, that does not exclude the use and implementation of additional metaphors and motifs in his atonement theory. I agree with Quinn and Williams that Abelard is not a pure exemplarist—there are objective and subjective elements present in Abelard's atonement theory. The remainder of this section will detail what, exactly, those objective and subjective elements are and how they are relevant to Abelard's ethics by looking at *Scito te Ipsum* and Abelard's Romans Commentary.

As Williams describes, according to Abelard, humans need a redeemer because they are under the dominion of sin.[21] There is an objective aspect of this dominion and a subjective aspect of this dominion. First, let us review the objective dominion, which is a direct result of original sin. Though Abelard's view on original sin deviates from the norm, he does hold that all human beings incur punishment as a result of original sin—the sin of Adam. He proposes that "sin is said to be that contempt of God or consent to evil from which little children and the naturally foolish are immune" (Sc. 56:

22–23).[22] In other words, sin in the strict sense cannot be said of everyone. He takes this view because, as he demonstrates in *Scito te Ipsum*, consent is needed for sin and consent requires reason. Therefore, humans without the ability to consent (those who lack the power of reason) are unable to sin. However, sin can also be discussed in terms of penalty. Abelard contends that when we speak of "original sin" we speak of sin in terms of penalty. He claims, "But when we say that little ones have original sin or that all of us, as the Apostle says, have sinned in Adam, the effect is as if to say that by his sin we have incurred the beginning of our punishment or the sentence of damnation" (Sc. 56: 30–32).[23] From this we gather that human beings are not born sinful, per se; they are born bearing the punishment for the first sin of Adam. So, the objective dominion of sin is the punishment we incur through the first sin of Adam.

Now what about the subjective dominion? As Williams explains, concupiscence is the subjective dominion of sin Abelard describes in the Romans Commentary.[24] Abelard understands concupiscence in the typical Augustinian way: disordered love. Human beings love the wrong things too much and the right things too little. This inordinate love results in turmoil—we know what is right but, for some reason, do not want it as we should. Thus, a lot of time is spent chasing after things that ultimately lead to our degradation. In other words, we are subject to the power of our own rogue desire, enslaved to ourselves. If we were to put this in grossly Aristotelian terms, we could say that humans are not naturally virtuous.

So far, we have gathered, with the help of Williams's exposition of the Romans Commentary, that there is an objective and subjective dominion of sin in Abelard's theory of atonement. This means that there also must be an objective and subjective redemption from sin, which is precisely what we find Abelard describing. The objective redemption is the notion that Christ died for the remission of sin—to remove the punishment for sin, which is damnation. This is accomplished through the Passion—the suffering and death of Christ on the cross. The subjective redemption depends upon an individual's transformation in Christ. For Abelard, this transformation hinges upon sanctifying our intention—our desire or love.[25] If the subjective dominion of sin suggests that people are enslaved by inordinate loves, then the subjective redemption of sin denotes a release from these inordinate loves. When someone is released from the subjective dominion of sin, she can love what she ought to. This is precisely what the subjective transformation entails, coming to love Christ and letting go of other loves that are impediments to relation with him. This does not mean that one will never struggle against carnal desire. Instead, it means that the love of Christ allows one to conquer those desires.

Now there are two questions that we might consider that help make more sense of this atonement theory. First, how is Christ's expiation for sin transferred to particular people? Second, why was it necessary for God to become man to accomplish all this—to atone for the punishment of original sin and to remove the dominion of concupiscence? Why couldn't one final, really awesome goat suffice? These questions also shed light on how transformation of motivations or intentions occurs in relationship and through love, *caritas*.

First, let us consider the matter of transference. How does a particular person gain access to the merits of Christ's sacrifice? Martin Luther has one possible answer: one is justified or made right with God by virtue of one's faith.[26] One gains the merits of Christ through accepting Jesus as one's personal Lord and savior. Another possible answer is the prevailing Roman Catholic sentiment of the Middle Ages: the sacraments. In baptism, one is justified; through reception of the Eucharist, one is joined to the sacrifice of Christ; in confirmation, one receives the gifts of the Holy Spirit; in confession, one receives the grace of God's mercy, etc. Though Abelard would not deny the importance of faith and the sacraments, he considers neither to be sufficient for transference of Christ's merits. As he sees it, faith is a feature common to the saved and the reprobate:

> But he imparts this grace equally to the reprobate and the elect by instructing each one equally about this, so that by the same grace of faith which they obtained, one is aroused to good works, and the other is rendered inexcusable through the negligence of his sluggishness. Therefore, this faith, which works in the first through love, and is of no effect, inactive, unfruitful, and inoperative in the other one, is the grace of God, which goes before each of the elect, so that he may begin to desire well; and again it follows the beginning of a good will, so that that will may persevere.
>
> (*Comm. Rom.* IV.9:21, 298–9).[27]

In other words, there seem to be a lot of Christians who claim to believe and accept Christ but have no corresponding transformation—they lay claim to the objective redemption but are still walking according to the flesh. The same seems to be the case with the sacraments. Many get baptized and show no signs of personal transformation. Abelard is clear that the sacraments themselves are not sufficient for salvation; someone can be deemed righteous even without the sacrament of baptism.

> For if someone already believes and loves before he is baptized—just like Abraham, concerning whom it is written, "Abraham believed God, and it was counted to him as righteousness," and perhaps Cornelius, whose merciful acts were accepted by God when he had not yet been baptized—and truly repents of his previous sins, just like the tax collector who went down from the temple justified—I do not hesitate to say that he is righteous or has righteousness (iustitia), which renders to each person what is his.
>
> (*Comm. Rom.* II.3.27, 170).

As I already suggested, in the case of faith and the sacraments, there is a seeming disconnect between the objective and subjective. Redemption in the objective domain does not denote redemption in the subjective domain. Peter could claim faith in the Gospel and still act nothing like Jesus. Peter could participate in sacramental life and still look nothing like Jesus. This disconnect between the objective and subjective redemption of sin makes salvation technical—it consists of believing the right things or performing certain religious rituals. As a result, soteriology and morality become distinct discussions. In other words, one can be saved without also being transformed.[28]

Abelard avoids these pitfalls by locating charity as the medium of transference. Charity is the effective means through which the merits of Christ are transferred to particular people and the means of subjective transformation. In other words, love is the agent of objective and subjective redemption—it removes the punishment of sin and the subjective dominion of sin, concupiscence. As a result, it is impossible to speak of removing the punishment for sin without also speaking of the subjective transformation of a particular person. In Abelard's theory of atonement, we see a synthesis of the soteriological and the moral. Moreover, redemption and transformation of particular people both depend upon the paschal mystery—Christ's passion, death, and resurrection.

Christ as Moral Exemplar

Now, we are finally positioned to consider why the sacrifice of Christ is able to accomplish the subjective transformation Abelard deems necessary for salvation. This is the perfect point to consider the second question I proposed as being worthy of consideration: Why did Christ need to become a person to enable this entire process? How come one final, really awesome goat could not suffice and accomplish the same effects? As it turns out, the answer to this question has a lot to do with why Christ can serve as a universal moral exemplar—the sort that actually motivates genuine change in a student of virtue.

Let us recall Herdt's claim from earlier. It contains two suggestions. First, a student of virtue must love their teacher—their exemplar. Second, a student of virtue must be loved by their teacher—their exemplar. If one of these pieces is missing, then the student will fail to cultivate the intrinsic motivation necessary for virtue—she won't do what is right for the right reasons and enjoy doing so. In pointing this out, Herdt underscores the fact that love is the bedrock for virtue. It is important to distinguish love and admiration, for love occurs only in the context of relationship. Without it, she insists, the student of virtue can accomplish nothing more than continence or forced compliance. By definition, forced compliance does not leave room for the possibility that one enjoys the good. In effect, forced compliance inherently falls short of the criteria for virtue or as MacIntyre puts it, produces "counterfeit virtue."

If we explore the notion of Christ as moral exemplar, he fits the bill in both of these significant ways. He is not merely a person we point to as worthy of imitation, like a saint or a winner of the Nobel Peace Prize. Quinn makes a similar point: "The love of God for us exhibited in the life of Christ is a good example to imitate, but it is not merely an example."[29] Instead, the act of suffering and dying for us makes clear that we are loved *by* him and provides an open invitation for relationship. As Abelard so often recalls in the Romans Commentary, Christ demonstrates his supreme love for all people through the willingness to suffer and die for us. Abelard is keen on quoting John 15:13 in substantiating this point:

> Concerning his ineffable charity surrounding us, he elsewhere says, *But God commends his charity towards us in that while we were still sinners, Christ died for us.* Likewise again, *He did not spare his own Son, but handed him over for us all. And the Son says through himself,* "No one has greater love than this, that he [should lay down] his own life," etc.
>
> (*Comm. Rom.* III. 7:6, 247–8).

The Gospel message—that God loves us—is communicated uniquely through the expression of sacrifice, an expression made possible through the Incarnation. If God did not become a man, he could not suffer and die as a man. Though this point is obvious, it is an important one. This communication of love would be impossible if God himself were not the sacrifice, which is precisely why a really awesome goat will not do it. Indeed, this is necessary for rousing us to our perfection in charity:

> And this is what he says: that the perfect charity for God and neighbor IN US, which the law teaches, justifies us. For that greatest kindness, which he showed to us, compels [us] truly to love Christ in the same way as God, in the same way as our neighbor. This [kindness] is the condemnation of sin in us, that is, the destruction of all guilt and defect through charity, generated in us by this greatest kindness.
>
> (*Comm. Rom.* III.8:4, 206)

In other words, God's love entails more than simply not punishing us. He loves us to the point of willing and providing the means necessary to actualize our supernatural perfection: the very gift of himself. Again, to put this in rough Aristotelian terms—love allows for the formation of virtuous intentions. This love is communicated to and roused within the faithful through the sacrifice of the cross.

Moreover, this loving sacrifice of Christ transcends the limitations of human love because it is extended universally. What I mean by this is that Christ does not designate this sacrifice for one person in the way that I would be sacrificing my life for one person if I jumped in front of a bullet for them. By virtue of His omniscience, Christ knows each of us and has died for each of us.

By virtue of His omnipresence, he was not bound by the same physical or practical limitations that limit other available moral exemplars. His attention is not finite. His presence is not restricted by geographic location or time. In this way, the love he extends is open to all willing to reciprocate it; it is truly catholic. Ultimately, perfect mentorship into the virtues is available through relationship with Christ. Thus, habituation in virtue becomes available to all those who come to know and love Christ.

Let's consider how this contrasts with an exceptionally virtuous teacher— one who lacks the omniscience and omnipresence of Christ. Such a teacher can't know every child in her school. She can't personally know every child in her district. She is plainly and simply limited in the scope of her knowledge because she can't know every child personally. Because she can't know every child personally, she can't come to love them personally. As a result, her availability to serve as a moral exemplar—one that meets the stipulations set forth by Jennifer Herdt above—is significantly restricted to those children that she knows personally and those children that she has the bandwidth to develop relationships with, considering her finite resource of time. If teachers and parents such as these were the only viable moral exemplars, genuine education into the virtues would be exceedingly rare and privileged enterprise, as it is in the Aristotelian framework. Christ, however, is not limited in the ways this teacher is limited. While the teacher is only available *qua mentor* to a select few, Christ is available *qua* mentor to all. This solves the elitist difficulty that we are unable to explain away in Aristotle: only a small lot of privileged people have the capacity to develop virtue because of their luck in finding a suitable mentor who is available to cultivate a relationship with them.

Abelard's exemplarism, the subjective dimension of his atonement theory, challenges this notion by emphasizing the unique position of Christ to transform human affections through the sacrifice of the cross—a transformation that is necessary for our sanctification and corresponding growth in virtue. The scope, power, and influence of the Gospel (and its capacity to inspire this response of love) are only limited by the authenticity and evangelizing power of the church. Indeed, while Christ's mentorship is open to all, he must first be known to some specific person to serve as their moral exemplar. This reveals both the awesome agent and painful hindrance Christianity has the potential to be. Nonetheless, the sacrifice of Christ and corresponding relationship offered through that sacrifice extend the availability of a supremely fitting and unconditionally loving moral exemplar to all.

Conclusions and Cautions

Bringing together both the privileged virtue thesis I outlined above and the exemplarism present in the subjective dimension of Abelard's atonement theory, we can see that Christianity offers a unique solution to the scarcity of the formative moral exemplars problem evident in Aristotle's elitism. Christ is a universally accessible moral exemplar who extends boundless, unconditional love. His life, troubled by the foreknowledge that he would suffer a brutal death, displays the vicissitudes of the human condition and the virtues that make human flourishing possible. He is the perfect mentor—one with a sound vision of the good life, worthy of our imitation, capable of relationship and reciprocal love. The consequences of that love, His perfect example, and its capacity to transform the desires of selfish, broken, and vicious humans are evidenced in the lives of the saints.

While access to genuinely exemplary moral exemplars is, perhaps, chiefly important among the external goods Aristotle identifies as necessary for virtue formation, we would be remiss to disregard the others as irrelevant in the Christian vision. As one of the first and most famed baptized Aristotelians, Aquinas is most helpful here. In his commentary on Aristotle's *Politics,* Aquinas gives a telling interpretation of Aristotle's assertion that only beasts and superhumans can live outside the political community (61253a29–30), a further clarification of his claim that human beings are political animals.[30] While Aristotle was being hyperbolic, Aquinas genuinely believes apparent superhumans can exist and even gives examples. He claims that superhumans are, "superior to other human beings, namely, in that they have a nature that is more perfect than other human beings in general, so that they can be self-sufficient without human company. Such was the case with John the Baptist and Saint Anthony the Hermit" (I.20.21).[31] In other words, Aquinas gives a few very rare examples of how exceedingly fervent love of God renders typical human dependencies irrelevant. In other words, acquired human virtue in Aquinas's Aristotelian, Christian vision is not rare, but it is acquired human virtue without the need for external goods like friends or access to adequate resources may be.[32] While there is so much more to explore here, it is not within the scope of this paper to consider it all. This point simply serves as a caution to beware of equating too many with the likes of John the Baptist and Saint Anthony the Hermit.

Moreover, while transformation of motivations and intentions is a necessary condition for virtue, it is but one of several. Habituation is still required to ensure that our inclinations and habits match the desires of our hearts. Augustine reflects on this mismatch in the *Confessions,* lamenting that his vices followed him into his conversion to Christianity:

> Yet even now the images of such things are alive in my memory, about which I have spoken at great length. The kind of life to which I was once accustomed impressed those images firmly upon me and they intrude upon my thoughts
>
> (*Conf.* IX.30.41).[33]

As Augustine recalls, his immense and ever-growing love of Christ did not, at once, extinguish his vices completely. That process requires a certain sort of asceticism, which he was able to pursue vigorously because of his love. However, perhaps transformation of intention is chronologically prior to proper habituation—a point MacIntyre emphasizes. For, a prolonged effort to act virtuously without corresponding virtuous affections procures vice—vice that will be pressed firmly upon us.

Notes

1 Herdt (2010), 28.
2 All references to and quotations from Aristotle's *Nichomachean Ethics* utilize Aristotle (2019).
3 As Matthew Cashen explains in (2016), 293–303, Aristotle distinguishes between internal and external goods. External goods are "external to the soul." (ibid., 294).
4 There is considerable debate within the secondary literature on Aristotle about the extent to which external goods are required for the good life and virtuous activity, more specifically. One dominant view in the debate is that external goods are necessary for eudaimonia insofar as they are instrumental in the cultivation of virtue. T. D. Roche explains this view in the *Cambridge Companion to the Nichomachean Ethics*: "the presence of external goods in a person's life makes only an indirect contribution to that person's eudaimonia, through either (i) providing the agent with means toward, or objects for, activities in accordance with virtue (e.g., as wealth may be used for acts of generosity or as friends serve as objects or recipients of generosity), or (ii) providing the agent with opportunities to expand the range of excellent activities (e.g., as good looks may afford a person extensive opportunities to exercise temperance, or as good children may contribute to one's social prestige, which, in turn, leads to political office where virtues are exercised on a grand scale), or (iii) providing the agent with resources to maintain attitudes needed for (a) the acquisition of the virtues or (b) the steady exercise of virtues one possesses" (39).
5 See Kristjánsson (2022).
6 This concept is often referred to as "moral luck." See Williams (1981).
7 Kristjánsson (2022), 104.
8 Meyer (2016).
9 See Lännström (2006).
10 "How to Seem Virtuous Without Actually Being So," 5
11 Ibid., 6
12 Ibid., 6
13 This is Alasdiar MacIntyre's central thesis (1999).
14 Herdt (2010).
15 I say this because if one only takes the subjective dimension of Abelard's atonement theory without the objective transaction that he clearly includes in his schema, he could be understood as advocating that personal holiness or works alone are sufficient for salvation.
16 Hastings posits this notion in (1919), 360. Gustaf Aulén suggests something similar in *Christus Victor* (Wipf & Stock, 1931), 96: "He was, indeed, so far in accord with the mindset of the period that all his thought lay on the moralistic level." It is worth noting that this caricature of his theory of atonement was likely popularized by Bernard of Clairvaux. For instance, Bernard claims, "This is the righteousness of man in the blood of the Redeemer: which this son of perdition, by his scoffs and insinuations, is attempting to render vain; so much so, that he thinks and argues that the whole fact that the Lord of Glory emptied Himself,

that He was made lower than the angels, that He was born of a woman, that He lived in the world, that He made trial of our infirmities, that He suffered indignities, that at last, He returned to His own place by the way of the Cross, that all this is to be reduced to one reason alone, viz., that it was done merely that He might give man by His life and teaching a rule of life, and by His suffering and death might set before him a goal of charity. Did He, then, teach righteousness and not bestow it? Did He show charity and not infuse it, and did He so return to His heaven?" in Letter LX, "Against Certain Heads of Abelard's Heresies," in The Complete Works of S. Bernard, Abbot of Clairvaux, trans. Joannes Mabillon, (John Hodges, 1904).

17 It is worth noting that some, such as Gustaf Aulen, claim that Luther's atonement theory is more akin to a "classic" view of atonement. He argues that Luther prescribes a Chritus Victor model of atonement, where Christ defeats death and sin through his passion, death, and resurrection. Consequently, we can share in that victory through faith.

18 Swinburne (1989), 162.

19 Williams (2004), 259.

20 Quinn (1993).

21 Williams (2004), 265–69.

22 All of the translations from *Scito te Ipsum* are taken from Luscombe (Oxford, 1971). Luscombe also provides a Latin-critical edition of the text in the same publication.

23 Abelard discusses this point in the Romans Commentary as well. See Book II in a Quaestio on sin following his exposition of Romans 5:14: "Since, therefore, we say that men are begotten and born with original sin and also contract this same original sin from the first parent, it seems that this should refer more to the punishment of sin, for which, of course, they are held liable to punishment, than to the fault of the soul and the contempt for God. For the one who cannot yet use free choice nor yet has any exercise of reason, as though he recognizes the author or deserves the precept of obedience, no transgression, no negligence should be imputed to him, nor any merit at all by which he might be worthy of reward or punishment, more than to those beasts, when they seem either to do harm or to help in something."

24 Williams (2004), 267–69.

25 I consider this at length in my dissertation, *Abelard's Affective Intentionalism, ProQuest, 2019.* To briefly explain, Abelard considers intention in a rather Augustinian way (though he is often attributed to Kant). Is it one's weightiest love? Our love determines the intentional object of our actions, and our love is what makes our actions praiseworthy and meritorious for salvation. This doesn't render bad actions with "good" intentions, meritorious. Rather, it renders "good" actions with bad intentions, undeserving of merit or praiseworthiness.

26 Martin Luther indicates this pretty explicitly in "On Christian Liberty": "But you ask how it can be the fact that faith alone justifies, and affords without works so great a treasure of good things, when so many works, ceremonies, and laws are prescribed to us in the Scriptures. I answer: before all things bear in mind what I have said, that faith alone without works justifies, sets free, and saves, as I shall show more clearly below" (1883, 108).

27 All of my quotes from the Romans Commentary follow Stephen Cartwright (Catholic University Press, 2012).

28 This notion of transformation accompanying redemption is a Pauline theme in his epistle to the Romans 12:2, "And do not be conformed to this world, but be transformed by the renewing of your mind, so that you may prove what the will of God is, that which is good and acceptable and perfect."

29 Quinn (1993), 296.

30 Aristotle (1998).
31 Aquinas (2007), 15.
32 It is important to distinguish between acquired and theological virtue here.
33 Augustine (1998).

References

Abelard, Peter. 2012. *Commentaria in Epistolam Pauli ad Romanos*. Translated by Stephen Cartwright. Washington D.C.: Catholic University Press.
Aulen, Gustaf. 2003. *Christus Victor: A Historical Study of The Three Main Types of The Atonement*, translated by A.G. Herbert. Eugene, Oregon: Wipf & Stock.
Aquinas, Thomas. 2007. *Commentary on Aristotle's Politics*, translated by Richard J. Regan, Indianapolis, IN: Hackett Publishing Company, Inc.
Aristotle, 1998. *Politics*. Translated by C. D. C. Reeve, Indianapolis, IN: Hackett Publishing Company, Inc.
Aristotle, 2019. *Nicomachean Ethics*. Third edition. Translated by Terence Irwin, Indianapolis, IN: Hackett Publishing Company.
Augustine, 1998. *Confessions*. Translated by Thomas Williams, Indianapolis, IN: Hackett Publishing Company.
Cashen, Matthew. 2016. "Aristotle on External Goods: Applying the 'politics' to the 'Nicomachean Ethics." *History of Philosophy Quarterly* 33, no. 4: 293–303.
Hastings, Rashdall. 1919. *The Idea of Atonement in Christian Theology*. London: Macmillian.
Herdt, Jennifer A. 2010. *Putting on Virtue : The Legacy of the Splendid Vices*. Chicago, IL: University of Chicago Press.
Kristjánsson, Kristján. 2022. *Friendship for Virtue*. New edition. New York, NY: Oxford University Press.
Lännström, Anna. 2006. *Loving the Fine: Virtue and Happiness in Aristotle's Ethics*. Notre Dame, IN: University of Notre Dame Press.
MacIntyre, Alasdiar. 1999. *Dependent Rational Animals Why Human Beings Need the Virtues*. Chicago, IL: Open Court.
Meyer, Susan Sauvé. 2016. "Aristotle on Moral Motivation." In *Moral Motivation: A History*, edited by Iakovos Vasiliou, Oxford: New York.
Quinn, Phillip. 1993. "Abelard on Atonement: Nothing Unintelligible, Arbitrary, Illogical, or Immoral About It." In *Reasoned Faith: Essays in Philosophical Theology in Honor of Norman Kretzmann*, edited by Eleonore Stump and Norman Kretzmann, Ithaca, NY: Cornell University Press.
Saint Bernard of Clairvaux. 1904. The Complete Works of S. Bernard, Abbot of Clairvaux. Translated by Joannes Mabillon. London: John Hodges.
Swinburne, Richard. 1989. *Responsibility and Atonement*. Oxford: Clarendon Press.
Williams, Bernard. 1981. *Moral Luck: Philosophical Papers, 1973–1980*. Cambridge: Cambridge University Press.
Williams, Thomas. 2004. "Sin, Grace, and Redemption." In *Cambridge Companion to Abelard, Cambridge*: Cambridge University Press.

13 The Exemplary Life of St. Antony

A Case for Intercessory Exemplarism

Brother John Baptist Santa Ana, O.S.B.

Introduction

Most major religions have a primary moral exemplar. Jesus Christ is looked to as the moral exemplar of Christianity; Muhammed is the exemplar of Islam; Siddhartha Gautama is the exemplar of Buddhism; etc. Some religions focus on a primary exemplar in addition to numerous subsidiary exemplars, while other religions prefer to focus exclusively on imitating the primary exemplar. This difference is especially poignant within flavors of Christianity. Icon veneration, wherein saints are honored, emulated, and supplicated, is ubiquitous among Orthodox Christians. However, many Evangelical Christians regard Christ as the sole moral exemplar. After all, unlike Muhammed or Siddhartha, Jesus is God incarnate, thus containing everything worth imitating and lacking nothing whatsoever. Some Evangelicals may worry that veneration of other (inferior) exemplars may distract and deter from proper emulation of Jesus. However, Paul writes, "Be imitators of me, as I am of Christ" (1 Cor 11:1, ESV). The context of this passage suggests that Paul is elevating himself to the level of an exemplar for the church of Corinth to imitate—a church that is morally depraved and in need of serious instruction. This raises the question of why it is not only permissible but advantageous for Christians to imitate exemplars other than Christ for the purpose of achieving moral perfection when Christ is the moral exemplar par excellence.

To answer this question, I will take a historical-theological approach, drawing and expounding on the early Christian hagiography: *Vita Antonii*. I will discuss how this text was received in antiquity and was instrumental in the conversion of St. Augustine. The example of St. Antony and the influence he had on Augustine will serve to illustrate how effective exemplarism often involves some measure of commonality between the exemplar and imitator—especially commonality in weakness or disadvantage. I will conclude by demonstrating how apparent weakness or disadvantage of the saints may render them more effective exemplars for certain individuals, as in the case of Antony and Augustine. Although Jesus Christ is the moral exemplar par excellence of the Christian religion, inferior exemplars such

DOI: 10.4324/9781032648392-17

as Antony and the saints remain effective for achieving moral perfection because their apparent weakness or disadvantage inclines individuals who share the same weakness or disadvantage to emulate them in their moral perfection.

Vita Antonii

The tradition of hagiography, that is, writing and reading about the lives of the saints, originates from Athanasius' *Vita Antonii* (*VA* henceforth).[1] This fourth-century biography centers around the life and teachings of Antony of Egypt, a proto-monk who fled into the desert to lead a life of prayer and asceticism. His tale is told as a vivid drama of supernatural trials, temptations, and victories, capturing the imaginations of countless individuals and swiftly becoming the bestseller of its time. One might liken *VA* to the latest Marvel movie in fourth-century Rome. However, *VA* proved to be more than mere entertainment, as it unleashed a wave of radical piety manifested in the rise of desert monasticism. The life of St. Antony became a model for early Christians to follow. Anyone battling against temptation toward worldly allurement could look to Antony as their source of inspiration and hope. Though his influence has largely diminished, today he is often remembered for his struggle and victory over fleshly temptation. These episodes are especially vivified in popular works of art such as the paintings of Michelangelo, Cézanne, Dalí, Rivera, and others. Paul Hindemith's Symphony, *Mathis der Maler*, pays special tribute to St. Antony, and he is even featured as the star of a controversial short film by Georges Mélièse.

VA was written by Athanasius in approximately 357 CE during his third exile, only a year after Antony's death.[2] The speculative timeframe of Antony's life and Athanasius' biography implies a sense of haste with which *VA* was written. Athanasius admits in his introduction:

> Since the season for sailing was coming to a close, and the letter-bearer was eager—for this reason, what I myself know (for I have seen him often) and what I was able to learn from him when I followed him more than a few times and poured water over his hands, I hastened to write to your piety.[3]

Here Athanasius offers his stamp of qualification for this undertaking being someone who knew Antony firsthand as one of his followers (though Athanasius himself was not a monk). To view Athanasius' swift composition of *VA* as a project peripheral to his previous tomes would be a mistake. Despite *VA*'s uniquely narrative construction, it is the natural progression or "triquel" of *Contra Gentes* and *De Incarnatione*, wherein Athanasius' vision of embodied atonement through Jesus Christ is manifested in Antony's appropriation of Christ's victory.[4] Therefore, *VA* ought to be read with a holistic lens to the Athanasian corpus.[5]

Athanasius believes that the supernatural aura of Antony is available to all who desire to be transformed by Christ from within. He makes clear his intent for writing VA at the beginning of his introduction: "so that you also might lead yourselves in imitation of him—[...] I know that even in hearing, along with marveling at the man, you will want also to emulate his purpose, for Antony's way of life provides monks with a sufficient picture for ascetic practice."[6] Athanasius writes with the expectation that his readers (monks) will wish to imitate Antony upon merely hearing about him, and that such a wish is a realistic goal within reach for every listener. This nonchalant invitation of imitation should be kept in mind as the fantastic plights of Antony unfold.

Antony was raised in an Egyptian Christian household until the premature death of his parents at around 18 or 20. Six months after their death, while at church, Antony is suddenly struck by the Gospel reading: "If you would be perfect, go, sell what you possess and give to the poor, and you will have treasure in heaven" (Matt 19:21). Antony receives these words as if Christ was speaking directly to him at that moment. Antony immediately leaves, gives all his possessions to the poor, and begins disciplining himself with prayer and asceticism by emulating the example of others:

> he considered carefully the advantage in zeal and in ascetic living that each held in relation to him. He observed the graciousness of one, the eagerness for prayers in another; he took careful note of one's freedom from anger, and the human concern of another. And he paid attention to one while he lived a watchful life, or one who pursued studies, as also he admired one for patience, and another for fastings and sleeping on the ground. The gentleness of one and the long-suffering of yet another he watched closely. He marked, likewise, the piety toward Christ and the mutual love of them all. And having been filled in this manner, he returned to his own place of discipline, from that time gathering the attributes of each in himself, and striving to manifest in himself what was best from all.[7]

This account of young Antony's sincere piety is worth appreciating, for it is the last glimpse of Antony as a relatively ordinary Christian. From this point onward, Antony's life will appear wildly fantastic, like that of a superhero after first discovering his/her hidden powers. What is worth noting is how exemplarism marks Antony's transition from mundanity to magnanimity.

Antony's pious enthusiasm is met by the devil, who engages him in contest. Among a series of spiritual assaults, the devil attempts to seduce Antony with "the softness of pleasure."[8] This is the famously depicted scene wherein the devil takes on the form of a succubus. Though angered and saddened, Antony overcomes his temptation by "thinking about the Christ and considering the excellence won through him, and the intellectual part of the soul."[9] Audibly admitting defeat, the devil flees from

Antony, but not for good; this is only "Antony's first contest against the devil—or, rather, this was in Antony the success of the Savior."[10] Any Pelagian interpretations of the text may be silenced here, as victory over sin and temptation is explicitly credited to Christ rather than the efforts of Antony.[11]

The devil will continue to barrage Antony with attacks—being whipped to near death, threatened by wild animals, and offered silver and gold for the taking; all this happens in the desert, which becomes the arena where Antony engages in battle against the devil. Although the devil is the one who seems to initiate conflict with Antony, it becomes apparent that the devil is the one who gradually goes on the defense. After all, the desert in Christian antiquity was viewed as demonic territory, making Antony the invader and forcing demons to retreat.[12] Like a bold warrior, Antony proves victorious after each "wrestling" match with the devil, not because of his own strength but because of that which God supplies in him.[13]

After 20 years of solitary prayer as a hermit, Antony is intruded upon once again. Only this time it is not the devil but his friends: "When many possessed the desire and will to emulate his asceticism, and some of his friends came and tore down and forcefully removed the fortress door, Antony came forth as though from some shrine, having been led into divine mysteries and inspired by God."[14] Antony's dramatic return to civilization in miraculously good health is received with awe and wonder. Both physically and spiritually, Antony "maintained utter equilibrium, like one guided by reason and steadfast in that which accords with nature."[15] Athanasius' description of Antony's emergence from the desert is a striking parallel to Porphry's description of Pythagoras' emergence from the desert.[16] This reveals how unabashed Athanasius is to appropriate classical wisdom literature in Christian theology. By writing *VA*, Athanasius joins the ranks of such authors as Xenophon and Plutarch, who also authored biographies of virtuous men for the sake of emulation.

A key nuance between Athanasius' Antony and other virtuous men, such as Porphry's Plotinus, is that Antony's hidden source of power derives from a personal being who is simultaneously immediate and transcendent. William Harmless, S. J. writes,

> Athanasius chooses his words carefully here: Antony's 'equilibrium' comes from 'reason.' Here the 'reason,' the *logos*, that guides Antony is not the philosopher's *logos*. For Athanasius, the Logos is a person, Christ, the Logos (or Word) who was in the beginning with God and was God, as the Bible says in John I:I. It is the same Christ the Logos who infuses the universe with its good order, its balance and harmony, and who deifies human beings, making them like himself.[17]

This key difference between Antony's biography and similar biographies from before completely changes the force of the exemplar, redirecting power away from the human exemplar to God. This makes imitation much more feasible since it is not exclusively by human effort that moral perfection is attained but by God, who avails Himself equally to all.

Having reached a height of moral perfection through prayer and asceticism in the desert, Antony begins his active ministry of teaching, healing, and instructing monks. When asked by eager monks to share what he knows from his arsenal of ascetic experience, Antony says, "the Lord has told us before, 'the Kingdom of God is within you.' All virtue needs, then, is our willing, since it is in us, and arises from us. For virtue exists when the soul maintains its intellectual part according to nature."[18] Antony suggests that the way to achieve moral perfection is through proper orientation of the will. When he talks about maintaining the intellectual part of the soul, he does not mean rigorous philosophical training as Hellenic culture would prescribe, but orienting the will toward God as it was made to be rather than toward bodily gratification. The dominant social attitude of Antiquity was that Greek *paideia* was requisite for moral perfection.[19] Athanasius subverts this assumption by suggesting that an unlettered (likely illiterate) man can become a moral exemplar on account of infused virtue from God.[20] However, this infused virtue must be *willed*, and for that reason, the process of attaining moral perfection may be understood as "co-working" or participating in the power of Christ.[21] For Antony, this participation occurs through prayer and ascetic discipline, which condition the will.

After approximately seven years of active ministry, Antony moves to the inner mountain as his final abode. His fame follows him there, and he is often visited by numerous individuals seeking knowledge or healing.

> Frequently the Lord heard the prayers he offered on behalf of many people. And Antony was neither boastful when he was heeded, nor disgruntled when he was not; he gave thanks to the Lord always. He encouraged those who suffer to have patience and to know that healing belonged neither to him nor to men at all, but only to God who acts whenever he wishes and for whomever he wills. The ones who suffered therefore received the words of the old man as healing, and learned not to dwell on their infirmities but to be patient. And the ones who were cured were taught not to give thanks to Antony, but to God alone.[22]

Whatever power people sought from Antony does not derive from him but from God, to whom Antony functions as a conduit. This supernatural holiness is reminiscent of the prophets of the Old Testament, who act as God's intercessors to His chosen people. Before dying around the age of a hundred and five, Antony strictly orders his monks to bury his body in an unknown location to avoid being honored with burial rites. Only a year after his death, in approximately 356 CE, Athanasius comments on the lasting effect that his example had in memorandum. However, one of the most salient will be 30 years later, when Augustine converts to Christianity.

Confessions Book VIII

Augustine makes clear the profound impact *VA* has on his conversion, but I have not found any scholars who explain why Antony is such an effective exemplar for Augustine. In this section, I will focus on aspects of Augustine's life that are relevant for understanding why Augustine is so compelled to imitate Antony.

Augustine's autobiography resembles Antony's biography insofar as it recounts the painstaking triumph over sin and temptation made possible only through divine intervention. However, *Confessions* differs from *VA* insofar as the protagonist (Augustine) is in no way portrayed in an exemplary fashion as Athanasius paints Antony. Casual readers of Augustine often accuse him of being excessively self-disparaging. Indeed, Augustine is not bashful when recounting how great a sinner he was, even as a little boy.[23] He confesses to lying, stealing, and cheating at an early age, concluding that there is no such thing as innocence of youth.[24] His most famous confession is perhaps the extended discourse on pear kleptomania.[25] As Augustine matures into a successful rhetorician, he confesses a fixation on vanity and worldly glory that leaves him bereft of genuine happiness.[26] Above all, Augustine repeatedly names lust as his ongoing vice. He says, "In fact, my feelings of sexual desire were formed out of the perversion of my will. While my will was in thrall to sexual desire, it grew into a habitual behavior: while I was capitulating to that habitual behavior, it grew into something I could not live without."[27] It seems reasonable to conclude that Augustine's habitual promiscuity developed over time into a sexual addiction that he became powerless over.[28]

In reading the *Confessions*, there are two prominent figures in Augustine's life who help pave the way for his conversion: Ambrose and Monica. Augustine meets Ambrose on his visit to Milan and is immediately taken by the bishop's gift for rhetoric—a gift Augustine also shares. Furthermore, Augustine treasures the fatherly affection Ambrose shows to him. Although Augustine acknowledges the providential influence Ambrose had on him, he remains reluctant for one reason:

> I considered Ambrose himself to be quite the lucky man in worldly terms, for the authorities revered him. The only thing about him that seemed burdensome to me was his celibate state. [...] how he struggled against the temptations inherent in his own greatness [...] I did not know how to guess.[29]

Despite Ambrose's admirable talent and kindness, Augustine's will remained obstinate to conversion.

Augustine's mother, Monica, is undoubtedly the most important figure in his life. After her death, he credits his conversion to her unceasing prayers. That said, Augustine spends a good deal of his life avoiding his mother's proselytizing.[30] When Augustine finally agrees to marry, his mother rejoices and arranges a match for him; but the young bride-to-be is two years away from marital age.[31] In the meantime, Augustine is compelled to deport his long-term mistress back to Africa, which breaks his heart (though he keeps their illegitimate son, Adeodatus, for himself). However, he quickly realizes that he can't forgo sex for two years and so takes a new mistress, abandoning his fiancé.[32] Needless to say, Augustine's love and respect for Monica is not enough to assuage his will and to keep him from repeatedly disappointing his mother.

Leading up to the culmination of Augustine's conversion, he says, "So now I shall now relate how you delivered me from the chains of sexual desire, by which I was so tightly constrained, and from my enslavement to worldly affairs; and I shall confess your name, O Lord, my helper and my redeemer."[33] One day, Augustine and his friends welcome into their house an unnamed man who happens to be a fellow African and Roman legionary. Upon seeing a copy of Paul's epistles, the man begins to tell them the story of Antony of Egypt. The legionary goes on to talk about his two friends who, upon reading the story of Antony, decided to give up their positions of high office, break off their engagements for matrimony, and become monks. Augustine suddenly feels convicted by these stories and begins to wage an interior battle with himself. He rushes out of the house into a garden to clear his head, where he meets Lady Chastity, who consoles and embraces him, saying "Are you not able to do what these men, even these women do? Surely these men and women would have no such power in themselves, instead of in the Lord their God? It was the Lord their God who granted me to them."[34] After this encounter with Lady Chastity, Augustine wanders off in seclusion, weeping and prostrating himself on the ground.

In his adolescence, Augustine had prayed, "Grant me chastity and celibacy, but not just yet!"[35] Now, having been inspired by the story of Antony and encouraged by Lady Chastity, Augustine finally brings himself to pray, "Why not 'now'?"[36] At that moment, Augustine hears a child singing, "Pick it up and read it, pick it up and read it!"[37] Reminded of the manner in which God spoke to Antony during the Gospel reading, Augustine returns to the house, picks up Paul's epistles, and reads the first verse that meets his eyes: "Not in orgies and drunkenness, not in sexual immorality and sensuality, not in quarreling and jealousy. But put on the Lord Jesus Christ, and make no provision for the flesh, to gratify its desires" (Rom 13:13–14). It is at this climactic turning point where Augustine gives his life completely to God. Augustine's friend joins him in converting, and Monica is the first to celebrate with them. Augustine will go on to follow in the footsteps of Ambrose in becoming ordained a priest and bishop.

Although several factors contribute to Augustine's conversion to Christianity, the catalyst that compels him to become a Christian is the story of Antony. A hint of comic irony should be appreciated here. Augustine's

222 Brother John Baptist Santa Ana, O.S.B

narrative is laid out with a series of signposts, pointing him toward the Christian faith, yet his will remains obstinate. Neither the eloquence of Ambrose, nor the affectionate pleas of his mother, nor the arguments asserted by Simplicianus and other Christian Neoplatonists suffice to convert Augustine. His conversion appears more impulsive than deductive—something that happens by way of intervention rather than sheer effort. What finally subdues his stubbornness is simply hearing a stranger recount the popular tale of an Egyptian monk. Something about Antony's life is so compelling for Augustine that he immediately imitates Antony by heeding to God's word in Scripture, forsaking his former ways, and living exclusively for Jesus Christ. What is it that makes Antony an effective exemplar for Augustine?

Effective Exemplarism

Having offered a brief summary of Antony and Augustine, I will now begin to formulate a theory for what constitutes effective exemplarism by making connections about the relationship between exemplar and imitator. The purpose of this section is to better understand moral exemplarism by using Antony and Augustine as a case study.

Imitation is a natural form of human behavior. Everyone imitates. This can be observed in children at an early age who watch others and do as they do, speak as they speak, and believe what they believe. However, a child must eventually become selective about who she imitates, for she cannot imitate everyone she meets. Imitating the speech of one person means not imitating the speech of another. Therefore, she will generally try to imitate whomever seems best among her options. This is precisely what young Antony does when he embarks on his practice of spiritual discipline, "gathering the attributes of each in himself, and striving to manifest in himself what was best from all."[38] The expected outcome of this behavior would be to always imitate the best individual or the individual's best qualities. However, this does not always happen because people select different role models to imitate, whether it be a favorite athlete, artist, or moral exemplar.

One reason why people select different role models to imitate lies in the fact that people have different perceptions, admirations, and scales of values. Therefore, the role model that seems best to her may not seem best to him. However, this does not explain why people continue to choose different role models in situations where the best individual can be determined by way of competition. For example, the Olympic gold medalist in skateboarding will have a large following of skaters who wish to imitate them. However, there will remain a contingent of skaters who prefer to imitate some other skater, albeit inferior to the best skater. Therefore, although excellence is one motive for imitation, it is not the only motive since some people choose to imitate those who are neither the best nor appear to be the best.

In addition to excellence, one reason why someone may wish to practice imitation is because of preexisting commonality. In other words, like is attracted to like. Thomas Aquinas says,

> Likeness, properly speaking, is a cause of love. But it must be observed that likeness between things is twofold. One kind of likeness arises from each thing having the same quality actually: for example, two things possessing the quality of whiteness are said to be alike. Another kind of likeness arises from one thing having potentially and by way of inclination, a quality which the other has actually.[39]

Aquinas identifies two kinds of likeness: (1) likeness according to actuality, and (2) likeness between potentiality and actuality. For example, a skater at the skatepark possesses the quality of skateboarding actually. Whereas an aspiring skater who observes skaters at the skatepark only possesses the potential quality of skateboarding. Aquinas asserts that there is cause for love or inclination in both scenarios. He continues,

> Accordingly the first kind of likeness causes love of friendship or well-being. For the very fact that two men are alike, having, as it were, one form, makes them to be, in a manner, one in that form: thus two men are one thing in the species of humanity, and two white men are one thing in whiteness. Hence the affections of one tend to the other, as being one with him; and he wishes good to him as to himself. But the second kind of likeness causes love of concupiscence, or friendship founded on usefulness or pleasure: because whatever is in potentiality, as such, has the desire for its act; and it takes pleasure in its realization, if it be a sentient and cognitive being.[40]

Those who share the first kind of likeness may be drawn to one another on account of the quality they actually share in common. For example, an Australian citizen may feel inclined to cheer for an Australian Olympic athlete simply because they are both from Australia. The same goes for those who potentially share a quality in common. However, Aquinas seems to imply that this love is unrequited; the person who only potentially possesses a quality is inclined toward the person who actually possesses a quality, but not necessarily vice versa. For example, an aspiring skater will wish to hang out with other skaters so that she might learn how to become like them. However, seasoned skaters may not wish to hang out with aspirants since they have nothing useful by which to reciprocate. The fact that Antony is highly sought after by numerous aspirants shows that Antony possesses some quality actually, and his followers only possess this quality potentially. Hence, they are inclined to Antony, while Antony, from his desert fort or inner mountain, is not necessarily inclined toward them.

Likeness helps make sense of how people go about selecting different exemplars for imitation. Some measure of excellence is prerequisite for being selected as an exemplar, since no one would consciously choose to imitate a person unless she appears to possess some sort of excellent quality. However, some people are more inclined to imitate a particular person on account of some likeness, e.g., ethnicity, gender, religious affiliation, etc. There are countless qualities in which likeness may be discovered. Moreover, some qualities are considered more significant than others. For example, when voting for a presidential candidate, the quality of the candidate's gender may have more significance for some voters than the quality of the candidate's political party. Therefore, the process of selecting an exemplar for imitation will differ drastically from one person to another based on whatever shared quality is considered to have more significance.

Augustine has an abundance of excellent exemplars to choose from. Ambrose is a righteous and accomplished bishop whom Augustine greatly admires. Additionally, they both share the quality of rhetoric in actuality. However, Augustine remains reluctant to imitate his celibacy. Monica shows the highest level of prayerful patience and love for Augustine. As mother and son, the two share much in common, such that Augustine says, "my life and hers had been as one."[41] And yet, Augustine pays no heed to his mother's pleas. The unforeseen exemplar whom Augustine is moved by is Antony. One reason for this is Antony's excellence in moral perfection. More significantly, Augustine recognizes a quality he shares with Antony, namely, temptation to lust. Both possess this quality in the same way that Augustine and Ambrose possess the quality of rhetoric. However, Augustine is moved to imitate the celibacy of Antony, but not Ambrose. Therefore, there must be something particularly significant to Augustine about Antony as someone who understands what it is like to be tempted by the same vice—to experience the same weakness.

Likeness in weakness can be highly significant. Many individuals who struggle with addiction regularly attend 12-step programs where they meet with others who share the same addiction. Similarly, individuals with social disadvantages often convene to support and encourage one another, as in the case of groups for women's rights. Shared weakness and/or disadvantage can be a cause for love or inclination. Furthermore, someone who possesses the quality of overcoming weakness potentially will be inclined toward someone who possesses the quality of overcoming weakness actually. For example, recovering alcoholics will be inclined to imitate an individual who possesses 25 years of sobriety. What makes 25 years of sobriety significant is the fact that a particular weakness has been overcome. Recovering alcoholics will not be inclined to imitate an individual who possesses 25 years of sobriety if that individual never struggled with alcohol in the first place. Whereas a recovering alcoholic with 25 years of sobriety is worthy of imitation precisely because he has attained mastery over his will by overcoming weakness, which gives hope to those who strive to achieve the same goal.

Hope pertains to the will. Aquinas describes the effect of hope as "a stretching forth of the appetite to such an object."[42] Hope assists the will with obtaining that which it desires. Aquinas lists four criteria for something to be an object of hope: (1) something that is good and therefore desirable, (2) something that is future and therefore not possessed at present, (3) something that is arduous and difficult to obtain, and (4) something that is possible to obtain.[43] Any object that does not meet these four criteria or does not appear to meet them cannot be hoped for. Sometimes an individual is incapable of hope for obtaining a desired object because it does not appear to meet the fourth criterion. For example, Peter does not swim to the bottom of the pool because he does not think it is possible for him. However, when Peter sees Pauline touch the bottom of the pool, suddenly Peter knows it is possible and attempts to actualize his desire. What Peter previously considers to be an impossible and even a scary undertaking becomes a matter of effortless delight with the assistance of hope. In this example, Pauline functions as an exemplar who stretches Peter's will to obtain his desire.

Hope is especially important for overcoming weakness or disadvantage since weakness or disadvantage decreases the likelihood of obtaining something. However, in order to know whether or not it is possible to overcome some weakness, someone with the same weakness must prove it is possible. Consider the example of UFC middleweight champion Israel Adesanya. In numerous sports interviews, he discusses the challenges of being a "skinny black guy" as opposed to a "big macho man."[44] Presumably, being "skinny" in mixed martial arts is considered a weakness, and being "black" a social disadvantage. However, after witnessing the success of Anderson Silva, Adesanya says, "If a skinny black guy can do this and just have this run, I'm a skinny black guy! I can do this and have this run!"[45] Adesanya is inspired to imitate Silva because he is an excellent fighter who shares the same putative weakness and disadvantage as Adesanya, thereby instilling Adesanya with hope.

When Augustine recounts his sexual deviance, he frames it within the context of an incorrigible will, saying, "I was bound: not by someone else's iron chains but by my own iron will."[46] Augustine's will is inflexible, lacking the hope needed to be stretched forth. He desires chastity as an object that is good in the future but arduous and difficult to obtain. However, he does not seem to believe it is possible for him. It might be possible for others like Ambrose, but Ambrose does not appear to share the same weakness as Augustine. It is only when Augustine hears of Antony, who experiences the same temptation yet overcomes his weakness and achieves chastity, that the fourth criterion is met, filling Augustine with hope and leaving him without excuse. Through Antony, Augustine comes to believe that chastity is actually within reach; indeed, she appears right in front of him, saying, "Are you not able to do what these men, even these women do?"[47] At last, Augustine obtains chastity thanks to the example of Antony, who shares in his own weakness.

Sola Jesus?

For all Christians, Jesus is the moral exemplar par excellence. There is no one who surpasses Jesus in virtue, since Jesus is fully God. Furthermore, by taking on human nature, Jesus subjects himself to disadvantage, weakness, temptation, and death. Therefore, everyone, insofar as they are human, may identify some quality they share in common with Jesus, and so be inclined to love and imitate Him. For these reasons, it may seem foolish for a Christian to imitate any exemplar other than Christ since all exemplars pale in comparison to Him. However, Christians have always imitated other moral exemplars, as in the case of Antony and Augustine or Paul and the church of Corinth. Obviously, Antony and Paul do not surpass Jesus in virtue, but they do surpass Jesus in weakness. If weakness can be a significant quality, then Christians who share the same weakness may be more inclined to imitate an exemplar who is weaker than Jesus.

Augustine was certainly familiar with Jesus from the Gospels. However, Augustine was not inclined to imitate Jesus in the same way he was inclined to imitate Antony. This is not because Jesus is an insufficient exemplar, but because Augustine's perception of Jesus is insufficient to be immediately moved by Him as an exemplar. Nowhere in the Gospels does Jesus appear to struggle with lust. Having a human nature, it seems plausible that Jesus was tempted to lust, but since nothing of the sort is recorded in the Gospels, Augustine is unable to perceive this particular likeness he has with Jesus.[48] Furthermore, Jesus was confined to the limitations of a human body, and therefore could not have experienced every possible variant of human weakness and disadvantage. Jesus did not experience what it is like to be a woman in a patriarchal society, nor to be addicted to methamphetamine, nor to suffer from Alzheimer's. Therefore, individuals with these particular disadvantages or weaknesses may struggle to perceive likeness with Jesus, opting to imitate an exemplar whose likeness is more apparent. However, this does not render Jesus as an unrelatable exemplar, but one who, through divine omniscience, perfectly understands every instance of human weakness and disadvantage without firsthand experience. The author of Hebrews writes, "For we do not have a high priest who is unable to sympathize with our weaknesses, but one who in every respect has been tempted as we are, yet without sin" (Heb 4:15). Although numerous instances of human weakness and temptation are unaccounted for in the Gospels, Jesus is nonetheless intimately cognizant of every aspect of human frailty, and therefore an exemplar who sympathizes with our weakness, though we do not perceive these qualities in Him.

While Christian imitation of various exemplars is sensible, the fear remains that imitating any exemplar other than Christ can result in failure to imitate Christ Himself. This fear seems warranted, which is why it is of utmost importance for Christians to look for exemplars worthy of imitation and to be in regular fellowship within Christian communities. In circumstances where these are hard to come by, countless volumes of lives of the saints exist to expose Christians to godly exemplars. Still, the question remains whether or not even good exemplars can distract a Christian from imitating Christ. When considering the life of Antony, it becomes apparent how Antony resembles Jesus. Jesus routinely prays to the Father in seclusion, which Antony imitates. Jesus is led into the desert, where Antony follows Him. Jesus is tempted by the devil to indulge in bodily gratification and worldly power, as is Antony. Jesus teaches, heals, and disciples others, as does Antony. Many of Antony's wise maxims are simply quotations from Christ Himself. Therefore, successfully imitating Antony will inevitably result in imitating Christ. One might say that Augustine truly imitates Christ through imitating Antony. Thus, Antony functions as an intercessory exemplar for Augustine.

Intercessory exemplarism is especially appropriate for the Christian religion on account of the Judeo-Christian doctrine of the image of God. Athanasius says, "when the soul has put off every stain of sin with which it is tinged, and keeps pure only what is in the image, then when this shines forth, it can truly contemplate as in a mirror the Word, the image of the Father, and in him meditate on the Father, of whom the Savior is the image."[49] Through the grace of participation, humans are conferred with a likeness that reflects God's image (who is the Son, Jesus Christ) enabling humans to draw near to God through contemplation and reflect God's image (Jesus Christ) to others. As the image of the Son is perfected in a human being, it becomes more radiant. Athanasius portrays Antony as the ideal image of the Son, functioning as a spotless mirror that reflects the Son's likeness, illuminating the image of the Son in whomever Antony encounters.[50] However, it is vital to remember that Antony was not born a spotless mirror but, despite his own weakness, *becomes* a spotless mirror on account of God's work within Antony and his cooperative prayer and asceticism.[51] Every human person is made to the image of the Son with a dynamic capacity to increase in likeness to the Son through the grace of participation.

Participation in God comes with implications for human relationships. Athanasius goes so far as to say that true imitation of Christ involves sharing with others what God shares with us:

> What has accrued to us from God Himself by grace, these things we may impart to others, without making distinctions, but largely towards all extending our kind service. For only in this way can we anyhow become imitators, and in no other, when we minister to others what comes from Him.[52]

What one human receives from participating in God naturally flows outward to other human beings. Once again, the mirror analogy is helpful for visualizing how the Son's likeness is reflected by spotless mirrors. By reflecting the Son's luminosity to others, a human being, in imitating the Son, becomes more like Him, and thus more luminous, resulting in an ever-increasing cycle of luminosity. This is Athanasius' understanding of intercessory exemplarism. Just as Christ, the exemplar, intercedes on behalf of the Father for us, we are called to imitate Him and become exemplars who intercede on His behalf for others.

Conclusion

If a reader could take away three things from this chapter, this is what I would like them to be. First, for readers of *Confessions*, I hope this chapter offers a reasonable explanation for Augustine's unexpected impetus to suddenly convert and how Antony's story plays a central role in freeing Augustine from, as he puts it, "a cruel slavery that had me in shackles."[53] Few scholars, if any, have drawn a connection between Augustine and Antony's triumph over sexual temptation. I hope this small, yet significant connection contributes toward further Augustinian/Athanasian discussions.

Second, I have attempted to offer an apology for why it is not only permissible but also advantageous for Christians to have moral exemplars other than Jesus, provided that they function as intercessory exemplars on behalf of Jesus, the exemplar par excellence. I believe this argument, as I have constructed it, can have ecumenical merit, especially among interdenominational conversations about the communion of saints. To idolize any saint over Jesus is problematic for all Christians. However, to ignore the resource of exemplars that the saints have to offer stifles opportunities of becoming more like Christ through imitation of them while truncating the doctrine of the image of God.

Third, those who have any kind of weakness or disadvantage should not preclude themselves from becoming exemplars. In fact, being weak or disadvantaged can make someone more effective as an exemplar. The best details in the lives of the saints are not their triumphs but their shortcomings, or perhaps their triumphs in light of their shortcomings. This, at least, is how Augustine felt when he heard the life of Antony. This is also what inspires Paul to tell the church of Corinth, "Therefore I will boast all the more gladly of my weaknesses, so that the power of Christ may rest upon me. For the sake of Christ, then, I am content with weaknesses, insults, hardships, persecutions, and calamities. For when I am weak, then I am strong" (II Cor 12:9–10).

Notes

1 Harmless (2004), 59–60.
2 Behr (2005), 253–254. This chapter agrees with recent historical analysis in affirmation of Athanasius as the original author of *VA*.
3 Athanasius (1980).
4 Behr (2011), 41.
5 Anatolios (1998), 166.
6 Athanasius (1980), intro.
7 Athanasius (1980), 4.
8 Ibid., 34.
9 Ibid., 34.
10 Athanasius, *VA*, 35.

11 Anatolios (1998), 180.
12 Chitty (1966), 6.
13 Athanasius, *VA*, 10.
14 Ibid., 14.
15 Ibid., 14.
16 Harmless (2004), 71.
17 Harmless (2004), 90–91.
18 Athanasius, *VA*, 20.
19 Urbano (2008), 887.
20 Ibid., 893.
21 Anatolios (1998), 177, 183.
22 Athanasius, *VA*, 56.
23 Augustine (2014), 1:19.
24 Ibid., 1:30.
25 Ibid., 2:9–17.
26 Ibid., 6:9–10.
27 Ibid., 8:10.
28 Ibid., 7:5.
29 Ibid., 6:3.
30 Augustine, *Confessions*, 5:15.
31 Ibid., 6:23.
32 Ibid., 6:25.
33 Ibid., 8:13.
34 Ibid., 8:27.
35 Augustine, *Confessions*, 8:17.
36 Ibid., 8:28.
37 Ibid., 8:29.
38 Athanasius, *VA*, 4.
39 Aquinas (2008–2016), q.27, a. 3, co.
40 Ibid., q. 27, a. 3, co.
41 Augustine (2016), 9:30.
42 Thomas Aquinas, *Summa Theologiae* I-II, q. 40, a. 2, co.
43 Ibid., q. 40, a. 1, co.
44 Edwards (2018).
45 MMA fighting on SBN (2023), 16:50.
46 Augustine, *Confessions*, 8:10.
47 Ibid., 8:27.
48 The impeccability of Christ is debated among theologians. See Aquinas, *Summa Theologiae* III, q. 41, a. 1, obj. 3.
49 Athanasius (1971).
50 For more on Athanasius' use of mirror, see Hamilton (1980), 14–18.
51 Anatolios (1998), 202–03.
52 Athanasius (1994).
53 Augustine, *Confessions* 8:10.

References

Anatolios, Khaled. 1998. *Athanasius: The Coherence of His Thought*. New York, NY: Routledge.

Aquinas, Thomas. 2008–2016. *Summa Theologiae I-II*. Translated by Benzinger Brothers, Scotts Valley, CA: Nov Antiqua.

Athanasius, 1971. "Contra Gentes, 34." Translated by Robert W. Thomson, *Athanasius: Contra Gentes and De Incarnatione*. Oxford: Oxford University Press.

Athanasius. 1980. "Vita Antonii, Intro." Translated by Robert C. Gregg, *Athanasius: The Life of Antony and The Letter to Marcellinus.* New York, NY: Paulist Press.

Athanasius, 1994. "Contra Arianos III. 19." Translated by John Henry Newman, *The Church Fathers—Nicene and Post-Nicene Fathers, Second Series Vol. 4.* Peabody, MA: Hendrickson Publishers Marketing, LLC.

Augustine. 2014. *Confessions.* Translated by Carolyn J.-B. Hammond, LCL 26, edited by Jeffery Henderson, Cambridge, MA: Loeb Classical Library.

Augustine. 2016. *Confessions.* Translated by Carolyn J.-B. Hammond, LCL 27, edited by Jeffery Henderson, Cambridge, MA: Loeb Classical Library.

Behr, John. 2005. *Nicene Faith: Part One True God of True God.* New York, NY: St Vladimir's Seminary Press.

Behr, John. 2011. *On the Incarnation: Greek Original and English Translation.* Yonkers, NY: St. Vladimir's Seminary Press.

Chitty, Derwas J. 1966. *The Desert a City: An Introduction to the Study of Egyptian and Palestinian Monasticism under the Christian Empire.* New York, NY: St. Vladimir's Seminary Press.

Edwards, Jim. 2018. mmanytt, February 27th, 2018, https://www.mmanytt.com/exclusive/israel-adesanyas-career-inspired-skinny-black-guy-anderson-silva-kicking-ass/

Hamilton, Andrew. 1980. "Athanasius and the Simile of the Mirror." *Vigiliae Christianae* 34, no. 1: 14–18. North-Holland Publishing Company.

Harmless, S. J. William. 2004. *Desert Christians: An Introduction to the Literature of Early Monasticism.* New York, NY: Oxford University Press.

MMA fighting on SBN. 2023. "UFC 230: Israel Adesanya Post-Fight Press Conference -MMA Fighting," accessed on July 30th, 2023, 16:50, https://youtu.be/JY41DDXrf7M.

Urbano, Arthur. 2008. "'Read It Also to the Gentiles': The Displacement and Recasting of the Philosopher in the Vita Antonii." *Church History* 77: 4. American Society of Church History.

14 A Triadic Model of How to Become Like the Saints

Grace Hibshman

Introduction

The last four months of her life, medieval mystic St. Catherine of Siena neither ate nor drank anything except the Body and Blood of her Lord Jesus Christ. She died at the age of 33 after a life of intense asceticism. She often slept for only half an hour every other day and abstained from all food except water and the occasional raw vegetable. As a child, she was known to lead her playmates in flagellating themselves as they said the rosary together (Undset 1954).

The Church often portrays the saints as examples of what we should try to become. However, it is not clear how we should engage with the examples of saints like Catherine, whose spirituality is bound up with practices that are inappropriate for most people. If what it looks like for us to be holy is different from what it looks like for her, then what role can her example play in the cultivation of our sanctity?

Virtue ethicists have long tried to understand how moral exemplars can help us acquire virtue. Unfortunately, their models of moral emulation are not especially suited to modeling how the lives of saints help us become like the saints, or at least, so I argue, is true of the models of Aristotle, Linda Zagzebski, and Julia Annas. The core difficulty is that it is not clear what role an exemplar's particular features play in the process of emulation. If we try to copy an exemplar's exact behaviors, motives, reasons, or whatnot (e.g., Catherine's fasting), then we will likely end up trying to have traits that are inappropriate in our own context. On the other hand, if we don't try to replicate any particular features of the exemplar, then it's not clear how the exemplar is helping us acquire virtue.

My goal in this paper is to offer a model of how the lives of the saints can help us become holy that avoids this difficulty. Whereas in models of moral emulation, the aspiring practitioner of virtue becomes like the moral exemplar by directly imitating some feature of the exemplar, on my model a penitent becomes like a saint in an indirect way by engaging in a certain kind of three-way relationship with God and the saint. The saint, including their unique way of being holy, has an active role in this special, three-way

DOI: 10.4324/9781032648392-18

relationship. However, engaging in this kind of relationship doesn't require the penitent to try to directly imitate any particular feature of the saint. So, the triadic model preserves the relevance of the saint's particular way of being holy to the process of becoming like the saint, but it does so without requiring the fraught activity of directly imitating the saint's specific features.

But in addition to its theoretical merits, my model explains actual practices of venerating the saints. In fact, I argue that something like my model appears to underlie hymnography surrounding the saints in the Eastern Christian liturgical tradition. Tracing this feature of the tradition serves the double purpose of illustrating how one might go about putting my triadic model into practice as well as some of the mechanisms by which the model works. I conclude with applications of the model to non-Christian and non-theistic settings.

Models of Moral Emulation

Aristotle famously supposed that we acquire virtue through habituation (*Nicomachean Ethics*, bk II). On his view, it is by first doing what the virtuous person would do that we learn to not only do *what* the virtuous person would do but also do it in the *way* that virtuous person would do it, i.e., at the right times, to the right extent, with reference to the right objects, toward the right people, with the right motive, etc. Even if we start out doing virtuous actions for less than virtuous reasons, or in less than virtuous ways, Aristotle thought that it is through doing virtuous actions that we learn to do them virtuously and so acquire virtue. For example, even if we start out abstaining from excessive drink simply to impress, Aristotle would contend that it is by abstaining in this less than temperate way that we learn to abstain as the temperate person would, i.e., for the right reasons, while taking proper pleasure in the act of abstinence itself, out of a stable disposition to abstain in relevantly similar contexts, etc. (*Nichomachean Ethics*, 2.3.1, 2.4.3–4). Analogous pictures hold for courage, justice, generosity, and the rest of the virtues.

If we tried to use Aristotle's model to emulate St. Catherine, then we would try to learn to be holy like her by doing the holy things that she did. But what are those things? Assuming, as hagiographies of her life suggest, that her fasting was a holy thing for her to do, "doing the holy things she did" could mean starving ourselves as she did; or, operating on a lower-level granularity, it could mean engaging in any form of bodily penance to which we feel called; or, operating on an even lower level of granularity, it could mean any form of self-denial, or some combination. Construing her example on a lower level of granularity makes imitating her example seem less problematic, but it also makes it harder to understand what role her example plays in the cultivation of our sanctity. If imitating her abstinence amounts to something as abstract as any form of self-denial, then it is not clear what her example teaches us about holiness that, say, a biblical command to be self-sacrificing does not.

This problem is at least partly addressed by the neo-Aristotelian models of emulation developed by Linda Zagzebski (2017, ch. 5) and Julia Annas (2011, ch. 3), both of which augment Aristotle's picture of how we transition from merely doing what the virtuous person would do to doing it in the way that a virtuous person would. The central mechanism of Zagzebski's model is the practice of imaginatively taking up the perspective of moral exemplars. It is intuitive to Zagzebski that imagining ourselves having a certain feeling can cause us to actually experience the feeling, especially if we want to. One example she offers is that of a woman who falls in love with a man by wistfully imagining what it would be like to fall in love with him (C:\Users\user\Downloads\82017, 136). Zagzebski infers that imagining what it would be like to have the motives of moral exemplars can move us to actually have their motives, especially if our imagining is conjoined with admiration for them and a desire to be like them. With time, we can make having these motives a habit, which, once acquired, disposes us to perform the same kinds of actions as moral exemplars. Moral exemplars facilitate this process by giving us a window into what it would be like to have virtuous motives, thus inspiring us to want to have them.

The central mechanism of Annas' model is the transmission of practical reasons from the moral exemplar to the aspiring practitioner of virtue. Following Aristotle, Annas compares the acquisition of virtue to the acquisition of a skill, like pipe-laying, for example (2011, 19). She observes that in order to teach an apprentice, the expert needs to not only show the apprentice *how* he lays pipes but also explain *why* he lays them the way he does, what is essential to the arrangement and what is optional, what goal is being accomplished by a particular arrangement, etc. The apprentice acquires the skill of pipe-laying by internalizing these reasons so that he can apply them to pipe-laying problems he has never seen before. If the apprentice can only reproduce by rote the exact same arrangements that his mentor has already shown him, then he hasn't yet learned how to lay pipes. Annas supposes that we emulate moral exemplars through a similar process. In order to learn virtue, we need to not only observe *how* moral exemplars act but also understand *why* they act that way. We have acquired virtue when we have internalized their practical reasons so that we can apply their kind of reasoning to new situations. If we can only parrot back exact imitations of moral exemplars, we have not acquired virtue.

Both Zagzebski's motives-first model and Annas' reasons-first model at least partly solve the problem of needing to know how granularly to imitate the actions of moral exemplars. Instead of specifying how closely to follow the behavior of exemplars, their accounts specify how to acquire exemplary motives or practical reasons, both of which, once acquired, dispose their bearers to consequently perform exemplary actions. Deciding exactly which actions to perform is left as an exercise for the aspiring practitioner of virtue once they have acquired the right motives or reasons.

Nonetheless, if we tried to use their models to emulate the holiness of St. Catherine of Siena, for example, we would run into a number of difficulties. First, it's not clear *which* of her motives we should try to cultivate. She was holy, but not necessarily all of her purported motives were holy. Even if they were, just because they were part of what it looked like for *her* to be holy doesn't necessarily imply that they are part of what it looks like for *us* to be holy. Many saints, including Catherine, had special vocations that required them to make choices that would be inappropriate or harmful for most people to make. There is also the complication that the "holy" parts of a saint's life, like Catherine's zeal for fasting, are not easily separable from the "merely" incidental ones (e.g., Catherine's personality, her family life, the culture of 14th century Catholicism in Siena, etc.). After all, grace perfects nature. Some have even argued that the characteristic of passionate asceticism of many female mystics from Catherine's time, while perhaps still part of their sanctity, may have been a form of mental illness, such as anorexia.[1] But even if we restrict ourselves to motives that would be appropriate for us to have if we could manage to acquire them, it's still not clear that we should try to emulate them, at least not on a very high level of granularity. Trying to imitate the motives of such extraordinary saints as Catherine could easily lead to despair, bitterness, or self-righteousness. We might have more success if we started out by emulating those whose holiness is within a more realistic striking range for us.[2]

We could avoid these difficulties if we construed St. Catherine's motives from a low level of granularity, as a form of loving God or some other sufficiently abstract generality. However, that would lead us back to our old problem of needing to know at what level of granularity to emulate the saints. We've moved the goalpost from actions to motives. Construing the saints' motives on a low level of granularity makes imitating them seem unproblematic, but if our motives are only supposed to vaguely resemble theirs and resemble them by having qualities that we already know that we should have, like being less self-absorbed, then it is hard to understand what role their particular example plays in the development of our sanctity. We could try to follow Zagzebski's model by imaginatively taking up their perspective on a very low level of granularity, but in doing so, we would be taking up a very abstract version of their perspective, one that is largely formed by our preconceived notions of what it looks like to love God or whatnot. A similar argument can be made about the practical reasoning of saints.

A Triadic Model of How to Become Like the Saints

Aristotle's, Zagzebski's, and Annas' models of emulation are all dyadic in the sense that they can be described in terms of just two parties, the understudy and the exemplar. On their models, the understudy finds an exemplar that they would like to resemble, identifies features of the exemplar to imitate, and engages in a process to acquire those features themselves. Alternatively, we can conceive of the process whereby we come to resemble the saints as a triadic process, one that cannot be described without reference to at least three parties: the penitent, the saint, and God. Instead of conceiving of the saint's holiness as an attribute they possess, we can construe it as a two-way relationship between the saint and God. On this model, a penitent tries to acquire a similar two-way relationship with God as the saint's relationship with God by engaging in a certain kind of three-way relationship with God and the saint.

This three-way relationship functions in a variety of ways. Christ is mediated to the penitent through the saint's unique personhood. Observing the way that God has worked through the saint, the penitent asks God to work in their life just as he has worked in the life of the saint: that they would be united to God, that the Spirit would live in them and they in Christ, etc. Adding another layer of relationality, the penitent can do this through the saint by asking the saint to intercede with God and make this petition on their behalf. The saint can then ask God on behalf of the penitent that he would satisfy the penitent's desire and work in them as he worked in the saint, effecting in the penitent the same life in him that the saint already enjoys. Having received grace from God (perhaps through the saint's intercession), the penitent can more fully participate with the saint in joint love and worship of God. Furthermore, the penitent can honor and love the saint for the love of God, drawing closer to the saint as they draw closer to God, and drawing closer to God as they draw closer to the saint. Through this process taken as a whole, the saint is enfolded into the penitent's relationship with God, the penitent is enfolded into God's relationship with the saint, and God is enfolded into the saint's relationship with the penitent. Christ is mediated in and through all parts of the process, and all parts of the process are mediated in and through Christ.

As we will see in the next section, liturgical tradition offers us glimpses into the mechanisms by which this process works. Nonetheless, my triadic model cannot definitively spell out all of the mechanisms by which God transforms people when they enter into relationship with him and his saints, in part because these are parts of the Christian faith typically regarded as mysteries. So, to some extent, these must be taken on faith. Like standard models of moral emulation, the triadic model thus leaves unexplained some details of how we come to resemble those whom we aspire to resemble. Unlike standard models of moral emulation, however, these details are not ones that we must know in order to employ the model, and the triadic model has an explanation as to how these details are sorted out. Whereas those employing standard models of moral emulation must presumably know *which* motives, reasons, or behaviors to imitate, penitents employing the triadic model do not need to know how God is going to go about transforming them when they enter into relationship with him and his saints. That part of the model is outsourced to God's discretion. Of course, penitents need to know something about how to enter into relationship with God in order to employ the model; however, there are whole liturgical traditions to guide penitents through this part of the process. Moreover, even imperfect attempts to enter into relationship with God give God room to respond and begin his transformative work. Unlike imitating virtuous reasons, motives, or behaviors, entering into relationship with God is the sort of thing that one accomplishes to some extent just in virtue of trying.

The successful living out of the triadic model will culminate in the penitent's enjoying union with God. The penitent will thereby in fact come to resemble the saints in their union with God. Unlike models of moral emulation, however, on my triadic model the penitent does not do so by directly imitating specific features of the saint they are trying to become like. In this way, the triadic model resembles what it looks like to apply one of the dyadic models at a low level of granularity, i.e., wherein the understudy tries to imitate the exemplar only in a very general way, by loving God, for example. Consequently, the triadic model inherits immunity to the risks that come with trying to directly imitate an exemplar on too close a level of granularity. However, unlike high-level applications of the dyadic models, in the triadic model, the particularity of the saint's unique way of being holy retains a clear role in the cultivation of the penitent's sanctity. Through the communion of the saints, the penitent enters into a direct, living relationship with the saint. In addition, the saint has a direct and living relationship with God, the particularities of which impact how God receives and chooses to act on the saint's intercession on the penitent's behalf. Depending on the saint's role in salvation history, the particularities of the saint's relationship with God might even shape how God chooses to relate to his people as a whole, including the penitent, or, relatedly, how the penitent is able to relate to God. The details of how God has worked in the life of the saint can give the penitent knowledge of God's character. In addition, the saint may mediate facets of God's splendor that God has made, especially manifest in the saint's unique hypostasis. Knowledge of the saint's personhood and relationship with God can in turn move the penitent to respond to God's initiative in their life, which is a key part of how, on the triadic model, the penitent comes to resemble the saint. In these ways, the triadic model preserves the relevance of the saint's particular way of being a saint to the process of becoming like the saint, but it does so without requiring the penitent to directly imitate the saint's specific features.

As I have been describing throughout, the triadic model is in some ways similar to the models of moral emulation in the virtue ethics literature and in other ways dissimilar to them. Whether the similarities are great enough to make my model count as a model of "emulation" in a technical sense, I leave as a question of semantics. What's important for my purposes is that I have found a model of how engaging with a saint's particular way of being holy can help us become more like the saint, and this model avoids the problem I identify in the models of moral emulation in the literature.

Support for the Triadic Model within the Liturgical Tradition of Eastern Christianity

But while I have outlined some theoretical merits of the triadic model, it remains to be seen whether my model fits comfortably with actual practices of venerating the saints. In this section, I give evidence that the Eastern Christian liturgical tradition seems to assume something like my triadic model. The hymnography of this tradition does not say what one would expect it to if a purely dyadic model were operative. For example, prayers to the saint do not say, "O Saint So-and-so, you are such-and-such a way. I want to be that way too." Instead, prayers to and about the saints tend to follow a two-part, *anamnesis-epiclesis* structure. In the first part, they describe something about the saint's life. Then, in the second part, they respond to the example of the saint's life by turning to God in a way that is related to the saint, or alternatively, by asking the saint to do so on our behalf. These prayers thereby guide worshipers into a triadic relationship with God and his saints, giving us glimpses along the way into how this three-way relationship can reshape our own two-way relationships with God.

Having its origin in Eucharistic prayers, an *anamnesis-epiclesis* structure is typical of prayers of blessing in the Eastern Christian liturgical tradition. The *anamnesis* remembers features of who God is and how He has worked in the past, presenting this relational backdrop as warrant for the petition in the *epiclesis*. As an example, consider one of the epicycles of *anamnesis* and *epiclesis* found in the Great Blessing of Waters celebrated on the Feast of Theophany:

> ...Thou art our God, who hast renewed through water and Spirit our nature grown old through sin. Thou art our God, who hast drowned sin through water in the days of Noah. Thou art our God who, through the waters of the sea, at Moses' hand hast set free the Hebrew nation from the bondage of Pharoah. Thou art our God who hast cleft the rock in the wilderness: the waters gushed out, the streams overflowed, and Thou hast satisfied Thy thirsty people. Thou art our God who by water and fire through Elijah hast brought back Israel from the error of Baal. [*anamnesis*] Therefore, do Thou Thyself, O Master, now as then sanctify this water by Thy Holy Spirit. (*3 times*) Grant to all those who touch it, who anoint themselves with it or drink it, sanctification, blessing, cleansing, and health...[*epiclesis*] (*Festal Menaion*, 357)

The *anamnesis* in this blessing does not present the lives of Noah, Moses, and Elijah as examples for us to imitate, nor does the *epiclesis* ask God to make us like them. Instead, their lives serve as precedents of a different kind. They confirm the church's faith that God will indeed work "now as then" through the water the church is ritually blessing. In addition, the church treats the events in the lives of Noah, Moses, and Elijah as typological moments in the history of God's people, allowing them to shape the church's poetic imagination of its relationship to water in the scheme of salvation. Immediately after the Great Blessing, the priest and the faithful engage in rituals that reference these and other water narratives in Scripture. The priest dunks a crucifix in the water three times and sprinkles the newly blessed holy water onto the walls of the church. The faithful ritually kiss the crucifix, drink the water, and receive a sprinkling of it on their heads. Through these prayers and rituals, the church enfolds the work of Christ and the lives of the faithful into the narratives of the lives of Noah, Moses, Elijah, and others.

An *anamnesis-epiclesis* structure is paradigmatic of prayers of blessing, especially Eucharistic blessing; however, its influence permeates the liturgical tradition at every level. Consider the following Theophany hymn addressed to John the Forerunner:

> With thine hand hast Thou Touched the immaculate head of the master (*3 times*). And with the finger of that hand, Thou hast shown him to us[3]: [*anamnesis*] on our behalf, O Baptist, stretch out that same hand over Him, for Thou hast great boldness before Him. [*epiclesis*] To thee He bore witness, that Thou art greater than all the prophets. With thine own eyes hast Thou beheld the Holy Spirit descending in the form of a dove. [*anamnesis*] Lift up those same eyes towards Him, O Baptist, and make Him merciful towards us. Come and stand with us (*3 times*) Setting the seal upon our song and beginning our feast. [*epiclesis*] (*Festal Menaion*, 332–333)

This hymn recalls three physical gestures John the Baptist made at Christ's Theophany in the Jordan River: the saint's stretching out his hand toward Christ, his touching Christ's head in baptism, and his lifting up his eyes toward the Spirit in the form of a dove. The first two especially reshape God's relationship with his people. The act of baptizing Christ brings Christ into a new kind of union with his creation, and the act of pointing us to Christ (both literally and figuratively) brings the church into a new kind of relationship with God, who has now been made manifest in the flesh. Each time the hymn remembers one of John's gestures, it asks the saint to relate to God in the same way, performing the same concrete movements, but this time in intercession on the Church's behalf, incorporating them into his prior relationship with God. The hymn then invites the saint into the congregation's own relationship with God, asking him to stand with them and seal their song.

Encouraging the congregation to join with a saint in their worship of God is a common trope in Eastern Christian hymnography. For example, consider another theophany hymn.

> The waters saw Thee, O God: The waters saw Thee and were afraid. For the cherubim cannot lift their eyes upon Thy glory, nor can the seraphim gaze upon Thee: but standing by Thee in fear, the first carry Thee

and the second glorify Thy might. [*anamnesis*] With them, O Merciful Lord, we proclaim Thy praises and we say: O God who hast appeared, have mercy on us. [*epiclesis*] (*Festal Menaion*, 362–363)

In this hymn, the *epiclesis* responds to the activities of the heavenly hosts described in the *anamnesis* by repeating the seraphim's requests for God's mercy. In so doing, it not only leads the faithful in imitating the heavenly hosts, but, adding another layer of communion, it also leads them in joining *with* the seraphim in their choir of praise.

In addition to putting the words of the saints in the mouths of the faithful, hymns often stimulate identification between the faithful, Christ, and the saints by asking the faithful to take up the first-person perspective of those in the events they are celebrating or to address them in the second-person, or paradoxically, to even do both simultaneously. For example, the Theophany hymnography contains a dialogue between Christ and John the Baptist in which Christ says,

'O John the Baptist, who from the womb has known Me the Lamb, minister to Me in the river, serving Me with the angels. Stretch out thy hand and touch My undefiled head; and when thou seest the mountains tremble and Jordan turn back, [*anamnesis*] do thou cry aloud with them: O lord who hast been made flesh of a Virgin for our salvation, glory to Thee.' [*epiclesis*] (*Festal Menaion*, 312)

When the choir sings the epiclesis, they not only join with John the Baptist and the Jordan river and the mountains as they praise Christ in the second person, but since the choir quotes Christ, who is quoting John, the choir simultaneously takes up Christ's first-person perspective as he addresses John in the second person. As the perspectival layers pile up, we lose track of whose voice in which we are speaking and catch a glimpse of the communion between us, God, his saints, and all creation.

Whereas in the hymns we've seen so far, the *epiclesis* concretely reflects the *anamnesis*, more commonly, the connection is looser and more abstract. For example, in the two hymns below, the first connects the *epiclesis* to the *anamnesis* primarily through wordplay, whereas the second culminates in a general, all-purpose *epiclesis* common to many hymns.

O Thou who baptized in the waters of the river Him that taketh away the sins of the world, [*anamnesis*] do Thou, with the streams of thine intercessions dry up, O blessed John the Forerunner, the abyss of my evil deeds. [*epiclesis*] ("General Service to John, Precursor, Prophet, and Baptist of the Lord," Ode 8)

O Baptist and Forerunner, strengthened by the divine grace of Christ thou hast shown us the lamb that takes away all the sin of the world;

and with joy thou hast this day brought two disciples to him. [*anamnesis*] Entreat Him that peace and great mercy may be given to our souls. [*epiclesis*] (*Festal Menaion*, 389)

The most common exception to the *anamnesis-epiclesis* pattern I have identified are hymns that are missing an *epiclesis*; however, these hymns can be construed as fitting the pattern if we attend to the surrounding liturgical context. In this liturgical tradition, hymns are sung in a call-and-response fashion with interjected psalms verses or short refrains, the most common being "Alleluia!", "Have mercy on me, O God, have mercy on me", "Holy St. ____, pray to God for us.", "Glory to Thee, O Lord, glory to Thee!", and "Glory to the Father, and to the Son, and to the Holy Spirit both now and ever and unto ages of ages. Amen." We can construe these God-ward responses between hymns as supplying the missing *epiclesis*.

I have only addressed the hymns of one feast day, namely Theophany. However, my analysis is at least some evidence that Eastern Christian hymnography to and about the saints follows an *anamnesis-epiclesis* structure wherein the church responds to the lives of the saints by engaging in various three-way relationships with God and those saints. I infer that the triadic model fits well with at least traditional Eastern Christian practices of venerating the saints. If this is right, then liturgical prayers like the ones we've seen may serve as guides for engaging in the kind of three-way relationship at the heart of the triadic model.

The prayers I've analyzed also offer us clues about some of the mechanisms by which the triadic model works. As we've seen, the hymns present the lives of the saints as precedents for how God acts, paradigms for restructuring our poetic imagination of the world, stories into which we can imbed our own life narratives, schemas of God's economy of salvation, and pivotal moments in the history of God's relationship to the church. Each of these ways of understanding our relationship with the saints gives us a glimpse into how our relationship with them can work on us, reshaping our own two-way relationship with God. But there is still so much more to explore in this regard, and ultimately, much of it may remain a mystery to us.

Conclusion

It has long puzzled ethicists that we can fail to be virtuous precisely by trying to be virtuous. Michael Stocker (1976) famously offers the vivid example of a person who visits their friend in the hospital, not for the love of the friend herself, but simply because they want to be virtuous. I have suggested that we can fail to resemble the saints precisely by trying to be like them. Alternatively, we can come to resemble the saints, not by imitating them directly, but rather by engaging in a certain kind of three-way relationship with them and God, a relationship in which the saints' particular ways of being holy are operative and serve as precedents for us, but aren't exactly examples for us *per se.*

The engine of the triadic model is the Christian vision of the communion of the saints. Nonetheless, pieces of this model could be adapted to non-Christian and even non-religious settings. For example, one could jettison the robustly Christian commitments of the model and merely augment Zagzebski's and Annas' mechanisms of moral emulation with prayers that God (or Yahweh or Allah) would help one acquire the motives or reasons of one's moral exemplars, including non-religious moral exemplars. A completely non-religious adaption would call for more thorough revision, but even secular ethicists could perhaps benefit from developing models of moral emulation that are more heavily relationships-first, as mine is. To my knowledge, no one in the literature has yet tried to understand moral emulation primarily as a process of entering into ever deeper relationship with moral exemplars.

Notes

1 See Bell (1985) and Bynum (1991, Chapter 4).
2 For empirical support of similar claims, see Hyemin et al. (2017).
3 This is a reference to John the Baptist's gesture in the traditional festal Icon of Christ's Theophany in the Jordan, which in turn is a metaphor for the saint's role as the forerunner who points ahead to Christ.

References

Annas, Julia. 2011. *Intelligent Virtue.* Oxford: Oxford University Press. https://doi.org/10.1093/acprof:oso/9780199228782.001.0001

Bell, Rudolph. 1985. *Holy Anorexia.* Chicago, IL: University of Chicago Press.

Bynum, Caroline Walker. 1991. *Fragmentation and Redemption: Essays on Gender and the Human Body in Medieval Religion.* New York, NY: Zone Books.

Han, Hyemin, Jeongmin Kim, Changwoo Jeong, and Geoffrey L. Cohen. 2017. "Attainable and Relevant Moral Exemplars Are More Effective than Extraordinary Exemplars in Promoting Voluntary Service Engagement." *Frontiers in Psychology* 8: 283.

Kallistos, Ware, and Mother Mary. 1990. *The Festal Menaion.* Pennsylvania, PA: St. Tikhon's Seminary Press.

Stocker, Michael. 1976. "The Schizophrenia of Modern Ethical Theories." *Journal of Philosophy* 73, no. 14: 453–66.

Undset, Sigrid, and Kate Austin-Lund. 1954. *Catherine of Siena.* New York, NY: Sheed and Ward.

Zagzebski, Linda. 2017. *Exemplarist Moral Theory.* New York, NY: Oxford University Press.

Afterword

Linda Zagzebski

Moral and spiritual exemplars have profoundly improved human lives for thousands of years. All the major religions have exemplars, and it is impossible to imagine how any religion could exist for more than a short time without them. What makes exemplars so deeply admirable is that they are persons who assimilate the learning of the head to the wisdom of the heart, and they impart their wisdom in the most direct way one human being can affect another—through the desire to emulate them. In a stirring introduction to his commentary on the Katha Upanishad, Eknath Easwaran quotes G.K. Chesterton, who once said that to understand the Gospels, we have only to look at St. Francis of Assisi. Easwaran then says that to grasp the meaning of the Bhagavad Gita, we need to look no farther than Mahatma Gandhi, who made it a guide for every aspect of his life.[1]

Imitating a person is the natural way we learn almost everything. Often it takes no effort at all, but if what we are learning is difficult, attention and concentration are called for, and we might need to sift through the features of the exemplar to distinguish those that are truly admirable from those that are not. If the exemplar exemplifies perfection or something close to perfection, attempts at emulation might be ineffective or even counterproductive. We do better when the person we are emulating is not too much better than we are. I imagine that that is why Chesterton proposed imitating St. Francis rather than Jesus, and Easwaran proposed imitating Gandhi rather than the sage Veda Vyasa, the legendary author of the Bhagavad Gita.

In the early 2000s, I worked on a Christian form of my moral theory that I later called exemplarism, in which God is the supreme exemplar. That became my book, *Divine Motivation Theory* (2004). I intended that book for Christian philosophers and theologians. Later, I developed the theory into a general moral theory without any theological commitments that I called *Exemplarist Moral Theory* (2017). I was happy to see that it got attention from psychologists and education theorists, as well as moral philosophers. The theory is radical because it proposes a theoretical structure that can be derived from observation of exemplary persons, identifiable through the emotion of admiration that survives critical reflection over time.

One problem that I fear makes the idea of exemplars less influential than it deserves to be is that we live in a culture suspicious of exemplars, or any persons who are commonly thought to be better than the rest of us. About a 100 years ago, Max Scheler identified the phenomenon of *ressentiment*, a term coined by Nietzsche, who used it to attack Christian moral ideals, but which Scheler blamed on the egalitarianism of the age. We do not want to think that there are people who are morally superior, whose existence makes us feel shabby in comparison. We like to see the mighty fall; we like to find out that St. Teresa of Calcutta had defects that some people think excuse them from admiring her. One line of research I would love to see come out of this book is research on the psychology of resisting admiration of exemplars. Why does the media search for hypocrisy among the saintly? Why is hypocrisy the vice that leaves people gleeful, while dishonesty, cruelty, and extreme narcissism get a yawn?

I welcome Eric Yang's collection for advancing the study of exemplars in philosophical theology, psychology, and spiritual development. One feature I have seen in it that I think is an important advance is the study of exemplary communities. I believe that further research on exemplary communities is important because we live in a society in which communities are weak and often barely functional. Because of extreme belief polarization, some groups of people are defined more by what they are against than by what they are for. Research on healthy, admirable communities need not focus on small, saintly communities whose structure makes them inapplicable to the social conditions most people live in. What is it about a community that permits its members to live flourishing lives without rancor, violence, and continuous disagreement? To avoid being the worst, they do not have to be the best. They just have to arouse our admiration, and they should be similar enough to our own social structures that we can see practical steps for making our communities more like theirs.

I also hope to see more work connecting moral theory with narrative ethics and the place of admiration in ethics. I gave my own theory in *Exemplarist Moral Theory*, but there is no reason to think that my theory is the only way to do it. I believe that exemplars are important for theory as well as practice. The more interdisciplinary connections between mainstream philosophical ethics, theology, and psychology, the better. This volume is an important step in that direction, and I am grateful for it.

Note

1 Easwaran (2009), 8.

Bibliography

Easwaran, Eknath. 2009. *Essence of the Upanishads*. Tomales, CA: Nilgiri Press.

Index

Note: Page numbers followed by "n" refer to notes.